高职高专经济贸易类专业规划教材

浙江省“十一五”重点教材建设项目

外贸单证操作

主　编　章安平

副主编　范越龙　王　琼

参　编　杨永明

机　械　工　业　出　版　社

本书采取以工作过程为线索、职业能力培养为本位、任务驱动、项目导向的教材编写模式。本书依据外贸单证工作流程，分为申请开证业务操作、审证和改证业务操作、制作商业发票和装箱单操作等 12 个工作项目。每个工作项目都包括学习目标、导入项目、示范操作、知识支撑和实训项目等内容。每个工作项目都依据学习目标设计了一个典型的项目活动载体，布置了相应工作任务，进行了示范操作，提供了知识支撑，最后还提供了对应的实训项目。

本书既可以作为经济贸易类专业的教材，又可以作为外贸单证从业人员的培训教材，也可以作为外贸从业人员的业务参考书。

图书在版编目（CIP）数据

外贸单证操作/章安平主编．—北京：机械工业出版社，2010．12（2017.7 重印）
高职高专经济贸易类专业规划教材 浙江省“十一五”重点教材建设项目
ISBN 978-7-111-32708-0

Ⅰ．①外… Ⅱ．①章… Ⅲ．①进出口贸易－原始凭证－高等学校：技术学校－教材 Ⅳ．①F740．44

中国版本图书馆 CIP 数据核字（2010）第 243927 号

机械工业出版社（北京市百万庄大街 22 号 邮政编码 100037）
策划编辑：孔文梅 责任编辑：张 亮
封面设计：鞠 杨 责任印制：李 飞

北京富生印刷厂印刷

2017 年 7 月第 1 版第 6 次印刷
184mm×260mm・12．25 印张・296 千字
15 001—18 000 册
标准书号：ISBN 978-7-111-32708-0
定价：29．00 元

凡购本书，如有缺页、倒页、脱页，由本社发行部调换

电话服务 网络服务
服务咨询热线：010－88379833 机 工 官 网：www．cmpbook．com
读者购书热线：010－88379649 机 工 官 博：weibo．com/cmp1952
教育服务网：www．cmpedu．com

金 书 网：www．golden－book．com

前　言

教高【2006】16号文件《教育部关于全面提高高等职业教育教学质量的若干意见》明确指出，高等职业院校要积极与行业企业合作开发课程，根据技术领域和职业岗位（群）的任职要求，参照相关的职业资格标准，改革课程体系和教学内容；建立突出职业能力培养的课程标准，规范课程教学的基本要求，提高课程教学质量；改革教学方法和手段，融“教、学、做”为一体，强化学生能力的培养；与行业企业共同开发紧密结合生产实际的实训教材，并确保优质教材进课堂。

有鉴于此，本人结合“外贸单证操作”国家级精品课程的建设，联合具有多年外贸单证从业经验的外贸单证专家，在外贸单证员岗位工作任务和职业能力分析的基础上，共同开发课程标准，以外贸单证员工作过程为线索，共同编写了这本《外贸单证操作》项目教材。本书具有以下三个主要特点：

一、创新教材编写模式

本书是在对外贸单证员岗位工作任务和职业能力分析的基础上，依据与外贸单证专家组共同开发的外贸单证员岗位职业标准，打破了以知识体系为线索的传统编写模式，采用了以外贸单证员工作过程和工作任务为线索，体现工学结合、任务驱动、项目导向的项目教材编写模式。

二、业务环节系统、全面

本书系统介绍了外贸单证操作的各个环节，涵盖申请开证业务操作、审证和改证业务操作、制作商业发票和装箱单操作、制作订舱委托书和办理订舱操作、制作出境货物报检单和办理报检操作、制作和申领原产地证操作、制作和办理报关单证操作、制作投保单和办理保险操作、制作附属单据操作、制作汇票操作、审单操作、交单收汇和单证归档操作12个工作环节。本书依据外贸单证操作的12个工作环节，安排12个工作项目。每个工作项目都安排学习目标、导入项目、示范操作、知识支撑和实训项目五部分内容。每个工作项目都依据学习目标设计一个典型的项目活动载体，布置相应工作任务，进行示范操作，提供知识支撑，最后还提供对应的实训项目。

三、业务内容来自实际

本书包括七套外贸单证操作案例，涉及阀门、夹克、皮衣、轮胎、木材、白酒、数控车床等七种外贸商品。这七套外贸单证操作案例都是来源于外贸企业的真实业务案例，其中，四套是典型的出口单证业务案例，三套是典型的进口单证业务案例；结算方式涉及L/C、T/T、D/P等；贸易术语涉及FOB、CFR、CIF和CPT等。学生进行这七套外贸单证操作案例的实训操作犹如进行实际业务操作，能大大提高其外贸单证操作能力，从而实现培养外贸单证员的实训目标。

为了紧贴外贸业务实际，本书中的合同、单证等一般都仿照真实文件的外观样式，所述内容如不慎与真实生活中的人物、组织或事件有雷同之处，实属巧合，谨此声明。

本书由浙江金融职业学院章安平担任主编并统稿，参加编写的人员有：章安平（课程标准、项目一、二、三、四、五、六、七、八、十一）、范越龙（项目九）、王琼（项目十）、杨永明（项目十二）。

为方便教学，本书配备电子课件等教学资源。凡选用本书作为教材的教师均可索取，请发送邮件至 cmpgaozhi@sina.com，咨询电话：010-88379375。

本书既可以作为经济贸易类专业的教材，又可以作为外贸单证从业人员的培训教材，也可以作为外贸从业人员的业务参考书。

本书在编写过程中得到了浙江中成进出口有限公司江龙正副总经理、杭州银行宁波分行国际业务部蔡红波总经理等外贸单证专家的大力支持，在此表示衷心的感谢。

由于编写时间较紧、任务重，书中难免出现一些疏漏和错误，真诚欢迎各界人士批评指正，以便再版时予以修正，使其日臻完善。

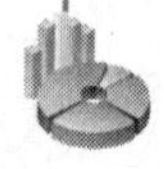

章安平

目　录

课 程 标 准

课程名称：外贸单证操作
适用专业：国际贸易实务、国际商务等经济贸易类专业
学分数：4 学分
课时数：72 学时

一、课程性质和作用

“外贸单证操作”是国际贸易实务、国际商务等经济贸易类专业的一门专业核心课程。本课程主要培养具有较强职业能力、专业知识和良好职业素质的外贸单证员。通过本课程的学习，学生能制作和办理各种外贸单据，能审核信用证和各种外贸单据，能分析和处理各种外贸单证问题。本课程的铺垫课程是“外贸基础”和“国际结算操作”。

二、课程设计理念和特点

（一）设计理念

本课程采用以外贸单证员岗位职业标准为依据，以职业能力为本位，以工作过程为主导，以校企合作为路径，融“教、学、考、做”为一体的工学结合课程建设模式。

（二）设计特点

本课程的设计体现了系统性、开放性、职业性和实践性等四个特点。①系统性体现在对课程的教学内容、活动载体、教学团队、教学场所、教学方法、考核体系等各环节进行了系统的设计；②开放性体现在本课程的双元课程建设主体，由校内专任教师和外贸企业外贸单证业务专家共同进行课程建设；③职业性体现在课程培养定位于外贸单证员职业人和以外贸单证员岗位职业标准为依据；④实践性体现在本课程实施做中教、做中学和做中考的项目教学模式。

三、课程设计思路

本课程的设计思路是，在工学结合课程建设模式的指导下，首先校内专任教师和行业兼职教师共同分析外贸单证员的工作过程和任务，共同开发外贸单证员岗位职业标准；然后依据职业标准，以职业能力为本位，开发课程内容，设计项目活动载体，编写项目教材；同时，建设双师结构的课程教学团队，在校内外实训基地开展以学生为主体，融“教、学、考、做”为一体，以工作任务为驱动的项目教学；最后，实施过程考核与结果考核相结合、校内考核与企业考核相结合、课程考核与职业考证相结合的多样化课程评价体系。

四、课程建设目标

通过在外贸单证实训室的仿真操作和在外贸企业的全真操作，使学生熟练掌握外贸单证的制作、办理和审核等专业知识，能熟练进行申请开证、审证、制作和办理外贸单证、审单

等业务操作，培养学生一丝不苟的工作作风和善于沟通与团队合作的工作品质，考取外贸单证员职业证书，为今后从事外贸单证岗位工作和其他外贸岗位工作奠定扎实基础。

五、课程内容和要求

本课程的具体内容和要求见表 0-1。

表 0-1　课程内容和要求

序号	工作项目	能力要求	知识要求	课时
1	申请开证业务操作	1.1　能根据外贸合同填写开证申请书 1.2　能办理申请开证手续	•掌握信用证业务流程和开证申请书内容 •熟悉信用证当事人和申请开证步骤	4
2	审证和改证业务操作	2.1　能根据外贸合同审出 L/C 中的问题条款 2.2　能提出信用证修改意见	•掌握信用证各栏目内容和 UCP600 改证相关条款 •熟悉审证的依据和步骤、改证的原则和步骤	6
3	制作商业发票和装箱单操作	3.1　能找出 L/C 条款或合同条款中关于商业发票和装箱单的相关条款 3.2　能根据 L/C 条款或合同条款准确制作商业发票 3.3　能根据 L/C 条款或合同条款准确制作装箱单	•掌握商业发票的定义和作用、UCP600 中关于商业发票和装箱单的条款 •熟悉装箱单的种类和作用	8
4	制作订舱委托书和办理订舱操作	4.1　能根据 L/C 条款或合同条款制作订舱委托书 4.2　能根据 L/C 条款或合同条款办理订舱手续	•熟悉托运操作流程、集装箱的装箱方式 •了解托运的注意事项	6
5	制作出境货物报检单和办理报检操作	5.1　能根据 L/C 条款和/或合同条款准确填制出境货物报检单 5.2　能准确填制报检委托书	•掌握报检和法定报检 •熟悉商检机构种类和出口货物检验检疫的一般流程 •了解电子转单、电子通关和检验检疫证书	6
6	制作和申领原产地证操作	6.1　能根据 L/C 条款和/或合同条款准确填制一般原产地证 6.2　能根据 L/C 条款和/或合同条款准确填制普惠制原产地证	•熟悉原产地证的含义、作用和种类	6
7	制作和整理报关单据操作	7.1　能准确填制出口收汇核销单 7.2　能准确填制报关单 7.3　能准确缮制报关委托书	•熟悉报关的期限和流程、报关单的填制要求 •了解报关流程和报关单位	8
8	制作投保单和办理保险操作	8.1　能根据 L/C 条款或合同条款填写投保单 8.2　能根据 L/C 条款或合同条款办理保险手续	•中国保险条款海运货物保险、UCP600 的保险相关条款 •熟悉航空货物运输保险、保险除外责任和责任起讫、保险金额和保费的计算、保险单的种类 •了解协会保险条款	4
9	制作附属单据操作	9.1　能根据 L/C 条款或合同条款缮制受益人证明 9.2　能根据 L/C 条款或合同条款缮制船公司证明 9.3　能根据 L/C 条款或合同条款缮制装运通知等	•熟悉装运通知、受益人证明内容 •了解船公司证明、船籍和航程证明、船龄证明等单据的内容	6
10	制作汇票操作	10.1　能准确填制 L/C 项下汇票 10.2　能准确填制托收项下汇票	•掌握汇票的定义、当事人、背书和承兑 •熟悉汇票的种类 •了解出票、提示、付款、拒付、追索等其他票据行为	6

（续）

序号	工作项目	能力要求	知识要求	课时
11	审单操作	11.1 能审核商业发票 11.2 能审核装箱单 11.3 能审核运输单据 11.4 能审核保险单据 11.5 能审核产地证 11.6 能审核汇票 11.7 能审核其他单据	• 掌握审单原则和 UCP600 相关条款 • 熟悉审单方法、常见的单据不符点	8
12	交单收汇和单证归档操作	12.1 能按信用证或外贸合同条款进行交单 12.2 能处理不符单据 12.3 能按业务的要求将各类单证归档	• 掌握信用证结算方式下的交单收汇操作方法 • 熟悉电汇、托收结算方式下的交单收汇操作方法和单证归档要求	4
合计				72

六、实施建议

（一）教学团队

本课程建议采用校内专任教师和行业兼职教师共同组建“双师结构”课程教学团队，行业兼职教师与校内专任教师比例达到 1:1；建议校内专任教师到外贸单证相关部门开展挂职锻炼，提升外贸业务操作能力，培养双师素质教师；建议行业兼职教师来源应包括外贸企业单证部、银行国际结算部、国际货运代理公司、商检局、海关等部门；建议“双师结构”课程教学团队共同开发课程、共同编写教材、共同备课、共同授课、共同命题，全程参与课程建设。

（二）教学场所

本课程建议全部都放在校内实训室和校外实习基地上课和考试，实现教学场所与职业场所的一体化，使学生非常容易找到强烈的职业归属感，以提高其学习效率。建议本课程应配套至少 1 个外贸单证实训室和多个校外外贸单证实习基地；建议外贸单证实训室要配备 1 个外贸单证操作软件和一定数量具有上网功能的电脑；建议校外外贸单证实习基地应涵盖不同类型、不同区域的外贸单证相关企业，具体校内实训室设备数量和校外实习基地数量因学生数量而定。

（三）教学方法

本课程建议采用以学生为主体，职业能力培养为本位，以工作过程和工作任务为主线，任务驱动，融“教、学、考、做”为一体的项目教学法。教学通过项目导入、学生操作、教师示范、归纳总结、能力实训等五个环节循序渐进，让学生以职业人身份进行业务操作，突出学生主体地位，打破了在教室进行教学的传统固有模式，全部安排在校内外贸单证实训室与校外外贸实习基地，实现课堂与实习地点一体化教学模式，让学生在做中学，让教师在做中教，融“教、学、做”为一体。

校外外贸单证实习基地数量充足时，建议还可同时采用工学交替教学法，通过前期在校内实训室学习和训练后，再安排一定课时到校外外贸单证实习基地进行外贸单证实战训练，实现工学交替。

在教学中还要与外贸单证员职业考证紧密结合，实施课证融合教学法，把考证内容融入到教学内容中，使学生学会本课程之后，就能较顺利地取得外贸单证员职业证书。

（四）教学评价

本课程采用多样化的考核方式，采用过程考核与结果考核相结合、校内考核与企业考核相结合。建议考核分数比例见表 0-2。

表 0-2　建议考核分数

考 核 内 容	考核成绩的比例（%）
平时成绩	10
上机实训成绩	20
工学交替成绩	30
期末上机考核成绩	40
合　计	100

（五）课程资源

要注重建设和开发本课程的课程标准、电子教材、项目活动载体、教学单元设计、学习指导、多媒体课件、实训实习项目库、习题集、案例集、试题库等教学资源，并建设课程网站，使教师和学生能够通过课程网站教学平台开展高效、灵活的教与学的活动。

项目一

申请开证业务操作

能力目标

能根据外贸合同填制开证申请书并办理申请开证手续。

知识目标

掌握信用证的业务流程和开证申请书的内容，熟悉信用证的当事人和申请开证步骤。

2010 年 4 月 19 日，浙江龙江机械有限公司与日本 Takashi Machinery Ltd. 就进口 2 台数控车床 CNC Lathe，签订如下进口合同。

CONTRACT

Contract No: TM20100066　　**Date of Signature:** April 19, 2010

The Buyer: Zhejiang Longjiang Machine Co., Ltd.

Address: No. 88, Wenhui Road, Hangzhou, China

Tel: 0086-571-86739270　Fax: 0086-571-86739271

The Seller: Takashi Machinery Co., Ltd.

Address: No.108, Aza Shinbo, Ohaza Yamaya, Ojiya City, Niigata Pref., Japan

Tel: 0081-258-82-4309　Fax: 0081-258-83-1367

This Contract is made by and between the Buyer and Seller, whereby the Buyer agrees to buy and the Seller agrees to sell the under-mentioned commodity according to the terms and conditions stipulated below:

1. **Description of commodity:** Microstar TNC-L09 CNC Lathe
2. **Quantity:** 1 set
3. **Unit Price:** JPY5800000.00 /set CFR Shanghai, China
4. **Total Value:** JPY5800000.00 (Say JPY Five Million Eight Hundred Thousand Only)
5. **Country of Origin and Manufacturer:** Japan/ Takashi Machinery Co., Ltd.
6. **Time of Shipment:** Within 1 month after the Seller received the L/C.
7. **Port of Shipment and Destination:** From any port in Japan to Shanghai, China
8. **Insurance:** To be covered by the Buyer.

（续）

9. Packing: The goods shall be packed suitable for long distance ocean transportation and well protected against dampness, moisture, shock, rust and rough handling. The Seller shall be liable for any damage to the commodity on account of improper for any rust damage attributable to inadequate or improper protective measure taken by the Seller, and in such case or cases any losses and/or expenses incurred in consequence thereof shall be borne by the Seller. **10. Shipping Mark:** TM20100066 Shanghai, China **11. Terms of Payment:** The Buyer shall open 100% L/C at sight in favor of the Seller and remaining valid for negotiation in Japan for further 15 days after the effected shipment. Advising bank: Bank of China, Tokyo Branch SWIFT: BKCHJPJT×××× **12. Documents:** a. Full set of clean on board ocean Bills of Lading, blank endorsed, marked "freight prepaid" and "contract no.", made out to order, and notify the Buyer. b. Signed Commercial Invoice, indicating contract No., shipping mark No. in 1 original and 3 copies c. Packing List with indication of both gross and net weights, measurements and quantity of each item packed in 1 original and 2 copies d. Certificate of Quality and Quantity issued by the Manufacturer in 1 original and 2 copies e. Certificate of Japanese Origin issued by Chamber of Commerce & Industry in Japan in 1 original and 1 copy. f. Seller's certified copy of the Fax dispatched to the Buyer within 3 days after the shipment date, advising the contract No., name of commodity, quantity, gross and net weight, invoice value, name of vessel, shipment date, and ETA. g. Certificate of Treatment issued by J.P.Q.A. if packing is made with wooden case, or, one original Certificate of Non-wooden Packing Declaration if packing is not made with wooden case. **13. Banking Charges:** All banking charges outside the opening bank are for the Seller's account. **14. Other Terms:** (omitted) This contract is made in two originals, one original for each party in witness thereof. **THE BUYER:** Zhejiang Longjiang Machine Co., Ltd. 龙江 **THE SELLER:** Takashi Machinery Co., Ltd. 山本桥一

【任务 1】根据进口合同填写开证申请书

2010 年 4 月 23 日，浙江龙江机械有限公司外贸单证员季华需根据以上进口合同的要求填写开证申请书，并向其开户行——中国农业银行浙江省分行国际业务部（地址：杭州市庆春路 30 号，邮编：310003）办理申请开证手续。要求采用 SWIFT 电报方式开证，所有单据要注明开证日期、信用证号码和开证行名称。中国农业银行浙江省分行给予浙江龙江机械有限公司的开证授信额度为 100 万美元。

IRREVOCABLE DOCUMENTARY CREDIT APPLICATION

To: Date:

( ) Issue by airmail ( ) With brief advice by teletransmission ( ) Issue by teletransmission ( ) Issue by express	Credit No. Date and place of expiry
Applicant	Beneficiary
Advising Bank	Amount: Say:

（续）

<table>
<tr><td>Partial shipments
(　) allowed
(　) not allowed</td><td>Transshipment
(　) allowed
(　) not allowed</td><td rowspan="3">Credit available with______________
By (　) sight payment　(　) acceptance
(　) negotiation　(　) deferred payment at
against the documents detailed herein
(　) and beneficiary’s draft(s) for ___ % of invoice value
at________________ sight
drawn on______________</td></tr>
<tr><td colspan="2">Loading on board:
not later than:
For transportation to:</td></tr>
<tr><td colspan="2">(　) FOB (　) CFR (　) CIF (　) other terms</td></tr>
<tr><td colspan="3">Documents required: (marked with ×)
1. (　) Signed commercial invoice in ______ copies indicating L/C No. and Contract No. ______.
2. (　) Full set of clean on board Bills of Lading made out to order and blank endorsed, marked “freight [　] to collect / [　]prepaid” notifying ______ .
(　) Airway bills/cargo receipt/copy of railway bills issued by ______ showing “freight [　]to collect/[　] prepaid” [　] indicating freight amount and consigned to ______ .
3. (　) Insurance Policy/Certificate in ______ for ______ of the invoice value blank endorsed, covering ______ .
4. (　) Packing List/Weight Memo in ______ copies indicating quantity, gross and net weights of each package.
5. (　) Certificate of Quantity and/or Quality in ______ copies issued by ______.
6. (　) Certificate of ____Origin in____ copies issued by ______.
7. (　) Beneficiary’s certified copy of fax send to the applicant within ______ days after shipment advising L/C No., name of vessel, date of shipment, name, quantity, weight and value of goods.
(　) Other documents, if any.</td></tr>
<tr><td colspan="3">Description of goods:</td></tr>
<tr><td colspan="3">Additional instructions:
1. (　) All banking charges outside the opening bank are for beneficiary’s account.
2. (　) Documents must be presented within ______ days after date of shipment but within the validity of this credit
(　) Other terms, if any.</td></tr>
</table>

STAMP OF APPLICANT:

【任务 2】办理申请开证手续

浙江龙江机械有限公司向中国农业银行浙江省分行国际业务部提交开证申请书和相关材料，办理申请开证手续。

【任务 1】根据进口合同填写开证申请书

外贸单证员季华根据合同和其他信息填写开证申请书。

1. 申请书抬头

在申请书抬头（To）后面填写开证行：Agricultural Bank of China, Zhejiang Branch。

2. 申请日期

本栏目（Date）填写申请日期：April 23, 2010。

3. 信用证开立方式

采用电开，即 SWIFT，在 Issue by teletransmission 前打“×”。

注意：根据银行开证申请数填写操作习惯，在正确选择项前要打“×”，而不是打“√”。

4. 开证申请人

本栏目（Applicant）填写开证申请人，即进口合同买方的名称和地址：Zhejiang Longjiang Machine Co., Ltd.，No. 88, Wenhui Road, Hangzhou, China。

5. 受益人

本栏目（Beneficiary）填写受益人，即进口合同卖方的名称和地址：Takashi Machinery Co., Ltd.，No.108, Aza Shinbo, Ohaza Yamaya, Ojiya City, Niigata Pref., Japan。

6. 通知行

本栏目（Advising Bank）填写通知行名称、地址和 SWIFT 号码，若卖方没有提供，则由开证行指定。本业务填写：Bank of China, Tokyo Branch，SWIFT: BKCHJPJT××××。

7. 金额

本栏目（Amount）填写信用证的大小写金额：JPY5800000.00，Say：JPY Five Million Eight Hundred Thousand Only。

8. 分批装运

根据进口合同规定，不允许分批装运，在 not allowed 前打“×”。

9. 转运

根据进口合同规定，不允许转运，在 not allowed 前打“×”。

10. 装运港

本栏目（Loading on board）填写装运港：Any port in Japan。

11. 目的港

本栏目（For transportation to）填写目的港：Shanghai, China。

注意：若有转运港，则在目的港后加 via，如 Liverpool, U.K. via Hong Kong。

12. 最迟装运日期

本栏目（not later than）填写最迟装运日期：May 31, 2010。

13. 贸易术语

本栏目填写所采用的贸易术语，在 CFR 前打“×”。

注意：若所采用的贸易术语不是 FOB、CFR 或 CIF，则在 other terms 前打“×”，然后写上具体的贸易术语，如 CIP。

14. 指定银行和付款方式

在 Credit available with 后填写指定银行，并选择对应的付款方式。本业务根据进口合同的规定，在 Credit available with 后填写 any bank in Japan，并在 negotiation 前打“×”。

15. 汇票条款

若需要出具汇票，则本栏目需填写汇票金额、期限和付款人。本业务的汇票金额填写发票金额的 100%，期限填写 at sight。付款人填写 issuing bank。

16．单据条款

根据进口合同的要求或实际需要选择所需提供的单据。本业务选择商业发票、海运提单、装箱单、数量和质量证明、一般原产地证、装运通知。并按照合同要求在“Other documents, if any”前的括号内打“×”，然后填写“Certificate of Treatment issued by J.P.Q.A. if packing is made with wooden case, or, one original Certificate of Non-wooden Packing Declaration if packing is not made with wooden case.”。

17．货物描述

本栏目（Description of goods）填写货物描述：Microstar TNC-L09 CNC Lathe, 1 set, JPY5800000.00/set CFR Shanghai, China; Country of Origin and Manufacturer: Japan/Takashi Machinery Co., Ltd.; Shipping Mark: TM20100066/Shanghai, China。

18．特殊条款

选择常规费用条款：All banking charges outside the opening bank are for beneficiary's account。

根据合同要求，规定装运日期后 15 天内交单：Documents must be presented within 15 days after date of shipment but within the validity of this credit。

并在“Other documents, if any”前的括号内打“×”，然后填写“All documents must indicate the L/C no., date of issue and the name of issuing bank.”。

19．信用证效期和交单地点

交单地点一般情况下在受益人所在国，信用证效期一般是最迟装运日期加交单期，本业务填写：June 15, 2010, in Japan。

20．签章

申请书内容填写准确后，对正面和背面分别进行盖章签名：

浙江龙江机械有限公司
龙　江

填制好的开证申请书如下。

IRREVOCABLE DOCUMENTARY CREDIT APPLICATION

To: Agricultural Bank of China, Zhejiang Branch　　Date: April 23, 2010

(　) Issue by airmail (　) With brief advice by teletransmission (×) Issue by teletransmission (　) Issue by express	Credit No. Date and place of expiry June 15, 2010, in Japan
Applicant Zhejiang Longjiang Machine Co., Ltd. No. 88, Wenhui Road, Hangzhou, China	Beneficiary Takashi Machinery Co., Ltd. No.108, Aza Shinbo, Ohaza Yamaya, Ojiya City, Niigata Pref., Japan
Advising Bank Bank of China, Tokyo Branch SWIFT: BKCHJPJT××××	Amount: JPY5800000.00 Say: JPY Five Million Eight Hundred Thousand Only

（续）

<table>
<tr><td>Partial shipments
（ ）allowed
（×）not allowed</td><td>Transshipment
（ ）allowed
（×）not allowed</td><td rowspan="3">Credit available with any bank in Japan
By（ ）sight payment （ ）acceptance
（×）negotiation （ ）deferred payment at
against the documents detailed herein
（×）and beneficiary's draft(s) for 100 % of invoice value at ××× sight
drawn on issuing bank</td></tr>
<tr><td>Loading on board:
not later than
For transportation to:</td><td>any port in Japan
May 31, 2010
Shanghai, China</td></tr>
<tr><td colspan="2">（ ）FOB（×）CFR（ ）CIF（ ）other terms</td></tr>
<tr><td colspan="3">Documents required: (marked with ×)
1.（×）Signed commercial invoice in 1 original and 3 copies indicating Contract No. TM20100066 and shipping mark no.
2.（×）Full set of clean on board Bills of Lading made out to order and blank endorsed, marked "freight [ ] to collect / [×]prepaid" and "contract No." notifying the applicant
（ ）Airway bills/cargo receipt/copy of railway bills issued by ______ showing "freight [ ]to collect/ [ ] prepaid" [ ] indicating freight amount and consigned to ______
3.（ ）Insurance Policy/Certificate in ________ of the invoice value blank endorsed, covering ______.
4.（×）Packing List/Weight Memo in 1 original and 2 copies indicating gross and net weights, measurements and quantity of each item.
5.（×）Certificate of Quantity and/or Quality in 1 original and 2 copies issued by the Manufacturer.
6.（×）Certificate of Japanese Origin in 1 original and 1 copies issued by Chamber of Commerce & Industry in Japan.
7.（×）Beneficiary's certified copy of fax send to the applicant within three days after shipment date advising contract No., name of commodity, quantity, gross and net weight, invoice value, name of vessel, shipment date, and ETA.
（×）Other documents, if any
Certificate of Treatment issued by J.P.Q.A. if packing is made with wooden case, or, one original Certificate of Non-wooden Packing Declaration if packing is not made with wooden case.</td></tr>
<tr><td colspan="3">Description of goods:
Microstar TNC-L09 CNC Lathe, 1 set, JPY5800000.00/set CFR Shanghai, China;
Country of Origin and Manufacturer: Japan/Takashi Machinery Co., Ltd.;
Shipping Mark: TM20100066/Shanghai, China</td></tr>
<tr><td colspan="3">Additional instructions:
1.（×）All banking charges outside the opening bank are for beneficiary's account.
2.（×）Documents must be presented within 15 days after date of shipment but within the validity of this credit
（×）Other terms, if any
All documents must indicate the L/C No., date of issue and the name of issuing bank.</td></tr>
</table>

STAMP OF APPLICANT: 浙江龙江机械有限公司

龙江

然后，在开证申请书的背面，对开证申请人承诺书进行盖章签名。

【任务 2】办理申请开证手续

外贸单证员季华将填写好的申请开证所需的开证申请书、合同副本以及自动进口许可证（因为数控冲床进口须办理自动进口许可证）交中国农业银行浙江省分行国际业务部，办理申请开证手续。由于申请的金额没有超过 100 万美元的开证授信额度，无须提供开证保证金。

知识支撑

一、信用证定义和特点

1. 定义

根据UCP600（Uniform Customs and Practice for Documentary Credits, ICC Publication No.600，跟单信用证统一惯例，国际商会第 600 号出版物）规定，Credit means any arrangement, however named or described, that is irrevocable and thereby constitutes a definite undertaking of the issuing bank to honour a complying presentation. 信用证意指一项约定，无论其如何命名或描述，该约定不可撤销并因此构成开证行对于相符交单予以兑付的确定承诺。

其中，相符交单（Complying Presentation）是指与信用证条款、本惯例的相关适用条款以及国际标准银行实务一致的交单。承付（Honour）是指：①即期付款，如果信用证为即期付款信用证；②承诺延期付款并在承诺到期日付款，如果信用证为延期付款信用证；③承兑受益人开出的汇票并在汇票到期日付款，如果信用证为承兑信用证。

2. 特点

（1）跟单信用证是一种银行信用，开证行承担第一性的付款责任。

在跟单信用证业务中，开证行一旦开出信用证，就承担了第一性的付款责任。只要受益人在规定的期限内交单，并做到“单单相符，单证相符”，开证行就必须毫不延误地履行付款责任。因此，跟单信用证是一种银行信用。

（2）跟单信用证是一项独立文件，它不依附于贸易合同而存在。

根据UCP600规定，信用证虽然依据贸易合同开立，但一经开出，便成为独立于贸易合同之外的一项文件，不再受合同的约束。贸易合同是进出口商之间的契约，只对进出口双方有约束力，而信用证则是开证行与受益人之间的法律文件，开证行、受益人和其他参与信用证业务的银行受信用证的约束。

（3）跟单信用证业务是纯单据业务，银行处理单据而非货物、服务及其他行为。

根据UCP600规定，在信用证业务中，有关各方处理的是单据，而不是与单据有关的货物、服务及其他行为。银行只根据表面相符的单据付款，而对任何单据的形式、完整性、准确性、真实性以及伪造或法律效力等概不负责。所以，在单证相符的情况下，开证申请人付款后，发现货物与单据不一致，也只能由开证申请人自己凭买卖合同向受益人交涉。相反，即使货物相符，但单据与信用证规定不符，开证行也有权拒付。

二、跟单信用证的当事人

1. 开证申请人

开证申请人（Applicant）又称开证人，通常是指进口商或买方。他填写开证申请书并签字，请求往来银行开出以国外出口商或卖方为受益人的信用证。

2．开证行

开证行（Issuing Bank）是应开证申请人请求代表申请人开出信用证的银行。一般情况下，开证行是开证申请人的账户行。若双方没有账户往来关系，信用证中往往会增加一个与开证申请人有账户往来关系的银行，即开证申请人的银行（Applicant Bank）。

3．受益人

受益人（Beneficiary）是指信用证上所指定的有权使用信用证并获得付款的人，即出口商或卖方。受益人和开证行是信用证这份合约的缔约双方。一旦受益人接受信用证，该合约即告生效。

4．通知行

通知行（Advising Bank）是指应开证行的委托将信用证通知指定受益人的银行，往往是出口方的银行。通知行的责任是审核信用证表面的真实性和开证行的资信状况，它的权利是收取信用证通知手续费。如果开证行或开证申请人直接把信用证寄给受益人，受益人应把信用证拿到银行，以证实信用证的真实性和开证行的资信状况，以免上当受骗。

5．保兑行

保兑行（Confirming Bank）是指经开证行授权或应其请求而在信用证上加上它的保兑的通知行或任何其他银行。信用证一经保兑行保兑，受益人就获得开证行和保兑行的双重付款保证。保兑行与开证行一样，承担第一性付款责任。

6．议付行

议付行（Negotiating Bank）是指由开证行指定的愿意购买该信用证项下的汇票或单据（即押汇）的银行，往往是由通知行担当议付行。

7．付款行

付款行（Paying Bank）是开证行指定的根据信用证付款的银行。若信用证要求出具汇票，它就是汇票付款人，有时开证行自己就是付款行。付款行一旦付款，就是最终付款，对出票人和/或善意持票人不能追索。

8．承兑行

承兑行（Accepting Bank）是承兑信用证上规定的承兑远期汇票并在到期日付款的银行。

9．偿付行

偿付行（Reimbursing Bank）是开证行的代理人，它可以是开证行的分行，也可以是第三方银行。按照开证行给予的指示或授权，根据某一特定的信用证，它承付付款行或承兑行或议付行的索偿。如偿付行并不偿付，那么，开证行必须自行偿付。在这种情况下，开证行将对付款行或承兑行或议付行由于偿付行并不偿付而遭受的利息损失负责。

三、信用证业务流程

以即期议付信用证为例，信用证结算方式的业务程序，大体要经过以下几个环节：（见图 1-1）

（1）买卖双方签订销售合同，并在合同中订明使用信用证结算方式。

（2）进口商按照合同规定向当地银行提出申请，还要缴纳若干押金或提供其他担保。

（3）开证行将信用证开给出口商所在地的分行或代理行，并请他们办理信用证通知事宜。

（4）通知行核对信用证上印鉴或密押无误后将信用证通知受益人。

（5）受益人将信用证与贸易合同核对无误后，立即备货装运，并取得运输单据。

（6）备齐信用证所规定的单据，在信用证有效期内向当地银行交单议付，或向信用证明确指定的议付银行交单议付。

（7）议付行将单据与信用证核对无误后，按汇票金额扣除邮程利息后付款给受益人。

（8）议付行将汇票和单据寄给开证行或其指定的银行索偿。

（9）开证行或其指定银行审核单证无误后，偿付给议付行。

（10）开证行通知进口商付款。

（11）开证申请人向开证行付款赎取单据。

（12）开证申请人凭提单向船公司提货。

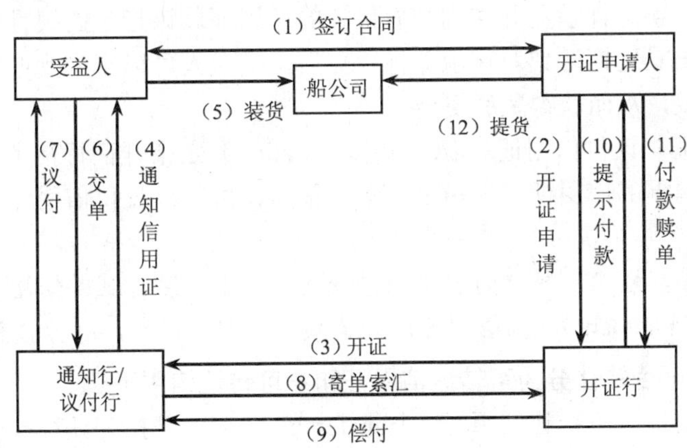

图 1-1　信用证业务流程图

四、信用证的开证形式

信用证一般包括信开和电开两种基本开证形式。信开信用证是指开证行用书信格式缮制并通过邮寄方式送达通知行的信用证。目前，这种开证方式较少使用。

电开信用证是指开证行用电信方式（SWIFT 报文）开立和通知的信用证，分为全电开信用证和简电开信用证。

（1）全电开信用证是以电文形式开出的完整信用证，这种信用证是有效的，可以凭以交单收款，采用 MT700/701 的 SWIFT 报文开立。

（2）简电开信用证是将信用证金额、有效期等主要内容用电文预先通知受益人，采用 MT705 的 SWIFT 报文开立。其目的是让受益人早日备货。但由于内容不完整，在简电开信用证中往往会注明“随寄证实书”（Mail Confirmation to Follow）。简电开信用证是无效的，受益人要注意在证实书未收到之前，千万不能仓促出货，万一证实书内容与简电开信用证有出入，有可能无法正常收款。

五、信用证种类

1．根据信用证付款方式的不同分为即期付款信用证、延期付款信用证、承兑信用证和议付信用证

（1）即期付款信用证。即期付款信用证（L/C by Sight Payment）是指开证行指定一家银行或自己即期付款的信用证。该指定的银行称为付款行，即期付款信用证一般要求受益人递交以付款行为付款人的即期汇票。由于某些国家对汇票要征收印花税，因此即期付款信用证有时也不要求受益人递交汇票。

（2）延期付款信用证。延期付款信用证（L/C by Deferred Payment）是指开证行指定一家银行或自己进行延期付款的信用证。延期付款信用证的付款期限一般是海运提单日或交单日后一段期间（At ××× days after B/L date or the date of presentation）。延期付款信用证不要求受益人出具汇票。

（3）承兑信用证。承兑信用证（L/C by Acceptance）是指开证行指定一家银行或自己对受益人递交的远期汇票进行承兑并在到期后付款的信用证。该指定的银行称为承兑行。承兑信用证要求受益人出具远期汇票。在承兑行承兑后，受益人可以拿未到期的银行承兑汇票去另一家银行进行贴现，从而获得融通资金。

（4）议付信用证。议付信用证（L/C by Negotiation）是指开证行指定一家银行购买该信用证项下的汇票或单据的信用证。该指定的银行称为议付行。议付信用证一般要求受益人出具即期或远期汇票。

另外，在实践中，还有一种同时使用两种或两种以上付款方式的信用证，即混合付款信用证（L/C by Mixed Payment），如信用证部分金额采用即期付款，部分金额采用延期付款。

2．根据信用证可否转让分为可转让信用证和不可转让信用证

（1）可转让信用证。可转让信用证（Transferable L/C）是指开证行授权有关银行在受益人（即第一受益人）的要求下，可将信用证的全部或一部分金额转让给第三者（即第二受益人）使用的信用证。可转让信用证只限转让一次，如果允许分批装运，在总和不超过信用证金额的前提下，可分别转让给几个第二受益人；如果不允许分批装运，则只能转让给一个第二受益人。可转让信用证主要适用于中间商贸易。

（2）不可转让信用证。不可转让信用证（Untransferable L/C）是指受益人无权转让给其他人使用的信用证。如果信用证未注明“可转让”，均为不可转让信用证。

3．其他形式的信用证

（1）循环信用证。循环信用证（Revolving L/C）是按照信用证条款，其金额可以恢复至原金额而无需进行任何具体修改的一种信用证。为了便于向同一供货商持续、重复采购，往往使用循环信用证。就这种信用证来说，开证行只开一张信用证，它适用于在每一确定的日历时间，可用一笔固定金额。货物是按规定的间隔时间分批交货。当受益人提用了信用证金额，原来的信用证金额还可用于下一个日历时间。其循环的方式主要有三种：

1）自动循环：信用证金额在其被提用后立即恢复至原金额。

2）半自动循环：在某一特定时间内开证行并未送达停止恢复原金额通知，信用证金额恢复至原金额。

3）非自动循环：即只是在收到开证行恢复原金额通知时将信用证金额复原。

（2）红条款信用证。红条款信用证（Red clause L/C）又称为预支信用证（Anticipatory L/C），是指开证行授权指定银行向受益人预付全部或部分信用证金额，由开证行保证偿还利息的信用证。这是一种装船前的资金融通，意在帮助出口商生产或采购所出售的货物。

（3）背对背信用证。背对背信用证（Back to Back L/C）是指受益人要求原证的通知行或其他银行以原证为基础，另开一张内容相似的新信用证。对背信用证通常是由于中间商为转售他人货物谋利或两国不能直接进行交易，需通过第三国商人而开立。

（4）对开信用证。对开信用证（Reciprocal L/C）是指两张信用证的开证申请人互以对方为受益人开立的信用证。两证的受益人和开证申请人对调，两证的开证行和通知行对调，两证的金额可相等也可不等，两证可同时生效也可先后生效。对开信用证适用于易货贸易、来料来件加工和补偿贸易。

六、开立信用证的程序

进口商在合同规定的时间向银行办理申请开立信用证手续如下：

（1）填写开证申请书。进口商根据银行规定的开证申请书格式，一般填写一式三份，一份由银行结算部门留存，一份由银行信贷部门留存，一份由开证申请人留存。填写开证申请书，必须按合同条款的具体规定，写明对信用证的各项要求，内容要明确、完整，无词意不清的记载。开证申请书（Irrevocable Documentary Credit Application）的格式和内容各银行印制的都差不多，大同小异。

（2）开证申请人承诺书。开证申请书的背面是开证申请人承诺书，是开证申请人对开证行的声明，用以明确双方责任，内容如下：

开证申请人承诺书

致：×××银行

我公司已依法办妥一切必要的进口手续，兹谨请贵行为我公司依照本申请书所列条款开立不可撤销的跟单信用证，并承诺如下：

一、同意贵行依照国际商会第___号出版物《跟单信用证统一惯例》办理该笔信用证项下的一切事宜，并同意承担由此产生的一切责任。

二、及时提供贵行要求我公司提供的真实、有效的文件及资料，接受贵行的审查监督。

三、在贵行规定的期限内支付该信用证项下的各种款项，包括货款及贵行和有关银行的各项手续费、电信费、杂费、利息以及国外受益人拒绝承担的有关银行费用等。

四、在贵行信用证单据通知书规定期限内，书面通知贵行办理对外付款/承兑/确认延期付款/拒付手续。否则贵行有权自行确定对外付款/承兑/确认延期付款/拒付，并由我公司承担由此引起的一切责任和后果。

五、我公司如因单证有不符之处而拟拒绝付款/拒绝承兑/拒绝确认延期付款时，将在贵行单据通知书规定的期限内提出书面拒付，并附拒付理由书一式两份，一次列明所有不符点。对单据存在的不符点，贵行有独立的最终认定权和处理权。经贵行根据国际惯例审核认为不属可据以拒付的不符点的，贵行有权主动对外付款/承兑/确认延期付款，我公司对此放弃抗辩权。

六、该信用证如需修改，由我公司向贵行提出书面申请。贵行可根据具体情况确定能否办理修改。我公司保证支付因信用证修改而产生的一切费用。

七、经贵行承兑的远期汇票或确认的延期付款，我公司无权以任何理由要求贵行止付。

八、按上述承诺，贵行在对外付款时，有主动借记我公司在贵行的账户款项。若发生任何形式的垫付，我公司将无条件承担由此产生的债务、利息和费用等，并按贵行要求及时清偿。

九、在收到贵行开出信用证、修改书的副本之后，及时核对，如有不符之处，将在收到副本后的两个工作日内书面通知贵行。否则，视为正确无误。

十、该信用证如因邮寄、电信传递发生遗失、延误、错漏，贵行概不负责。

十一、本申请书一律用英文填写。如有中文填写而引发的歧义，贵行概不负责。

十二、因开证申请书字迹不清或词意含混而引起的一切后果均由我公司负责。

（续）

十三、如发生争议需诉讼，同意由贵行所在地法院管辖。 十四、我公司已对开证申请书及承诺书各印就条款进行审慎研阅，对各条款含义与贵行理解一致。 同意受理 银行盖章 负责人 或授权代理人	 申请人（盖章） 法定代表人 或授权代理人 年　月　日

（3）提交有关合同的副本及附件。为了最大限度地回避风险，除开证申请书外，银行还会要求开证申请人提供其他相关资料，如进口合同副本、进口许可证、与贷款相关文件等。

（4）开证抵押。如果开证行对开证申请人所交材料审查通过后，还会要求申请人提供押金，即保证金。从理论上讲，申请人提供不动产作抵押，或以动产及财产权利作押，以及提供其他银行的保函都是可以的，但实际中多是要求以现金作押。保证金可以用现汇，也可从申请人的存款中扣除，拨入保证金账户。具体交纳保证金的数额与申请人的资信、货物的市场销售等情况有关，有时高达90%～100%，有时仅百分之几，甚至免收。如果申请人同时也是另一份信用证的受益人，则可以要求用出口信用证项下的权益代替押金。银行如果觉得出口信用证下的收汇有把握，而且金额超过申请开立的用于进口的信用证金额，也可以接受申请人要求，以正本出口信用证作抵押。此外，如果申请人提供其他银行的有效保函，保证承担因开证而引起的各项义务，则开证行也可以免除抵押的要求。

大多数要求开立跟单信用证的客户都会在一段时间内进行多笔交易，因而也将多次申请开证。若每进行一笔业务都开展一次资信调查，则手续较为繁杂。因此银行往往根据资信调查情况规定一个授信额度，此额度是免保开证的最高限额，有了授信额度之后，在授信金额范围内开证可不收保证金，超过授信额度时才收取保证金。国外保证金通常不计利息。

◆ 实训项目 1-1

2010 年 8 月 12 日，浙江安妮进出口有限公司与中国香港 U.A.C.C. (Pacifique) S.A.就进口非洲楝木，签订如下进口合同。

PURCHASE CONTRACT

CONTRACT NO.: ANNIE10029　　　　DATE:August 12, 2010

THE BUYER: Zhejiang Annie Import and Export co., Ltd.
1298 Huaxing Road, Hangzhou, China
Tel: 0086-571-89991351　　Fax: 0086-571-89991352

THE SELLER: U.A.C.C. (Pacifique) S.A.
18th Floor, Tacwood Plaza, 32 Des Voeux Road, Central, Hong Kong
Tel: 00852-2581-3097　　Fax: 00852-2581-3099

This Contract is made by and between the Buyer and Seller, whereby the Buyer agrees to buy and the Seller agrees to sell the under-mentioned commodity according to the terms and conditions stipulated below:

（续）

DESCRIPTION OF GOODS	QUANTITY	UNIT PRICE	AMOUNT
Sapelli Log Diameter:60-80cm Length: 5m and up Grade: Slicing grade Origin: Cameroon	$150m^3$	FOB Douala, Cameroon EUR370.00/m^3	EUR55500.00
Total	$150m^3$		EUR55500.00
Total Contract Value: Say EURO Fifty Five Thousand Five Hundred Only.			

PORT OF LOADING: Douala, Cameroon

PORT OF DESTINATION: Zhangjiagang, China

SHIPMENT: Cargo should be shipped in the container not later than October 1, 2010. Partial shipment is not allowed and transshipment is allowed.

INSURANCE: Covered by the Buyer.

PAYMENT: L/C at sight, issued before August 28, 2010, the documents must be presented within 21 days after the date of shipment.

DOCUMENTS:

1. Signed Commercial Invoice in quintuplicate indicating L/C No.

2. Packing List in quintuplicate indicating the diameter, length and measurement of each log.

3. Full set of clean 'on board' ocean Bills of Lading made out to order and blank endorsed, marked 'freight collect' and notify applicant.

4. Certificate of Origin in triplicate issued by the manufacturer.

5. One original and two copies of phytosanitary certificate issued by the competent government quarantine authority of the export country.

INSPECTION AND CLAIMS:

1. After arrival of the goods at the port of destination, if any discrepancies are found regarding the specifications or the quantity/weight or both, except those for which either the insurance company or the shipping company is responsible , the Buyer shall, within 60 days after discharge of the goods at the port of destination ,have the right either to reject the goods or to claim against the Seller on the strength of the relevant certificate issued.

2. Any and all claims shall be regarded as accepted if the Seller fails to reply within 30 days after receipt of the Buyer's claim.

SETTLEMENT OF CLAIMS:

In case the Sellers are liable for the discrepancies and a claim is made by the Buyers within the period of claim as stipulated in Clause INSPECTION AND CLAIMS of this contract, the sellers shall settle the claim upon the agreement of the Buyers in the following ways:

1. Agree to rejection of the goods and returned to the Buyer the value of the goods so rejected in the same currency as contracted herein, and to bear all direct losses and expenses in connection therewith including interest accrued, banking charges, freight, insurance premium, inspection charges, storage, stevedore charges and all other necessary expenses required for the custody and protection of the rejected goods.

2. Devaluate the goods according to the degree of inferiority, extent of damage and amount of losses suffered by the Buyers.

3. Replace the defective goods with new ones, which conform to the specifications, quality as stipulated in this contract, and bear all expenses incurred to and direct losses sustained by the Buyers.

FORCE MAJEURE:

The seller shall not be held responsible for the delay in delivery or non-delivery of the goods due to Force Majeure. However the sellers shall advise the Buyers immediately of the occurrence and within fourteen days thereafter, the seller shall send by airmail to the buyers for their acceptance a certificate of the accident issued by the Competent Government Authorities of the place where the accident occurs as evidence thereof. Under such circumstances the sellers, however, are still under the obligation to take all necessary measures to hasten the delivery of the goods. In case the accident lasts for more than six weeks, the buyer shall have the right to cancel the contract.

LATE DELIVERY AND PENALTY:

In case of delayed delivery, except for force majeure cases, the Sellers shall pay to the Buyers for every week of delay a penalty amounting to 0.5% of the total value of the goods whose delivery has been delayed. Any fractional part of a week is to be considered a full week. The total amount of penalty shall not, however, exceed 5% of the total value of the goods involved in the late delivery and is deducted from the amount due to the Sellers by the paying bank at the time of negotiation, or by the Buyers direct at the payments. In case the period of delay exceeds ten weeks after the stipulated delivery date, the Buyers have the right to terminate this contract but the

（续）

Sellers shall not thereby be exempted from the payment of penalty.

ARBITRATION:

All disputes in connection with this contract or the execution thereof shall be settled friendly through negotiations. In case no settlement can be reached through negotiation, the case should then be submitted for arbitration to the Foreign Trade Arbitration Commission of the China Council for the Promotion of International Trade, Beijing, in accordance with the provisional rules of procedures of the Foreign Trade Arbitration Commission of the China Council for the Promotion of International Trade. The arbitration shall take place in Beijing and the decision rendered by the said authorities for revising the decision. The arbitration fee shall be borne by the losing party. Or the arbitration may be settled in the third country mutually agreed on by both parties.

This contract is made in two original copies and becomes valid after signature, one copy to be held by each party.

ACCEPTED AND CONFIRMED BY (SELLER):	FOR AND ON BEHALF OF (BUYER):
U.A.C.C. (Pacifique) S.A.	ZHEJIANG ANNIE IMPORT & EXPORT CO., LTD.
Jackie Wang	蔡海峰
------------------------------	------------------------------

【任务 1】填写开证申请书

2010 年 8 月 18 日，浙江安妮进出口有限公司外贸单证员马金春需根据与 U.A.C.C. (Pacifique) S.A.签订的进口合同 ANNIE10029 的要求和信息，填写开证申请书并向中国农业银行浙江省分行办理申请开证手续：①付款方式是采用自由议付；②通知行是 BANK OF CHINA (HONG KONG) LIMITED；③除发票和汇票以外的单据接受第三方单据；④所有单据显示信用证号码。中国农业银行浙江省分行给予浙江安妮进出口有限公司的开证授信额度为 80 万美元。

IRREVOCABLE DOCUMENTARY CREDIT APPLICATION

To: Date:

<table>
<tr><td colspan="2">(　) Issue by airmail
(　) With brief advice by teletransmission
(　) Issue by teletransmission
(　) Issue by express</td><td>Credit No.

Date and place of expiry</td></tr>
<tr><td colspan="2">Applicant</td><td>Beneficiary</td></tr>
<tr><td colspan="2">Advising Bank</td><td>Amount:
Say:</td></tr>
<tr><td>Partial shipments
(　) allowed
(　) not allowed</td><td>Transshipment
(　) allowed
(　) not allowed</td><td rowspan="3">Credit available with______________________
By (　) sight payment　(　) acceptance
(　) negotiation　(　) deferred payment at
against the documents detailed herein
(　) and beneficiary's draft(s) for ___ % of invoice value
at______________________ sight
drawn on__________________</td></tr>
<tr><td colspan="2">Loading on board:
not later than
For transportation to:</td></tr>
<tr><td colspan="2">(　) FOB (　) CFR (　) CIF (　) other terms</td></tr>
<tr><td colspan="3">Documents required: (marked with ×)
1. (　) Signed commercial invoice in ____ copies indicating L/C No. and Contract No. ______.
2. (　) Full set of clean on board Bills of Lading made out to order and blank endorsed, marked "freight [　] to collect / [　]prepaid" notifying ______ .
(　) Airway bills/cargo receipt/copy of railway bills issued by ______ showing "freight [　]to collect/[　] prepaid" [　] indicating freight amount and consigned to ______ .</td></tr>
</table>

（续）

3.（　）Insurance Policy/Certificate in ______ for ______ of the invoice value blank endorsed, covering ______. 4.（　）Packing List/Weight Memo in ______ copies indicating quantity, gross and net weights of each package. 5.（　）Certificate of Quantity and/or Quality in ______ copies issued by ______. 6.（　）Certificate of ______ Origin in ______ copies issued by ______. 7.（　）Beneficiary's certified copy of fax send to the applicant within ______ days after shipment advising L/C No., name of vessel, date of shipment, name, quantity, weight and value of goods. （　）Other documents, if any.
Description of goods:
Additional instructions: 1.（　）All banking charges outside the opening bank are for beneficiary's account. 2.（　）Documents must be presented within ______ days after date of shipment but within the validity of this credit. （　）Other terms, if any.

STAMP OF APPLICANT:

【任务 2】办理申请开证手续

浙江安妮进出口有限公司外贸单证员马金春向中国农业银行浙江省分行国际业务部提交开证申请书和相关材料，办理申请开证手续。

◆　实训项目 1-2

2010 年 10 月 11 日，上海冬冬贸易公司与日本 Nibo Shuzo Co., Ltd.就进口甘薯烧酒，签订如下进口合同。

CONTRACT

CONTRACT NO.:DD10106　　DATE: Oct. 11, 2010

THE SELLER: Nibo Shuzo Co., Ltd.
　　88 Tategamihonmachi, Makurazaki City, Kagoshima-pref, Japan
　　Tel: 0081-993-72-1908　Fax: 0081-993-72-1904

THE BUYER: Shanghai Dongdong Trading Company
　　No. 9980 Renmin Rd. Shanghai, China
　　Tel:0086-21-90128765　Fax: 0086-21-90128766

This Contract is made by and between the Buyer and Seller, whereby the Buyer agrees to buy and the Seller agrees to sell the

(续)

under-mentioned commodity according to the terms and conditions stipulated below:

1. Description of Goods, Quantity, Unit Price and Amount

Description of Goods	Quantity	Unit Price	Amount
Shochu Genshu, Sweet Potato 36.8% 720ml per Bottle	7200 Bottles	CFR Shanghai JPY580/Bottle	JPY4176000
Total	7200 Bottles		JPY4176000
Total Contract Amount in Words:			

2. Country of Origin: Japan

3. Port of Loading: Shibushi, Japan

4. Port of Destination: Shanghai, China

5. Delivery Time: not later than November 20, 2010

6. Partial Shipment: prohibited **Transshipment**: prohibited

7. Packing: Packed in 720ml/Bottle

8. Payment: The buyer will pay to the seller by T/T 30% of the contract value within 15 days after signing this contract. The remaining 70% of the contract value will be paid to the seller by L/C within 1 month after the B/L date.

Advising bank: Deutsche Bank AG, Osaka Branch

Address: Sanno Park Tower 2-11-1, Nagatacho, Chivoda-ku, Tokyo 1006170, Japan

SWIFT: DEUTJPJT

9. Insurance: covered by the Buyer.

10. Documents:

1) Full set of negotiable clean on board ocean Bills of Lading, marked "freight prepaid" , made out to order and blank endorsed, notifying the buyer.

2) Invoice in quintuplicate indicating contract number and shipping mark.

3) Packing list in 5 copies with indication of both gross and net weights, measurements quantity of each item.

4) Certificate of Quality and Quantity, each in three sets, issued by the Manufacturers as specified in of Clause 12 hereof.

5) Original certificate 3 sets issued by the manufacturer.

6) A true copy of Fax to advise the Buyer of shipment immediately the goods are loaded on ship as specified in Clause 11 hereof.

11. Shipping Advice:

The seller shall advise the buyer, 15 days before the month of shipment, of the time the goods will be ready for shipment.

The seller shall, immediately upon the completion of the loading of the goods, advise by fax the buyer of the contract number, commodity, quantity, invoiced value, gross weight, name of vessel and the date of sailing etc..

12. Inspection and Claims:

1) After arrival of the goods at the port of destination, the buyer shall apply to the Entry-exit Inspection & Quarantine Bureau of The People's Republic of China (herein after called the Bureau) for a preliminary inspection of the goods in respect of their quality, quantity /weight. If any discrepancies are found by the Bureau regarding the specifications or the quantity /weight or both, except those for which either the insurance company or the shipping company is responsible, the Buyer shall, within 120 days after discharge of the goods at the port of destination, have the right either to reject the goods or to claim against the Seller on the strength of the inspection certificate issued by the Bureau.

2) Any and all claims shall be regarded as accepted if the Seller fails to reply within 30 days after receipt of the Buyer's claim.

13. Settlement of Claims:

In case the Sellers are liable for the discrepancies and a claim is made by the Buyers within the period of claim as stipulated in Clause 12 of this contract, the sellers shall settle the claim upon the agreement of the Buyers in the following ways:

1) Agree to rejection of the goods and returned to the Buyer the value of the goods so rejected in the same currency as contracted herein, and to bear all direct losses and expenses in connection therewith including interest accrued, banking charges, freight, insurance premium, inspection charges, storage, stevedore charges and all other necessary expenses required for the custody and protection of the rejected goods.

2) Devaluate the goods according to the degree of inferiority, extent of damage and amount of losses suffered by the Buyers.

3) Replace the defective goods with new ones, which conform to the specifications, quality as stipulated in this contract, and bear all expenses incurred to and direct losses sustained by the Buyers.

（续）

14. Force Majeure:

The seller shall not be held responsible for the delay in delivery or non-delivery of the goods due to Force Majeure. However the sellers shall advise the Buyers immediately of the occurrence and within 10 days thereafter, the seller shall send by airmail to the buyers for their acceptance a certificate of the accident issued by the Competent Government Authorities of the place where the accident occurs as evidence thereof. Under such circumstances the sellers, however, are still under the obligation to take all necessary measures to hasten the delivery of the goods. In case the accident lasts for more than six weeks, the buyer shall have the right to cancel the contract.

15. Late Delivery and Penalty:

In case of delayed delivery, except for force majeure cases, the Sellers shall pay to the Buyers for every week of delay a penalty amounting to 0.5% of the total value of the goods whose delivery has been delayed. Any fractional part of a week is to be considered a full week. The total amount of penalty shall not, however, exceed 5% of the total value of the goods involved in the late delivery and is deducted from the amount due to the Sellers by the paying bank at the time of negotiation, or by the Buyers direct at the payments. In case the period of delay exceeds ten weeks after the stipulated delivery date, the Buyers have the right to terminate this contract but the Sellers shall not thereby be exempted from the payment of penalty.

16. Arbitration:

All disputes in connection with this contract or the execution thereof shall be settled friendly through negotiations. In case no settlement can be reached through negotiation, the case should then be submitted for arbitration to the Foreign Trade Arbitration Commission of the China Council for the Promotion of International Trade, Beijing, in accordance with the provisional rules of procedures of the Foreign Trade Arbitration Commission of the China Council for the Promotion of International Trade. The arbitration shall take place in Beijing and the decision rendered by the said authorities for revising the decision. The arbitration fee shall be borne by the losing party. Or the arbitration may be settled in the third country mutually agreed on by both parties.

This contract is made in two original copies and becomes valid after signature, one copy to be held by each party.

THE SELLER:	THE BUYER:
NIBO SHUZO CO., LTD.	SHANGHAI DONGDONG TRADING COMPANY
TACHIRO HOMBO	王冬冬
------------------------------	------------------------------

【任务 1】填写开证申请书

2010 年 10 月 13 日，上海冬冬贸易公司外贸单证员张丽莉需根据与 Nibo Shuzo Co., Ltd. 签订的进口合同 DD10106 的要求和其他相关信息，填写以下开证申请书并向中国银行上海市分行办理申请开证手续，所有单据显示信用证号码、开证日期和开证行名称。中国银行上海市分行给予上海冬冬贸易公司的开证授信额度为 50 万美元。

IRREVOCABLE DOCUMENTARY CREDIT APPLICATION

To: Date:

<table>
<tr><td colspan="2">( ) Issue by airmail
( ) With brief advice by teletransmission
( ) Issue by teletransmission
( ) Issue by express</td><td>Credit No.

Date and place of expiry</td></tr>
<tr><td colspan="2">Applicant</td><td>Beneficiary</td></tr>
<tr><td colspan="2">Advising Bank</td><td>Amount:
Say:</td></tr>
<tr><td>Partial shipments
( ) allowed
( ) not allowed</td><td>Transshipment
( ) allowed
( ) not allowed</td><td rowspan="3">Credit available with______________________
By ( ) sight payment ( ) acceptance
( ) negotiation ( ) deferred payment at
against the documents detailed herein
( ) and beneficiary's draft(s) for _____ % of invoice value
at____________________ sight
drawn on____________________</td></tr>
<tr><td colspan="2">Loading on board:
not later than
For transportation to:</td></tr>
<tr><td colspan="2">( ) FOB ( ) CFR ( ) CIF ( ) other terms</td></tr>
</table>

（续）

<table>
<tr><td>Documents required: (marked with ×)
1.（ ）Signed commercial invoice in ______ copies indicating L/C No. and Contract No. ______.
2.（ ）Full set of clean on board Bills of Lading made out to order and blank endorsed, marked “freight [ ] to collect / [ ]prepaid” notifying ______.
（ ）Airway bills/cargo receipt/copy of railway bills issued by ______ showing “freight [ ]to collect/[ ] prepaid” [ ] indicating freight amount and consigned to ______ .
3.（ ）Insurance Policy/Certificate in ______ for ______ of the invoice value blank endorsed, covering ______ .
4.（ ）Packing List/Weight Memo in ______ copies indicating quantity, gross and net weights of each package.
5.（ ）Certificate of Quantity and/or Quality in ______ copies issued by ______.
6.（ ）Certificate of ______ Origin in ______ copies issued by ______ .
7.（ ）Beneficiary’s certified copy of fax send to the applicant within ______ days after shipment advising L/C No., name of vessel, date of shipment, name, quantity, weight and value of goods.
（ ）Other documents, if any.</td></tr>
<tr><td>Description of goods:</td></tr>
<tr><td>Additional instructions:
1.（ ）All banking charges outside the opening bank are for beneficiary’s account.
2.（ ）Documents must be presented within ______ days after date of shipment but within the validity of this credit
（ ）Other terms, if any.</td></tr>
</table>

STAMP OF APPLICANT:

【任务 2】办理申请开证手续

上海冬冬贸易公司外贸单证员张丽莉向中国银行上海市分行国际业务部提交开证申请书和相关材料，办理申请开证手续。

项目二

审证和改证业务操作

学习目标

能力目标

能根据外贸合同审出信用证中的问题条款，针对问题条款提出修改意见。

知识目标

掌握信用证的内容、UCP600 改证相关条款，熟悉审证的依据和步骤、改证的原则和步骤。

导入项目

2010 年 3 月 3 日，浙江大同进出口有限公司与德国的 Cark GmbH & Co.KG 签订了一份黄铜球阀出口的销售合同，具体内容如下：

SALES CONTRACT

NO. DT1000033　　　　DATE: March 3, 2010

THE SELLER: Zhejiang Datong Import and Export Co., Ltd.
No.902 Yile Road, Hangzhou, China
TEL: 0086-571-87772409　　FAX: 0086-571-87772407

THE BUYER: Cark GmbH & Co. KG
Domstrasse 55, D-20095 Hamburg,Germany
TEL: 0049-40-3410967　　FAX: 0049-40-3410966

This Contract is made by and between the Buyer and Seller, whereby the Buyer agrees to buy and the Seller agrees to sell the under-mentioned commodity according to the terms and conditions stipulated below:

1. ARTICLE NO., NAME OF COMMODITY, QUANTITY AND AMOUNT:

Commodity	Size	Quantity	Unit Price CIF Hamburg	Amount
Forged Brass Ball Valves, Article no. V10033, Full Port, Nickel Plated, BSP Thread	1/2”	4320sets	USD1.08/set	USD4665.60
	3/4”	4000sets	USD1.51/set	USD6040.00
	1”	2400sets	USD2.30/set	USD5520.00
	1-1/4”	1296sets	USD3.70/set	USD4795.20
	1-1/2”	960sets	USD4.90/set	USD4704.00
	2”	1152sets	USD8.80/set	USD10137.60
Total		14128sets		USD35862.40
TOTAL CONTRACT VALUE: SAY U.S. DOLLARS THIRTY FIVE THOUSAND EIGHT HUNDRED AND SIXTY TWO AND CENTS FORTY ONLY.				

（续）

2. PACKING:

Packed in carton, then in wooden pallet.

Shipping mark includes Cark, S/C no., port of destination and carton no.

Side mark must show the article no., the size of goods, the size of carton and sets per carton.

3. SHIPMENT:

Within 1 month upon receipt of the L/C which accord with relevant clauses of this Contract. Shipped from Shanghai, China to Hamburg, Germany. Transshipment is allowed and partial shipment is prohibited.

4. TERMS OF PAYMENT:

By Letter of Credit at sight, reaching the Seller before March 20, 2010.

5. INSURANCE:

To be covered by the Seller.

6. DOCUMENTS:

+ Invoice in triplicate.

+ Packing List in triplicate.

+ Full set of clean on board ocean Bill of Lading marked "freight prepaid" made out to order blank endorsed notifying the Buyer.

+GSP Certificate of Origin FORM A.

+ Seller's Certified Copy of Fax dispatched to the Buyer within three days after shipment advising L/C no., name, quantity and amount of goods, number of packages, name of vessel and voyage no., and date of shipment etc..

7. INSPECTION:

Inspections shall be performed according to the quality and technical standards, including initial inspection and recheck initial inspection.

Initial Inspection: The certificate of Quality issued by the China Entry-Exit Inspection and Quarantine Bureau shall be taken as the basis of delivery.

Recheck: The customers of the buyer shall have the right to recheck the product. The recheck standards shall be the technical requirements of specimen in the order or that the goods are true to the specimen. The recheck result whether the goods conform to the contractual stipulations shall be taken as the final proof. In the case of the recheck result which shows that the goods do not conform to the contractual stipulations, the seller shall undertake any claim issued by the buyer.

8. PERIOD OF OBJECTION:

In case that the buyer or the customers of the buyer consider that the quality, quantity, packaging, etc. of the goods does not conform to the contractual stipulations; they shall raise a written objection within six months beginning from the actual delivery date of the seller. The case of no objection raised within the period of objection shall be deemed as that the goods conform to the contractual stipulations.

9. LIABILITIES FOR BREACH OF CONTRACT:

（1）In case the contract goes into effect, any part shall not change, terminate or cancel it without reason, otherwise he or she shall compensate for all the economic losses suffered by the other part.

（2）In case the quality, packaging, etc. of the goods does not conform to the contractual stipulations, the seller shall compensate for all the economic losses suffered by the buyer, including all the losses caused due to the claim lodged by the customers of the buyer.

（3）Time limit of delivery: In case of eventual delay of delivery penalties will be as follow:

From the 6th to the 10th day of delay from the latest delivery date, shown in sales contract between buyer and its customers, the buyer has the right to ask as liquidation of damages and penalties 1% of the total amount of the contract each day or cancel the contract.

From the 11th to the 25th day of delay from the latest delivery date, shown in sales contract between buyer and its customers, the buyer has the right to ask as liquidation of damages and penalties 20% of the total amount of the contract or to undertake the freight cost or cancel the contract.

After 25 days delay from the latest delivery date shown in sales contract between buyer and its customers the buyer has the right to ask as liquidation of damages and penalties to undertake the freight cost and 30% of the total amount of the contract each day or cancel the contract.

10. FORCE MAJEURE:

The seller shall not held responsibility if they, owing to Force Majeure cause or causes, fail to make delivery within the time stipulated in the Contract or cannot deliver the goods. However, in such a case, the seller shall inform the buyer immediately by cable and if it is requested by the buyer, the seller shall also deliver to buyer by registered letter, a certificate attesting the existence of such a cause or causes.

11. SETTLEMENT OF DISPUTES:

All disputes in connection with this contract or the execution thereof shall be settled amicably by negotiation. In case no settlement can be reached, the case shall then be submitted to the China International Economic Trade Arbitration Commission for settlement by arbitration in accordance with the Commission's arbitration rules. The award rendered by the commission shall be final and binding on both parties. The fees for arbitration shall be borne by the losing party unless otherwise awarded.

This contract is made in two original copies and becomes valid after signature, one copy to be held by each party.

Signed by:

THE SELLER:	**THE BUYER:**
Zhejiang Datong Import and Export Co., Ltd.	Cark GmbH & Co. KG
桂大同	Jack Duncan

2010 年 3 月 18 日，浙江大同进出口有限公司外贸单证员桂小龙收到了中国银行浙江省分行（Bank of China, Zhejiang Branch）国际业务部的信用证通知函，告知 Cark GmbH & Co.KG 已经通过中国银行汉堡分行（Bank of China, Hamburg Branch）开来信用证。信用证通知书和信用证内容如下：

1. 信用证通知书

中 国 银 行 股份有限公司浙江省分行

BANK OF CHINA LIMITED
ZHEJIANG BRANCH
ADDRESS: 321 FENGQI ROAD, HANGZHOU　　ED09
CABLE:6892　　信用证通知书
TELEX:35019 BOCHZ CN　**NOTIFICATION OF DOCUMENTARY CREDIT**
SWIFT: BKCH CNBJ910
FAX:85010842　　2010/03/18

To: 致 ZHEJIANG DATONG IMPORT AND EXPORT CO., LTD.		WHEN CORRESPONDING　AD91005302299 PLEASE QUTOTE REF NO.	
ISSUING BANK 开证行 BANK OF CHINA, HAMBURG BRANCH		TRANSMITTED TO US THROUGH 传递行 REF NO. REIM BANK	
L/C NO.信用证号 LC-536-089075	DATED 开证日期 2010/03/17	AMOUNT 金额 USD35862.40	EXPIRY PLACE 有效地 LOCAL
EXPIRY DATE 效期 2010/03/17	TENOR 期限 30 DAYS	CHARGE 未付费用 RMB200.00	CHARGE BE 费用承担人 DATONG
RECEIVED VIA 来证方式 SWIFT	信用证是否有效 VALID	TEST/SIGN 印押是否相符 YES	CONFIRM 我行是否保兑 NO

DEAR SIRS，敬启者：

WE HAVE PLEASURE IN ADVISING YOU THAT WE HAVE RECEIVED FROM BANK OF CHINA, HAMBURG BRANCH A(N) LETTER OF CREDIT, CONTENTS OF WHICH ARE AS PER ATTACHED SHEET(S). THIS ADVICE AND THE ATTACHED SHEET(S) MUST ACCOMPANY THE RELATIVE DOCUMENTS WHEN PRESENTED FOR NEGOTIATION.

兹通知贵司，我行收到自上述银行信用证一份，现随附通知，贵司交单时，请将本通知书及信用证一并提示。

REMARK 备注：

PLEASE NOTE THAT THIS ADVICE DOES NOT CONSTITUTE OUR CONFIRMATION OF THE ABOVE L/C, NOR DOES IT CONVEY ANY ENGAGEMENT OR OBLIGATION ON OUR PART.

限制中行议付。

THIS L/C CINSISTS OF TWO SHEETS, INCLUDING THE COVERING LETTER AND ATTACHMENT(S).

本信用证连同面函及附件共 2 纸。

IF YOU FIND ANY TERMS AND CONDITIONS IN THE L/C WHICH YOU ARE UNABLE TO COMPLY WITH AND OR AND ERRORS, IT IS SUGGESTED THAT YOU CONTACT APPLICANT DIRECTLY FOR NECESSARY.

AMENDMENT(S) SO AS TO AVOID ANY DIFFICULTIES WHICH MAY ARISE WHEN DOCUMENTS ARE PRESENTED.

如本信用证中有无法办到的条款及/或错误，请与开证申请人联系，进行必要的修改，以排除交单时可能发生的问题。

THIS L/C IS ADVISED SUBJECT TO ICC UCP PUBLICATION NO.600.

本信用证之通知系遵循国际商会跟单信用证统一惯例第 600 号出版物办理。

YOURS FAITHFULLY,

FOR **BANK OF CHINA,ZHEJIANG BRANCH**

2. 信用证

MT 700 ISSUE OF A DOCUMENTARY CREDIT

SENDER		BANK OF CHINA, HAMBURG BRANCH
RECEIVER		BANK OF CHINA, ZHEJIANG BRANCH
SEQUENCE OF TOTAL	27 :	1 / 1
FORM OF DOC. CREDIT	40A:	IRREVOCABLE
DOC. CREDIT NUMBER	20 :	LC-536-089075
DATE OF ISSUE	31C:	100417
DATE AND PLACE OF EXPIRY	31D:	DATE 100317 PLACE IN CHINA
APPLICANT	50 :	CARK GMBH & CO. KG DOMSTRASSE 55, D-20095 HAMBURG, GERMANY
BENEFICIARY	59 :	ZHEJIANG DATONG IMPORT AND EXPORT CO., LTD. NO.902 YILE ROAD, HANGZHOU, CHINA
AMOUNT	32B:	CURRENCY USD AMOUNT 35862.40
AVAILABLE WITH/BY	41D:	ANY BANK IN CHINA, BY NEGOTIATION
DRAFTS AT ...	42C:	30 DAYS AFTER SIGHT
DRAWEE	42A:	BANK OF CHINA，NEW YORK
PARTIAL SHIPMENT	43P:	PROHIBITED
TRANSSHIPMENT	43T:	PROHIBITED
PORT OF LOADING/ AIRPORT OF DEPARTURE	44E:	SHANGHAI, CHINA
PORT OF DISCHARGE	44F:	HAMBURG, GERMANY
LATEST DATE OF SHIPMENT	44C:	100417
DESCRIPTION OF GOODS AND/OR SERVICES	45A:	FORGED BRASS BALL VALVES, ARTICLE NO. V10033, FULL PORT, NICKEL PLATED, BSP THREAD, SIZE QUANTITY UNIT PRICE AMOUNT 1/2" 4320SETS USD1.08/SET USD4665.60 3/4" 4000SETS USD1.51/SET USD6040.00 1" 2400SETS USD2.30/SET USD5520.00 1-1/4" 1296SETS USD3.70/SET USD4795.20 1-1/2" 960SETS USD4.90/SET USD4704.00 2" 1152SETS USD8.80/SET USD10137.60 TRADE TERMS: FOB SHANGHAI
DOCUMENTS REQUIRED	46A:	+ COMMERCIAL INVOICE SIGNED IN TRIPLICATE. + PACKING LIST IN TRIPLICATE. + GSP CERTIFICATE OF ORIGIN FORM A FROM PEOPLES'S REPUBLIC OF CHINA IN 1 COPY, IN THE SECOND COLUMN OF FORM A, GOODS CONSIGNED TO APPLICANT, THE THIRD PARTY'S FORM A IS ACCEPTABLE. + FULL SET (3/3) OF CLEAN 'ON BOARD' OCEAN BILLS OF LADING MADE OUT TO APPLICANT MARKED FREIGHT COLLECT AND NOTIFY APPLICANT. + INSURANCE POLICY/CERTIFICATE IN DUPLICATE ENDORSED IN BLANK FOR 110% INVOICE VALUE, COVERING ALL RISKS OF CIC OF PICC (1/1/1981). + CERTIFICATE'S CERTIFIED COPY OF FAX DISPATCHED TO THE BUYER WITHIN THREE DAYS AFTER SHIPMENT ADVISING L/C NO., NAME, QUANTITY AND AMOUNT OF GOODS, NUMBER OF PACKAGES, NAME OF VESSEL AND VOYAGE NO., AND DATE OF SHIPMENT.
ADDITIONAL CONDITION	47A:	+ THE NUMBER AND THE DATE OF THIS CREDIT MUST BE QUOTED ON ALL DOCUMENTS. + TELEGRAPHIC REIMBUESEMENT CLAIM PROHIBITED. + A DISCREPANCY FEE OF USD60.00 OR EQUIVALENT SHOULD BE DEDUCTED FROM THE PROCEEDS IF DOCUMENTS ARE PRESENTED WITH DISCREPANCY/IES. +BENEFICIARY'S CERTIFICATE IS REQUIRIED STATING THAT ORIGINAL GSP CERTIFICATE OF ORIGIN FORM A HAS BEEN SENT TO THE APPLICANT BY SPEED POST.
CHARGES	71B:	ALL CHARGES AND COMMISSIONS ARE FOR ACCOUNT OF BENEFICIARY.
CONFIRMATION INSTRUCTION	49 :	WITHOUT.
INFORMATION TO PRESENTING BANK	78 :	ALL DOCUMENTS ARE TO BE REMITTED IN ONE LOT BY COURIER TO BANK OF CHINA, HAMBURG BRANCH，TRADE SERVICES, RATHAUSMARKT 5, 20095 HAMBURG , GERMANY.

此时外贸单证员桂小龙的工作任务包括：

【任务 1】审证

外贸单证员桂小龙根据 DT1000033 出口合同，审核 LC-536-089075 信用证，找出问题条款。针对问题条款提出修改意见。

【任务 2】改证

外贸单证员桂小龙针对问题条款提出信用证修改意见。

【任务 1】审证

第一步：读懂 LC-536-089075 信用证条款。

外贸单证员桂小龙熟悉 LC-536-089075 信用证条款内容，特别是信用证开证日期、效期、交单地点、金额、交单期、装运期、单据要求等主要条款的含义。

第二步：根据 DT1000033 出口合同，审核 LC-536-089075 信用证找出问题条款。

对照出口合同条款，逐条审核信用证各条款，发现如下不符情况：

（1）信用证规定的效期与最迟装运期为同一天，即双到期。由于信用证未规定交单期，根据 UCP600 规定，交单期为装运日期后 21 天内交单，但不迟于信用证效期。受益人要在信用证效期内交单，则必须比效期提前几天装运，这就会使实际装运期早于合同规定的装运期，容易造成受益人装运延迟，对受益人不利；

（2）信用证中汇票的付款期限“AT 30 DAYS AFTER SIGHT”错误，正确的是“AT SIGHT”；

（3）信用证中规定禁止转运，与出口合同规定不一致；

（4）信用证货物描述栏目中，贸易术语 FOB SHANGHAI 错误，合同规定为 CIF HAMBURG；

（5）信用证海运提单条款中提单抬头“TO APPLICANT”对受益人非常不利，应该为“TO ORDER”；“FREIGHT COLLECT”应该为“FREIGHT PREPAID”；

（6）信用证费用条款“ALL CHARGES AND COMMISSIONS ARE FOR ACCOUNT OF BENEFICIARY.”不合理。因为开证行费用理应由开证申请人承担。

（7）信用证增加了普惠制产地证“FORM A”直接寄开证申请人的受益人证明单据。

【任务 2】改证

外贸单证员桂小龙对于以上审核出来的问题条款，分别按以下原则处理如下：

（1）对我方不利，但是在不增加或基本不增加成本的情况下可以完成，可以不改。

问题条款：

1）信用证中规定禁止转运，与出口合同规定不一致。

2）信用证增加了普惠制产地证“FORM A”直接寄开证申请人的受益人证明单据。

（2）对我方不利，又要在增加较大成本的情况下可以完成，若对方愿意承担成本，则不改；否则，要改。

问题条款：

1）信用证中汇票的付款期限“AT 30 DAYS AFTER SIGHT”错误，正确的是“AT SIGHT”。

2）信用证费用条款“ALL CHARGES AND COMMISSIONS ARE FOR ACCOUNT OF BENEFICIARY.”不合理。因为开证行费用理应由开证申请人承担。

（3）对我方不利，若不改会严重影响安全收汇，则坚决要改。问题条款如下：

1）信用证规定的效期与最迟装运期为同一天，即双到期。由于信用证未规定交单期，根据 UCP600 规定，交单期为装运日期后 21 天内交单，但不迟于信用证效期。受益人要在信用证效期内交单，则必须比效期提前几天装运，这就会使实际装运期早于合同规定的装运期，容易造成受益人装运延迟，对受益人不利。

2）信用证货物描述栏目中，贸易术语 FOB SHANGHAI 错误，合同规定为 CIF HAMBURG。

3）信用证海运提单条款中提单抬头“TO APPLICANT”对受益人非常不利，应该为“TO ORDER”；“FREIGHT COLLECT”应该为“FREIGHT PREPAID”。

最后，外贸单证员桂小龙提出的修改意见为：

1. 信用证规定的效期改为 2010 年 5 月 8 日，比最迟装运日期 2010 年 4 月 17 日晚 21 天，与交单期相匹配。 2. 信用证中汇票的付款期限“AT 30 DAYS AFTER SIGHT”错误，改为“AT SIGHT”。 3. 信用证货物描述栏目中，贸易术语 FOB SHANGHAI 错误，改为 CIF HAMBURG。 4. 信用证海运提单条款中提单抬头“TO APPLICANT”对受益人非常不利，改为“TO ORDER”；“FREIGHT COLLECT”改为“FREIGHT PREPAID”。 5. 信用证费用条款改为“ALL CHARGES AND COMMISSIONS OUTSIDE ISSUING BANK ARE FOR ACCOUNT OF BENEFICIARY.”。

一、信用证内容

以 SWIFT 开信用证为例，信用证内容一般由一份 MT700 报文组成（见表 2-1）。如果信用证内容超过 MT700 报文容量时，则由一份 MT700 报文和一至三份 MT701 报文（见表 2-2）组成。

表 2-1 MT 700 报文内容

M/O	Tag 代号	Field Name 栏目名称	Content/options 内容
M	27	Sequence of total 合计次序	1n/1n 1 个数字/1 个数字
M	40A	Form of documentary credit 跟单信用证类别	24x 24 个字
M	20	Documentary credit number 信用证号码	16x 16 个字
O	23	Reference to pre-advice 预告的编号	16x 16 个字
O	31C	Date of issue 开证日期	6n 6 个数字
O	40E	Applicable Rules 适用的惯例	4*35x 4 行×35 个字
M	31D	Date and place of expiry 到期日及地点	6n29x 6 个数字/29 个字
O	51a	Applicant bank 开证申请人的银行	A or D A 或 D
M	50	Applicant 开证申请人	4*35x 4 行×35 个字
M	59	Beneficiary 受益人	[/34x] 4*35x 4 行×35 个字
M	32B	Currency code, amount 币别代码、金额	3a15n 3 个字母/15 个数字
O	39A	Percentage credit amount tolerance 信用证金额加减百分率	2n/2n 2 个数字/2 个数字
O	39B	Maximum credit amount 最高信用证金额	13x 13 个字
O	39C	Additional amounts covered 可附加金额	4*35x 4 行×35 个字
M	41a	Available with…By… 付款方式和指定银行	A or D A 或 D
O	42C	Drafts at… 汇票期限	3*35x 3 行×35 个字
O	42a	Drawee 付款人	A or D A 或 D
O	42M	Mixed payment details 混合付款指示	4*35x 4 行×35 个字
O	42P	Deferred payment details 延期付款指示	4*35x 4 行×35 个字
O	43P	Partial shipments 分批装运	1*35x 1 行×35 个字
O	43T	Transshipment 转运	1*35x 1 行×35 个字
O	44A	Place of taking in charge/ of receipt 接管地/接收地	1*65x 1 行×65 个字
O	44E	Port of loading/Airport of departure 装运港/始发港	1*65x 1 行×65 个字
O	44F	Port of discharge/Airport of destination 卸货港/目的港	1*65x 1 行×65 个字
O	44B	Place of final destination/of delivery 最终目的地/交货地	1*65x 1 行×65 个字
O	44C	Latest date of shipment 最迟装运日期	6n 6 个数字
O	44D	Shipment period 装运期间	6*65x 6 行×65 个字
O	45A	Description of goods and/or services 货物和/或各种服务描述	50*65x 50 行×65 个字
O	46A	Documents required 应提交的单据	50*65x 50 行×65 个字
O	47A	Additional conditions 附加条件	50*65x 50 行×65 个字
O	71B	Charges 费用	6*35x 6 行×35 个字
O	48	Period for presentation 交单期	4*35x 4 行×35 个字
M	49	Confirmation instructions 保兑指示	7x 7 个字
O	53a	Reimbursement bank 偿付行	A or D A 或 D
O	78	Instructions to the paying/ accepting /negotiating bank 对付款/承兑/议付行之指示	12*65x 12 行×65 个字
O	57a	"advise through" bank 通过……银行通知	A，B or D A，B 或 D
O	72	Sender to receiver information 附言	6*35x 6 行×35 个字

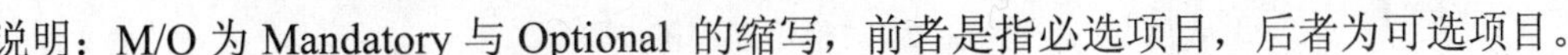
说明：M/O 为 Mandatory 与 Optional 的缩写，前者是指必选项目，后者为可选项目。

表 2-2　MT 701 报文内容

M/O	Tag	Field name	Content/Options
M	27	Sequence of total	ln/ln
M	20	Documentary credit number	16x
O	45B	Description of goods and/or service	100*65x
O	46B	Documents required	100*65x
O	47B	Additions conditional	100*65x

二、审证

通知行主要审核信用证的真实性和开证行的资信状况，出口企业外贸单证员主要审核信用证的内容，即信用证条款。

1．审核信用证通知书

在审证之前，出口企业外贸单证员要仔细阅读信用证通知书的内容。

（1）如果通知行认为开证行的资信状况差、信用等级低，出口企业可以采取两种应对措施：①要求开证申请人找一家信用可靠的银行对此信用证加保兑，使该信用证成为保兑信用证，以获得开证行和保兑行的双重付款保证；②要求开证申请人找一家信用可靠的银行重开信用证。

（2）如果通知行无法确认信用证的真实性，在信用证通知书上表示“押未核仅供参考”等内容时，则不能盲目开始准备生产货物，应催促通知行尽快确认信用证的真实性。

（3）如果通知行告知该信用证为预先通知信用证时，在信用证通知书上表示“未生效”，则要谨慎处理，因为预先通知信用证在法律上是无效的，只有开证行随后寄来信用证证实书之后才生效。

2．审核信用证

（1）审证依据：

1）外贸合同。信用证是依据外贸合同开立的，所以审查信用证条款是否与外贸合同的条款相符，是外贸单证员收到信用证后首先要做的工作。

2）UCP600。UCP600 是信用证各当事人都必须遵循的国际惯例，所以审核信用证时，应遵循 UCP600 的规定来确定是否可以接受信用证的某些条款。

3）业务实际情况。对于外贸合同中未作规定或无法根据 UCP600 来做出判断的信用证条款，外贸单证员应根据业务实际情况来审核。这里的业务实际情况，是指信用证条款对安全收汇的影响程度、进口国的法令和法规等。

（2）审证步骤如图 2-1 所示：

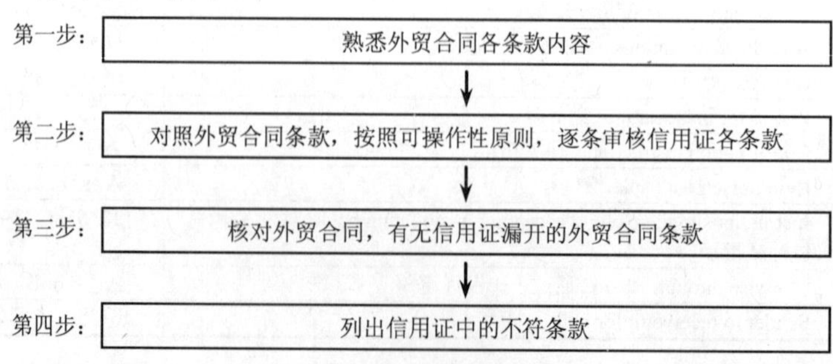

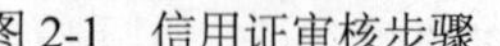

图 2-1　信用证审核步骤

（3）审证要点：

1）开证申请人和受益人的名称。开证申请人和受益人的名称是出口单证中必不可少的，若信用证开错应及时修改，以免影响安全收汇。

2）信用证金额。信用证金额的币别与数额必须与外贸合同相符。若信用证列有货物数量或单价的，应计算总值是否正确。

3）货物描述。审核信用证中货物的名称、货号、规格等内容是否与外贸合同一致。

4）信用证截止日和交单地点。按UCP600的规定，信用证必须规定一个交单的截止日。信用证规定截止日的同时一般也规定交单地点，它包括出口地、进口地和第三国三种情况。出口地交单对出口商最有利，进口地交单和第三国交单对出口商都不利，因为交单地点均在国外，容易产生迟交单和寄丢单的风险。为此，出口商应争取在出口地交单，若争取不到，应预先估计单据的邮寄时间，提前交单，以防逾期。

5）交单期。信用证还应规定一个运输单据出单日期后必须提交符合信用证条款的单据的特定期限，即“交单期”。若信用证没有规定交单期，按UCP600规定，交单期为不迟于装运期之后的21个日历日内交单，但是在任何情况下都不得迟于信用证的截止日。

6）装运期。若信用证中未规定装运期，则最迟装运期与信用证截止日为同一天，即通常所称的“双到期”。在实际业务操作中，应将装运期提前一定的时间，以便有合理时间来制单结汇。

7）运输条款。信用证运输条款中的装运港（地）和目的港（地）应与外贸合同相符，交货地点也必须与价格条款相一致。若信用证中未注明可否转运及/或分批，则视为允许转运及/或分批。对于分期支款或分期装运，按UCP600规定，如信用证规定在指定的时间段内分期支款或分期装运，任何一期未按信用证规定期限装运时，信用证对该期及以后各期均告失效。

8）保险条款。若来证要求的投保险别或投保金额超出了外贸合同的规定，除非信用证上表明由此而产生的超保费用由开证申请人承担并允许在信用证项下支取，否则应予修改。若保险加成过高，还需征得保险公司同意，否则应予修改。

9）单据条款。要仔细审核信用证中的单据条款，特别要注意一些软条款，如商业发票经买方复签生效、1/3正本提单直接寄给买方等。

10）银行费用条款。一般情况下，出口方银行费用由受益人承担，进口方银行的费用由开证申请人承担。关于银行费用承担，进出口双方应在谈判时加以明确。

三、改证

1．改证的常见情形

（1）开证申请人要求增加货物数量和金额。由于信用证项下的货物在开证申请人所在国很畅销，为了能够获得更多的货源，与受益人协商后，开证申请人向开证行提出增加货物数量和金额的改证申请。

（2）开证错误。因信用证条款与外贸合同条款不一致或存在软条款等开证错误，要求修改信用证。

（3）受益人要求展期。受益人由于各种原因无法如期装运要求展期，展期涉及装运期和信用证截止日。

2．改证的原则

对于审证后发现的信用证问题条款，受益人应遵循“利己不损人”原则进行。即受益人改证既不影响开证申请人的正常利益，又维护自己的合法利益。具体来讲，有以下五种常见的处理原则：

（1）对我方有利又不影响对方利益的问题条款，一般不改。

（2）对我方有利但会严重影响对方利益的问题条款，一定要改。

（3）对我方不利但在不增加或基本不增加成本的情况下可以完成的问题条款，可以不改。

（4）对我方不利又要在增加较大成本的情况下可以完成的问题条款，若对方愿意承担成本，则不改；否则，要改。

（5）对我方不利，若不改会严重影响安全收汇的问题条款，则坚决要改。

3．改证的业务流程

改证的业务流程见图 2-2。

（1）受益人给开证申请人发改证函，协商改证事宜。

（2）协商一致后，开证申请人填写改证申请书，向开证行提出改证申请。

（3）开证行同意后，向信用证的原通知行发信用证修改书，即 MT707。

（4）原通知行给受益人信用证修改通知书和信用证修改书，进行信用证修改通知。

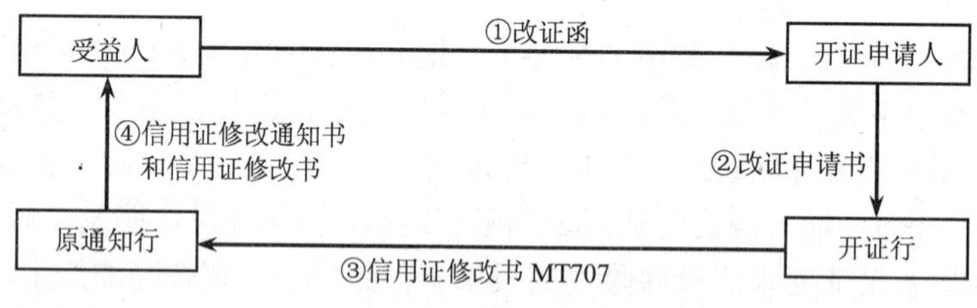

图 2-2　信用证改证的业务流程

4．改证操作与 UCP600

（1）改证通知与 UCP600 相关条款：

1）通知行通知信用证或其修改的行为表示其已确信信用证或修改的表面真实性，而且其通知准确地反映了其收到的信用证或修改的条款。

2）通知行可以通过另一银行（第二通知行）向受益人通知信用证及修改。第二通知行通知信用证或修改的行为表明其已确信收到的通知的表面真实性，并且其通知准确地反映了收到的信用证或修改的条款。

3）经由通知行或第二通知行通知信用证的银行必须经由同一银行通知其后的任何修改。

4）若一银行被要求通知信用证或修改但其决定不予修改，则应毫不延误地告知自其处收到信用证、修改或通知的银行。

5）若一银行被要求通知信用证或修改但其不能确信信用证、修改或通知的表面真实性，则应毫不延误地通知看似从其处收到指示的银行。如果通知行或第二通知行决定仍然通知信用证或修改，则应告知受益人或第二通知行其不能确信信用证、修改或通知的表面真实性。

6）通知修改的银行应将任何接受或拒绝的通知转告发出修改的银行。

（2）开证行、保兑行改证责任与 UCP600 相关条款开证行发出修改之时起，即不可撤销地受其约束。保兑行可将其保兑扩展至修改，并自通知该修改之时，即不可撤销地受其约束。但是，保兑行可以选择将修改通知受益人而不对其加具保兑。若如此，其必须毫不延误地将此告知开证行，并在其给受益人的通知中告知受益人。

（3）改证生效与 UCP600 相关条款：

1）除可转让信用证外，未经开证行、保兑行（如有的话）及受益人同意，信用证既不得修改，也不得撤销。

2）在受益人告知通知修改的银行其接受该修改之前，原信用证或含有先前被接受的修改的信用证的条款对受益人仍然有效。受益人应提供接受或拒绝修改的通知。如果受益人未能给予通知，当交单与信用证以及尚未表示接受的修改的要求一致时，即视为受益人已做出接受修改的通知，并且从此时起，该信用证被修改。

3）对同一修改的内容不允许部分接受，部分接受将被视为拒绝修改的通知。

4）修改中关于"除非受益人在某一时间内拒绝修改否则修改生效"的规定应不予理会。

实训项目

◆　实训项目 2-1

2010 年 6 月 8 日，浙江曼旎进出口有限公司与阿联酋 Emirates Clothes Trader 签订了一份男童夹克的出口合同，具体内容如下：

SALES CONTRACT

NO.: MN10066　　　　DATE: June 8, 2010

THE SELLER: Zhejiang Manni Import and Export Co., Ltd.
99 Xueyuan Sreet, Hangzhou, P.R.China
Tel: 0086-571-86739001　Fax: 0086-571-86739002

THE BUYER: Emirates Clothes Trader
P.O.Box33, No.12, Salahuddin Road, Dubai, U.A.E.
Tel: 00971-4-3535209　Fax: 00971-4-3535208

This Contract is made by and between the Buyer and Seller, whereby the Buyer agree to buy and the Seller agree to sell the under-mentioned commodity according to the terms and conditions stipulated below:

Commodity & specification	Quantity	Unit price	Amount
Boys Jacket, Style No. SS98 Shell: woven twill 100% cotton Lining: Woven 100% polyester As per the confirmed sample of May 10, 2010	5000pcs	CIFC5 Dubai, U.A.E. USD14.80/pc	USD74000.00
TOTAL	5000pcs		USD74000.00
TOTAL CONTRACT VALUE: SAY U.S. DOLLARS SEVENTY FOUR THOUSAND ONLY.			

SIZE/COLOR ASSORTMENT:　　Unit: piece

Size / Color	92	98	104	110	116	Total
White	440	700	700	360	300	2 500
Red	440	700	700	360	300	2 500
Total	880	1 400	1 400	720	600	5 000

More or less 5% of the quantity and the amount are allowed.

（续）

PACKING:

20 pieces of boys jackets are packed in one export standard carton, solid color and solid size in the same carton.

MARKS:

Shipping mark includes ECT, S/C No., style no., port of destination and carton No.

Side mark must show the color, the size of carton and pieces per carton.

TIME OF SHIPMENT :

In August, 2010.

PORT OF LOADING AND DESTINATION:

From Ningbo, China to Dubai, UAE

Transshipment is allowed and partial shipment is prohibited.

INSURANCE: To be effected by the seller for 110% of invoice value covering All Risks and War Risks as per CIC of PICC dated 01/01/1981.

TERMS OF PAYMENT :

By irrevocable Letter of Credit at sight, reaching the seller not later than June 22, 2010 and remaining valid for negotiation in China for further 15 days after the effected shipment. In case of late arrival of the L/C, the seller shall not be liable for any delay in shipment and shall have the right to rescind the contract and /or claim for damages.

DOCUMENTS :

+ Signed Invoice in triplicate, one original of which should be certified by Chamber of Commerce or CCPIT and legalized by UAE embassy/consulate in seller's country.

+ Full set (3/3) of clean on board ocean Bill of Lading marked "freight prepaid" made out to order blank endorsed notifying the applicant.

+ Insurance Policy in duplicate endorsed in blank.

+ Packing List in triplicate.

+ Certificate of Origin certified by Chamber of Commerce or CCPIT and legalized by UAE embassy/consulate in seller's country.

INSPECTION:

The certificate of Quality issued by the China Entry-Exit Inspection and Quarantine Bureau shall be taken as the basis of delivery.

CLAIMS:

In case discrepancy on the quality or quantity of the goods is found by the buyer, after arrival of the goods at the port of destination, the buyer may, within 30 days and 15 days respectively after arrival of the goods at the port of destination, lodge with the seller a claim which should be supported by an Inspection Certificate issued by a public surveyor approved by the seller. The seller shall, on the merits of the claim, either make good the loss sustained by the buyer or reject their claim, it being agreed that the seller shall not be held responsible for any loss or losses due to natural cause failing within the responsibility of shipowners of the underwriters. The seller shall reply to the buyer within 30 days after receipt of the claim.

LATE DELIVERY AND PENALTY :

In case of late delivery, the Buyer shall have the right to cancel this contract, reject the goods and lodge a claim against the Seller. Except for Force Majeure, if late delivery occurs, the Seller must pay a penalty, and the Buyer shall have the right to lodge a claim against the Seller. The rate of penalty is charged at 0.5% for every 7 days, odd days less than 7 days should be counted as 7 days. The total penalty amount will not exceed 5% of the shipment value. The penalty shall be deducted by the paying bank or the Buyer from the payment.

FORCE MAJEURE:

The seller shall not held responsible if they, owing to Force Majeure cause or causes, fail to make delivery within the time stipulated in the Contract or cannot deliver the goods. However, in such a case, the seller shall inform the buyer immediately by cable and if it is requested by the buyer, the seller shall also deliver to buyer by registered letter, a certificate attesting the existence of such a cause or causes.

ARBITRATION:

All disputes in connection with this contract or the execution thereof shall be settled amicably by negotiation. In case no settlement can be reached, the case shall then be submitted to the China International Economic Trade Arbitration Commission for settlement by arbitration in accordance with the Commission's arbitration rules. The award rendered by the commission shall be final and binding on both parties. The fees for arbitration shall be borne by the losing party unless otherwise awarded.

This contract is made in four original copies and becomes valid after signature, two copies to be held by each party.

Signed by:

THE SELLER:	**THE BUYER:**
Zhejiang Manni Import and Export Co., Ltd.	Emirates Clothes Trader
章曼旎	Colm McLoughlin

2010 年 6 月 25 日，浙江曼旎进出口有限公司外贸单证员王宁收到了杭州银行（Bank of Hangzhou）国际业务部的信用证通知函，告知 Emirates Clothes Trader 已经通过汇丰银行迪拜分行（HSBC Bank PLC，Dubai）开来信用证。信用证通知书和信用证内容如下。

1．信用证通知书

杭州银行

BANK OF HANGZHOU

信用证通知书

Notification of Documentary Credit

OFFICE: INT'L BUSINESS DEPT.

ADDRESS: 46 QINGCHUN ROAD, HANGZHOU, 310003,CHINA　　DATE: 2010-06-25

To: 致 ZHEJIANG MANNI IMPORT AND EXPORT CO., LTD.	Our Ref No.我行编号: AD2006869105555 Amount 金额 USD74000.00
Issuing Bank 开证行 HSBC BANK PLC，DUBAI, U.A.E.	Transmitted to us through 传递行 Transferred from 转让行
L/C No.信用证号 KKK101090	Issuing Date 开证日期 2010-06-25

Dear Sirs,敬启者：

We have pleasure in advising you that we have received from A/M a

兹通知贵公司，我行收自上述银行

(√) issuing by telex/SWIFT 电传/SWIFT 开立　　( ) ineffective 未生效

( ) issuing by mail 信开

( ) pre-advising of 预先通知　　( ) mail confirmation of 证实书

(√) original 正本　　( ) duplicate 副本

Letter of credit, contents of which are as per attached sheet(s).

This advise and the attached sheet(s) must accompany the relative documents when presented.

信用证一份，现随附通知。贵公司交单时，请将本通知书及信用证一并提示。

(√) Please note that this advice does not constitute our confirmation of the above L/C, nor does it convey any engagement or obligation on our part.

本通知并不构成我行对该信用证之保兑及其他任何责任。

( ) Please note that we have added our confirmation to the above L/C, which is available with ourselves only.

上述信用证已由我行加具保兑，并限向我行交单。

Remarks 备注：

This L/C consists of　　sheet(s), including the covering letter and attachment(s).

该信用证连同本面函及附件共　　页。

如该信用证中有无法办到的条款及/或错误，请与开证申请人联系进行必要的修改，以排除交单时可能发生的问题。

本通知费 CNY200

Yours faithfully

BANK OF HANGZHOU

杭州银行

AUTHORIZED SIGNATURE(S)

2．信用证

MT 700 ISSUE OF A DOCUMENTARY CREDIT

SENDER		HSBC BANK PLC，DUBAI,UAE
RECEIVER		BANK OF HANGZHOU, HANGZHOU, CHINA
SEQUENCE OF TOTAL	27：	1 / 1
FORM OF DOC. CREDIT	40A：	IRREVOCABLE
DOC. CREDIT NUMBER	20：	KKK101090
DATE OF ISSUE	31C：	100625
APPLICABLE RULES	40E：	UCP LATEST VERSION
DATE AND PLACE OF EXPIRY	31D：	DATE 100831 PLACE IN U.A.E.
APPLICANT	50：	EMIRATES CLOTHES TRADER P O BOX33, NO.12, SALAHUDDIN ROAD, DUBAI, U.A.E.
BENEFICIARY	59：	ZHEJIANG MANI IMPORT & EXPORT CORPORATION 99 XUEYUAN SREET, HANGZHOU, P.R.CHINA
AMOUNT	32B：	CURRENCY USD AMOUNT 74500.00
AVAILABLE WITH/BY	41D：	ANY BANK IN CHINA, BY NEGOTIATION
DRAFTS AT ...	42C：	60 DAYS AFTER SIGHT
DRAWEE	42A：	HSBC BANK PLC，NEW YORK
PARTIAL SHIPMTS	43P：	PROHIBITED
TRANSSHIPMENT	43T：	ALLOWED
PORT OF LOADING/ AIRPORT OF DEPARTURE	44E：	CHINESE MAIN PORT
PORT OF DISCHARGE	44F：	DUBAI, U.A.E.
SHIPMENT PERIOD	44D：	IN AUGUST, 2010
DESCRIPTION OF GOODS AND/OR SERVICES	45A：	5000PCS BOYS JACKET, SHELL: WOVEN TWILL 100% COTTON, LINING: WOVEN 100% POLYESTER, STYLE NO. SS98, AS PER S/C NO. MN10066 AT USD14.90/PC CIFC5 DUBAI, U.A.E. PACKED IN 20PCS/CTN.
DOCUMENTS REQUIRED	46A：	+ COMMERCIAL INVOICE SIGNED IN INK IN TRIPLICATE. ONE ORIGINAL OF WHICH SHOULD BE CERTIFIED BY CHAMBER OF COMMERCE OR CCPIT AND LEGALIZED BY U.A.E. EMBASSY/ CONSULATE IN BENEFICIARY'S COUNTRY. + PACKING LIST IN TRIPLICATE. + CERTIFICATE OF CHINESE ORIGIN CERTIFIED BY CHAMBER OF COMMERCE OR CCPIT AND LEGALIZED BY U.A.E. EMBASSY/ CONSULATE IN SELLER'S COUNTRY. + INSURANCE POLICY/CERTIFICATE IN DUPLICATE ENDORSED IN BLANK FOR 120% INVOICE VALUE, COVERING ALL RISKS AND WAR RISK OF CIC OF PICC (1/1/1981) INCL. WAREHOUSE TO WAREHOUSE AND I.O.P AND SHOWING THE CLAIMING CURRENCY IS THE SAME AS THE CURRENCY OF CREDIT. + FULL SET (3/3) OF CLEAN 'ON BOARD' OCEAN BILLS OF LADING MADE OUT TO APPLICANT MARKED FREIGHT PREPAID AND NOTIFY APPLICANT. + SHIPPING ADVICE SHOWING THE NAME OF THE CARRYING VESSEL, DATE OF SHIPMENT, MARKS, QUANTITY, NET WEIGHT AND GROSS WEIGHT OF THE SHIPMENT TO APPLICANT WITHIN 3 DAYS AFTER THE DATE OF BILL OF LADING.
ADDITIONAL CONDITION	47A：	+ DOCUMENTS DATED PRIOR TO THE DATE OF THIS CREDIT ARE NOT ACCEPTABLE. + THE COMMISSION WILL BE DEDUCTED FROM THE BILL AMOUNT. + THE NUMBER AND THE DATE OF THIS CREDIT AND THE NAME OF ISSUING BANK MUST BE QUOTED ON ALL DOCUMENTS.

（续）

		+ TRANSSHIPMENT ALLOWED AT HONGKONG ONLY. + SHORT FORM/CHARTER PARTY/THIRD PARTY BILL OF LADING IS NOT ACCEPTABLE. + SHIPMENT MUST BE EFFECTED BY 1×20'FULL CONTAINER LOAD. B/L TO SHOW EVIDENCE OF THIS EFFECT IS REQUIRED. + THE GOODS SHIPPED ARE NEITHER ISRAELI ORIGIN NOR DO THEY CONTAIN NEITHER ISRAELI MATERIALS NOR ARE THEY EXPORTED FROM ISRAEL, BENEFICIARY'S CERTIFICATE TO THIS EFFECT IS REQUIRED. + ALL PRESENTATIONS CONTAINING DISCREPANCIES WILL ATTRACT A DISCREPANCY FEE OF GBP40.00 PLUS TELEX COSTS OR OTHER CURRENCY EQUIVALENT. THIS CHARGE WILL BE DEDUCTED FROM THE BILL AMOUNT WHETHER OR NOT WE ELECT TO CONSULT THE APPLICANT FOR A WAIVER
CHARGES	71B:	ALL CHARGES AND COMMISSIONS ARE FOR ACCOUNT OF BENEFICIARY INCLUDING REIMBURSING FEE.
PERIOD FOR PRESENTATION	48:	WITHIN 5 DAYS AFTER THE DATE OF SHIPMENT, BUT WITHIN THE VALIDITY OF THIS CREDIT.
CONFIRMATION INSTRUCTION	49:	WITHOUT
REIMBURSING BANK	53A:	HSBC BANK PLC，NEW YORK
INFORMATION TO PRESENTING BANK	78:	ALL DOCUMENTS ARE TO BE REMITTED IN ONE LOT BY COURIER TO HSBC BANK PLC，TRADE SERVICES, DUBAI BRANCH, P O BOX 66, HSBC BANK BUILDING 312/45 Al SUQARE ROAD, DUBAI, UAE.

此时浙江曼旎进出口有限公司外贸单证员王宁的工作任务包括：

【任务 1】审证

外贸单证员王宁根据 MN10066 出口合同，审核 KKK101090 信用证，找出问题条款。

【任务 2】改证

外贸单证员王宁针对问题条款提出信用证修改意见。

◆ **实训项目 2-2**

2010 年 8 月 23 日，杭州维丰进出口有限公司与意大利 Sri Russa E Johns SPA 签订了一份腊感绵羊皮女上衣的出口合同，具体内容如下：

SALES CONTRACT

NO. WF10126 DATE:AUGUST 23, 2010

THE SELLER: Zhejiang Weifeng Import and Export Co., Ltd.

77 Fengtan Road, Hangzhou, China

TEL: 0086-571-81032136 FAX: 0086-571-81032137

THE BUYER: Sri Russa E Johns SPA

Add：55, Corso Matteotti 20121, Milan, Italy.

TEL: 0039-02-98280909 FAX: 0039-02-98280900

This Contract is made by and between the Buyer and Seller, whereby the Buyer agrees to buy and the Seller agrees to sell the under-mentioned commodity according to the terms and conditions stipulated below：

1．COMMODITY, QUANTITY, UNIT PRICE AND AMOUNT

Commodity & specification	Quantity	Unit price	Amount
Lamb Waxy Ladies' Jackets Style No. DE5, Color: Coffee Bean as per the sample of 080723	1400pcs	CPT Milan Airport, Italy USD58.00/pc	USD81200.00
TOTAL	1400pcs		USD81200.00
TOTAL CONTRACT VALUE: SAY U.S. DOLLARS EIGHTY ONE THOUSAND TWO HUNDRED ONLY.			

Labelling: SRJ supplied by the Buyer.

SIZE ASSORTMENT: Unit: piece

Size	38	40	42	44	46	48	Total
quantity	100	250	300	300	250	200	1 400

2．PACKING: 10pcs/carton.

Shipping mark made by the Seller.

3．SHIPMENT: Before 100930. Shipped from Hangzhou Airport, China to Milan Airport, Italy.

4．TERMS OF PAYMENT: 20% of the Amount payable by T/T within 7 days after the contract date; 80% of the Amount payable by L/C at 30 days after the AWB date.

5．INSURANCE: To be covered by the Buyer.

6．INSPECTION: the commodity must be inspected by the Buyer before delivery, then the buyer will issue the Certificate of Inspection.

7．OTHER TERMS: OMITTED.

This contract is made in two original copies and becomes valid after signature, one copy to be held by each party.

Signed by:

THE SELLER: THE BUYER:

Zhejiang Weifeng Import and Export Co., Ltd. Sri Russa E Johns SPA

杨光炜 Anna Bongiorni

8 月 27 日，杭州维丰进出口有限公司收到 Sri Russa E Johns SPA 电汇款 16 240 美元。

9 月 1 日，杭州维丰进出口有限公司外贸单证员叶丽收到了中国银行浙江省分行（Bank of China, Zhejiang Branch）国际业务部的信用证通知函，告知 Sri Russa E Johns SPA 已经通过中国银行米兰分行（Bank of China, Milan Branch）开来信用证。信用证通知书和信用证内容如下：

1．信用证通知书

中 国 银 行 股份有限公司浙江省分行

BANK OF CHINA LIMITED

ZHEJIANG BRANCH

ADDRESS: 321 FENGQI ROAD, HANGZHOU　　ED09

CABLE:6892　　**信用证通知书**

TELEX:35019 BOCHZ CN　**NOTIFICATION OF DOCUMENTARY CREDIT**

SWIFT: BKCH CNBJ910

FAX:85010842　　2010/09/01

To: 致 ZHEJIANG WEIFENG IMPORT AND EXPORT CO., LTD.		WHEN CORRESPONDING　AD91005305501 PLEASE QUTOTE REF NO.	
ISSUING BANK 开证行 BANK OF CHINA, MILAN BRANCH VIA SANTA MARGHERITA, NO.14/16 20121 MILAN, ITALY		TRANSMITTED TO US THROUGH 传递行 REF NO. REIM BANK	
L/C NO.信用证号 59340I015228	DATED 开证日期 2010/08/31	AMOUNT 金额 USD64960.00	EXPIRY PLACE 有效地 CHINA
EXPIRY DATE 效期 2010/09/30	TENOR 期限 AT 30 DAYS AFTER AWB DATE	CHARGE 未付费用 RMB200.00	CHARGE BE 费用承担人 WEIFENG
RECEIVED VIA 来证方式 SWIFT	信用证是否有效 VALID	TEST/SIGN 印押是否相符 YES	CONFIRM 我行是否保兑 NO

DEAR SIRS, 敬启者：

WE HAVE PLEASURE IN ADVISING YOU THAT WE HAVE RECEIVED FROM BANK OF CHINA, ROTTERDAM BRANCH A(N) LETTER OF CREDIT, CONTENTS OF WHICH ARE AS PER ATTACHED SHEET(S). THIS ADVICE AND THE ATTACHED SHEET(S) MUST ACCOMPANY THE RELATIVE DOCUMENTS WHEN PRESENTED FOR NEGOTIATION.

兹通知贵司，我行收到自上述银行信用证一份，现随附通知，贵司交单时，请将本通知书及信用证一并提示。

REMARK 备注：

PLEASE NOTE THAT THIS ADVICE DOES NOT CONSTITUTE OUR CONFIRMATION OF THE ABOVE L/C, NOR DOES IT CONVEY ANY ENGAGEMENT OR OBLIGATION ON OUR PART.限制中行议付。

THIS L/C CINSISTS OF TWO SHEETS, INCLUDING THE COVERING LETTER AND ATTACHMENT(S).

本信用证连同面函及附件共 2 页。

IF YOU FIND ANY TERMS AND CONDITIONS IN THE L/C WHICH YOU ARE UNABLE TO COMPLY WITH AND OR ERRORS, IT IS SUGGESTED THAT YOU CONTACT APPLICANT DIRECTLY FOR NECESSARY.

AMENDMENT(S) SO AS TO AVOID ANY DIFFICULTIES WHICH MAY ARISE WHEN DOCUMENTS ARE PRESENTED.

如本信用证中有无法办到的条款及/或错误，请与开证申请人联系，进行必要的修改，以排除交单时可能发生的问题。

THIS L/C IS ADVISED SUBJECT TO ICC UCP PUBLICATION NO.600.

本信用证之通知系遵循国际商会跟单信用证统一惯例第 600 号出版物办理。

YOURS FAITHFULLY,

FOR **BANK OF CHINA,ZHEJIANG BRANCH**

2. 信用证

MT 700		ISSUE OF A DOCUMENTARY CREDIT
SENDER		BANK OF CHINA, MILAN BRANCH, ITALY
RECEIVER		BANK OF CHINA, ZHEJIANG BRANCH
SEQUENCE OF TOTAL	27 :	1 / 1
FORM OF DOC. CREDIT	40A:	IRREVOCABLE
DOC. CREDIT NUMBER	20 :	59340I015228
DATE OF ISSUE	31C:	100831
DATE AND PLACE OF EXPIRY	31D:	DATE 100930 PLACE IN CHINA
APPLICANT	50 :	SRI RUSSA E JOHNS SPA 55, CORSO MATTEOTTI 20121, MILAN, ITALY
BENEFICIARY	59 :	ZHEJIANG WEIFENG IMPORT AND EXPORT CO., LTD. 77 FENGTAN ROAD, HANGZHOU, CHINA
AMOUNT	32B:	CURRENCY USD AMOUNT64960.00
AVAILABLE WITH/BY	41D:	BANK OF CHINA, ZHEJIANG BRANCH BY DEFERRED PAYMENT
DEFERRED PAYMENT. DETAILS AT ...	42D:	30 DAYS AFTER AWB DATE
PARTIAL SHIPMENT	43P:	PROHIBITED
TRANSSHIPMENT	43T:	PROHIBITED
PORT OF LOADING/ AIRPORT OF DEPARTURE	44E:	SHANGHAI AIRPORT, CHINA
PORT OF DISCHARGE	44F:	MILAN AIRPORT, ITALY
DESCRIPTION OF GOODS AND/OR SERVICES	45A:	1400 PIECES OF LAMB WAXY LADIES' JACKETS, STYLE NO. DE55, COLOR: COFFEE BEAN, AT USD58.00 PER PIECE, CIP MILAN AIRPORT, ITALY. AS PER ORDER NO. 77315.
DOCUMENTS REQUIRED	46A:	+ COMMERCIAL INVOICE SIGNED IN DUPLICATE. + PACKING LIST IN DUPLICATE. + ONE COPY OF GSP CERTIFICATE OF ORIGIN FORM A. + AIR WAYBILL MARKED ORIGINAL FOR SHIPPER CONSIGNED TO APPLICANT MARKED FREIGHT PREPAID AND NOTIFY APPLICANT. FAX COPY INSPECTION CERTIFICATE BY THE QC OF APPLICANT AS APPLICANT'S LEGAL REPRESENTIVE WHICH AUTOGRAPH SIGNATURE HELD BY US. + CERTIFICATE'S CERTIFIED COPY OF FAX DISPATCHED TO THE BUYER WITHIN THREE DAYS AFTER SHIPMENT DATE ADVISING L/C NO., NAME, QUANTITY AND AMOUNT OF GOODS, NUMBER OF PACKAGES, NAME OF CARRIER, FLIGHT NO. AND DATE.
ADDITIONAL CONDITION	47A:	+ THE NUMBER AND THE DATE OF THIS CREDIT MUST BE QUOTED ON ALL DOCUMENTS. + A DISCREPANCY FEE OF USD40.00 OR EQUIVALENT SHOULD BE DEDUCTED FROM THE PROCEEDS IF DOCUMENTS ARE PRESENTED WITH DISCREPANCY/IES. +BENEFICIARY'S CERTIFICATE IS REQUIRIED STATING THAT ORIGINAL GSP CERTIFICATE OF ORIGIN FORM A, ONE COPY COMMERCIAL INVOICE AND PACKING LIST HAVE BEEN SENT TO THE APPLICANT BY SPEED POST WITHIN ONE DAY AFTER THE FLIGHT DATE.
PERIOD FOR PRESENTATION	48 :	WITHIN 7 DAYS AFTER THE DATE OF SHIPMENT, BUT WITHIN THE VALIDITY OF THIS CREDIT.
CHARGES	71B:	ALL CHARGES AND COMMISSIONS ARE FOR ACCOUNT OF BENEFICIARY.
CONFIRMATION INSTRUCTION	49 :	WITHOUT.
INFORMATION TO PRESENTING BANK	78 :	ALL DOCUMENTS ARE TO BE REMITTED IN ONE LOT BY COURIER TO BANK OF CHINA, MILAN BRANCH, VIA SANTA MARGHERITA, NO.14/16 20121 MILAN, ITALY.

此时浙江维丰进出口有限公司外贸单证员叶丽的工作任务包括：

【任务 1】审证

外贸单证员叶丽根据 WF10126 出口合同，审核 59340I015228 信用证，找出问题条款。

【任务 2】改证

外贸单证员叶丽针对问题条款提出信用证修改意见。

项目三

制作商业发票和装箱单操作

能力目标

能找出信用证或外贸合同条款中关于商业发票和装箱单的相关条款，能根据信用证或外贸合同条款准确填写商业发票和装箱单相关栏目的内容。

知识目标

掌握商业发票的定义和作用、UCP600关于商业发票的条款，熟悉包装单据的种类和作用。

上接项目二的导入项目，2010年3月19日，浙江大同进出口有限公司外贸业务员采纳了外贸单证员桂小龙的合理改证建议，当天给Cark GmbH & Co.KG发改证函。Cark GmbH & Co.KG同意改证要求，向中国银行汉堡分行提出改证申请。3月25日，中国银行浙江省分行通知浙江大同进出口有限公司，中国银行汉堡分行的信用证修改书（Amendment to a documentary credit）已到。信用证修改书的内容如下：

MT 707		AMENDMENT TO A DOCUMENTARY CREDIT
SENDER		BANK OF CHINA，HAMBURG BRANCH
RECEIVER		BANK OF CHINA，ZHEJIANG BRANCH
SENDER'S REFERENCE	20:	LC-536-089075
RECEIVER'S REFERENCE	21:	NON
DATE OF ISSUE	31C:	100324
NUMBER OF AMENDMENT	26E:	01
BENEFICIARY(BEFORE THIS AMENDMENT)	59:	ZHEJIANG DATONG IMPORT AND EXPORT CO.，LTD. NO.902 YILE ROAD，HANGZHOU，CHINA
NEW DATE AND PLACE OF EXPIRY	31E:	DATE 100508 PLACE IN CHINA

（续）

NARRATIVE	79:	① UNDER FIELD 42C, THE TENOR OF DRAFT IS "AT SIGHT" INSTEAD OF "AT 30 DAYS AFTER SIGHT". ② UNDER FIELD 45A, "FOB SHANGHAI" AMENDS TO "CIF HAMBURG". ③UNDER FIELD 46A, THE CONSIGNEE OF B/L SHOULD BE "TO ORDER" NOT "TO APPLICANT": "FREIGHT COLLECT" AMENDS TO "FREIGHT PREPAID". ④ UNDER FIELD 71B, THE CHARGE CLAUSE AMENDS TO "ALL CHARGES AND COMMISSIONS OUTSIDE ISSUING BANK ARE FOR ACCOUNT OF BENEFICIARY." OTHER TERMS AND CONDITIONS REMAIN UNCHANGED. AMENDMENT FEE USD25.00 AND CABLE FEE USD30.00 ARE FOR A/C OF APPLICANT. SUBJECT TO UCPDC (2007 REVISION) ICC PUB. NO.600.

在接受改证后，信用证修改书成了原信用证的组成部分，并替代原信用证对应条款而使其失效。为了以后更好地操作业务，可以把信用证修改书替代原信用证对应条款而产生一份新的信用证：

MT 700		ISSUE OF A DOCUMENTARY CREDIT
SENDER		BANK OF CHINA, HAMBURG BRANCH
RECEIVER		BANK OF CHINA, ZHEJIANG BRANCH
SEQUENCE OF TOTAL	27:	1 / 1
FORM OF DOC. CREDIT	40A:	IRREVOCABLE
DOC. CREDIT NUMBER	20:	LC-536-089075
DATE OF ISSUE	31C:	100317
DATE AND PLACE OF EXPIRY	31D:	DATE 100508 PLACE INCHINA
APPLICANT	50:	CARK GMBH & CO. KG DOMSTRASSE 55, D-20095 HAMBURG, GERMANY
BENEFICIARY	59:	ZHEJIANG DATONG IMPORT AND EXPORT CO., LTD. NO.902 YILE ROAD, HANGZHOU, CHINA
AMOUNT	32B:	CURRENCY USD AMOUNT 35862.40
AVAILABLE WITH/BY	41D:	ANY BANK IN CHINA, BY NEGOTIATION
DRAFTS AT ...	42C:	AT SIGHT
DRAWEE	42A:	BANK OF CHINA，NEW YORK
PARTIAL SHIPMENT	43P:	PROHIBITED
TRANSSHIPMENT	43T:	PROHIBITED
PORT OF LOADING/ AIRPORT OF DEPARTURE	44E:	SHANGHAI，CHINA
PORT OF DISCHARGE	44F:	HAMBURG，GERMANY
LATEST DATE OF SHIPMENT	44C:	100417
DESCRIPTION OF GOODS AND/OR SERVICES	45A:	FORGED BRASS BALL VALVES, ARTICLE NO. V10033, FULL PORT, NICKEL PLATED, BSP THREAD

SIZE	QUANTITY	UNIT PRICE	AMOUNT
1/2"	4320SETS	USD1.08/SET	USD4665.60
3/4"	4000SETS	USD1.51/SET	USD6040.00
1"	2400SETS	USD2.30/SET	USD5520.00
1-1/4"	1296SETS	USD3.70/SET	USD4795.20
1-1/2"	960SETS	USD4.90/SET	USD4704.00
2"	1152SETS	USD8.80/SET	USD10137.60

TRADE TERMS: CIF HAMBURG

（续）

DOCUMENTS REQUIRED	46A:	+ COMMERCIAL INVOICE SIGNED IN TRIPLICATE. + PACKING LIST IN TRIPLICATE. + GSP CERTIFICATE OF ORIGIN FORM A FROM PEOPLES'S REPUBLIC OF CHINA IN 1 COPY, IN THE SECOND COLUMN OF FORM A, GOODS CONSIGNED TO APPLICANT, THE THIRD PARTY'S FORM A IS ACCEPTABLE. + FULL SET (3/3) OF CLEAN 'ON BOARD' OCEAN BILLS OF LADING MADE OUT TO ORDER MARKED FREIGHT PREPAID AND NOTIFY APPLICANT. + INSURANCE POLICY/CERTIFICATE IN DUPLICATE ENDORSED IN BLANK FOR 110% INVOICE VALUE, COVERING ALL RISKS OF CIC OF PICC (1/1/1981). + CERTIFICATE'S CERTIFIED COPY OF FAX DISPATCHED TO THE BUYER WITHIN THREE DAYS AFTER SHIPMENT ADVISING L/C NO., NAME, QUANTITY AND AMOUNT OF GOODS, NUMBER OF PACKAGES, NAME OF VESSEL AND VOYAGE NO, AND DATE OF SHIPMENT.
ADDITIONAL CONDITION	47A:	+ THE NUMBER AND THE DATE OF THIS CREDIT MUST BE QUOTED ON ALL DOCUMENTS. + TELEGRAPHIC REIMBUESEMENT CLAIM PROHIBTED. + A DISCREPANCY FEE OF USD60.00 OR EQUIVALENT SHOULD BE DEDUCTED FROM THE PROCEEDS IF DOCUMENTS ARE PRESENTED WITH DISCREPANCY/IES. +BENEFICIARY'S CERTIFICATE IS REQUIRIED STATING THAT ORIGINAL GSP CERTIFICATE OF ORIGIN FORM A HAS BEEN SENT TO THE APPLICANT BY SPEED POST.
CHARGES	71B:	ALL CHARGES AND COMMISSIONS OUTSIDE ISSUING BANK ARE FOR ACCOUNT OF BENEFICIARY.
CONFIRMATION INSTRUCTION	49:	WITHOUT
INFORMATION TO PRESENTING BANK	78:	ALL DOCUMENTS ARE TO BE REMITTED IN ONE LOT BY COURIER TO BANK OF CHINA HAMBURG BRANCH, TRADE SERVICES, RATHAUSMARKT 5, 20095 HAMBURG, GERMANY.

2010 年 4 月 2 日，浙江大同进出口有限公司接到黄铜球阀的供应商浙江玉环金山阀门有限公司通知，预计在 4 月 9 日能完成全部黄铜球阀的生产，具体备货情况见表 3-1。

表 3-1 备货情况

规格	数量/套	每箱数量/套	纸箱数/箱	每箱毛重/千克	每箱净重/千克	箱数/托盘/箱	毛重/托盘/千克	净重/托盘/千克	体积/立方米
1/2"	4 320	160	27	26.60	25.60	27	728.20	718.20	0.968
3/4"	4 000	100	40	24.00	23.00	40	970.00	960.00	0.968
1"	2 400	60	40	22.00	21.00	40	890.00	880.00	0.968
1-1/4"	1 296	36	36	20.50	19.50	36	748.00	738.00	0.968
1-1/2"	960	24	40	18.50	17.50	40	750.00	740.00	0.968
2"	1 152	16	72	21.50	20.50	36	784.00	774.00	1.936
合计	14 128		255						6.776

托盘的尺寸为 110 厘米×80 厘米×110 厘米=0.968 立方米

桂小龙应按照“正确、完整、及时、简洁和清晰”的制单要求，完成以下工作任务：

【任务 1】制作商业发票

桂小龙根据信用证和供应商的备货信息制作商业发票。商业发票的号码为 2010DT00101，日期为 2010 年 4 月 2 日。

<table>
<tr><td colspan="6"></td></tr>
<tr><td colspan="6">COMMERCIAL INVOICE</td></tr>
<tr><td rowspan="4">To:</td><td colspan="2" rowspan="4"></td><td colspan="2">Invoice No. :</td><td></td></tr>
<tr><td colspan="2">Invoice Date:</td><td></td></tr>
<tr><td colspan="2">S/C No. :</td><td></td></tr>
<tr><td colspan="2">S/C Date:</td><td></td></tr>
<tr><td>From:</td><td></td><td>To:</td><td colspan="3"></td></tr>
<tr><td>L/C No. :</td><td></td><td rowspan="2">Issued By:</td><td colspan="3" rowspan="2"></td></tr>
<tr><td>Date of Issue:</td><td></td></tr>
<tr><td>Marks and Numbers</td><td>Number and Kind of Package
Description of Goods</td><td>Quantity</td><td>Unit Price</td><td colspan="2">Amount</td></tr>
<tr><td></td><td></td><td></td><td></td><td colspan="2"></td></tr>
<tr><td colspan="2">TOTAL:</td><td></td><td></td><td colspan="2"></td></tr>
<tr><td>SAY TOTAL:</td><td colspan="5"></td></tr>
<tr><td colspan="6"></td></tr>
</table>

【任务 2】制作装箱单

桂小龙根据信用证和供应商的备货信息制作装箱单。

<table>
<tr><td colspan="5"></td></tr>
<tr><td colspan="5">PACKING LIST</td></tr>
<tr><td rowspan="4">To:</td><td colspan="2" rowspan="4"></td><td>Invoice No. :</td><td></td></tr>
<tr><td>Invoice Date:</td><td></td></tr>
<tr><td>S/C No. :</td><td></td></tr>
<tr><td>S/C Date:</td><td></td></tr>
<tr><td>From:</td><td></td><td>To:</td><td colspan="2"></td></tr>
<tr><td>L/C No. :</td><td></td><td rowspan="2">Issued By:</td><td colspan="2" rowspan="2"></td></tr>
<tr><td>Date of Issue:</td><td></td></tr>
</table>

（续）

Marks and Numbers	Number and Kind of Package Description of Goods	Quantity	Package	G.W	N.W	Meas.
	TOTAL:					
SAY TOTAL:						

示范操作

【任务 1】制作商业发票

1．发票名称

由于信用证中发票条款要求的单据名称是“COMMERCIAL INVOICE”，所以发票名称可以是 COMMERCIAL INVOICE，也可以是 INVOICE。

2．受单人或抬头名称和地址

根据 UCP600 第 18 条的规定，若信用证无另外规定，商业发票的受单人或抬头为开证申请人。因此本业务的发票抬头名称和地址按信用证的“50”栏目填写。

3．起运地和目的地

起运地按照信用证中的“44E”栏目内容填写。目的地按照信用证中的“44F”栏目内容填写。

4．唛头

凡是来证有指定唛头的（Shipping Marks），必须按规定制唛，可以在信用证规定唛头的基础上增加内容，但不可减少内容。唛头内容一般由名称的缩写、合同号（或发票号）、目的港、件号等几部分组成。如无唛头，可打上 N/M（No Mark）。本业务中，信用证没有规定唛

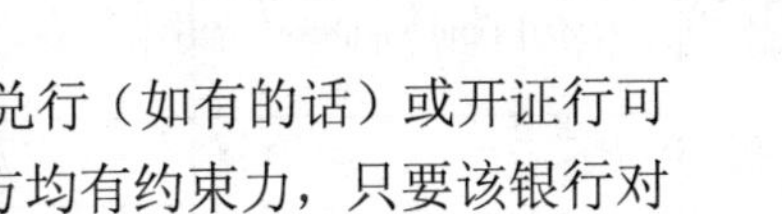

头内容，但出口合同规定了唛头内容。因此，根据出口合同，唛头为：

CARK
DT1000033
HAMBURG
CARTON NO.：1-255

5．货物描述

根据 UCP600 第 18 条的规定，发票中的货物描述必须与信用证规定的一致。本业务按信用证中的 45A 栏目内容填写。

6．数量、单价和金额

货物的数量要按实际出运货物数量填写，数量单位一定要与单价中的数量单位一致。单价由计价货币、单位数额、计量单位和价格术语四部分组成。金额要准确计算，认真复核。

根据 UCP600 第 30 条的规定，凡“约”、“大概”、“大约”或类似的词语用于信用证数量、单价和金额时，应理解为有关数量、单价和金额不超过 10%的增减幅度；在信用证未以包装单位件数或货物自身件数的方式规定货物数量时，只要总支取金额不超过信用证金额，货物数量允许有 5%的增减幅度。

根据 UCP600 第 18 条的规定，按指定行事的指定银行、保兑行（如有的话）或开证行可以接受金额大于信用证允许金额的商业发票，其决定对有关各方均有约束力，只要该银行对超过信用证允许金额的部分未作承付或者议付。

本业务的实际货物出运数量与信用证规定数量一致，因此数量、单价和金额都按信用证中“45A”栏目的内容填写。

7．发票号码、发票日期、信用证号码、合同号码等参考信息

这些信息根据出口合同和信用证的相关信息填写。

8．证明文句

信用证可要求在发票上加注各种证明文句，如分别标示加注运费、保险费和 FOB 金额，注明信用证号码、配额许可证号码等特定号码，加注非木质包装证明等。

本业务根据信用证“47A”栏目条款：“THE NUMBER AND THE DATE OF THIS CREDIT MUST BE QUOTED ON ALL DOCUMENTS. ”，须在发票中标出信用证号码 LC-536-089075 和开证日期 MARCH 17，2010。

9．出单人签名

根据 UCP600 第 18 条的规定，若信用证无另外规定，商业发票的出单人为受益人；商业发票可不必签字，但有时来证规定发票需要签字的，还是要签字，如 SIGNED COMMERCIAL INVOICE。在无手签要求的情况下，可以使用印鉴，但若来证要求“MANULLY SIGNED 或 SIGNED IN INK”，则必须手签。本业务只要求签字。

10．发票份数

发票有正副本之分，发票正副本份数的确定方法包括：①若信用证规定“发票若干份 Invoice in X copies”时，如发票三份，则提交至少一份正本发票；②若信用证规定“一份发票 One invoice”或“发票一份 Invoice in one copy”时，则需提交一份正本发票；③若信用证

规定“发票的一份 One copy of invoice”时，则提一份副本发票即为符合要求，当然也可提交一份正本发票。本业务要求出具三份，其中至少一份为正本。

以下是制作好的商业发票：

ZHEJIANG DATONG IMPORT AND EXPORT CO, LTD. NO.902 YILE ROAD, HANGZHOU, CHINA TEL: 0086-571-87772409 FAX: 0086-571-87772407 COMMERCIAL INVOICE					
To:	CARK GMBH & CO. KG DOMSTRASSE 55, D-20095 HAMBURG, GERMANY			Invoice No.: Invoice Date: S/C No.: S/C Date:	2010DT00101 APRIL 2, 2010 DT1000033 MARCH 3, 2010
From:	SHANGHAI, CHINA		To:	HAMBURG, GERMANY	
L/C No.:	LC-536-089075		Issued By:	BANK OF CHINA, HAMBURG BRANCH	
Date of Issue:	MARCH 17, 2010				
Marks and Numbers	Number and Kind of Package Description of Goods		Quantity (SETS)	Unit Price (USD/SET)	Amount (USD)
				CIF HAMBURG, GERMANY	
CARK DT1000033 HAMBURG CARTON NO: 1-255	FORGED BRASS BALL VALVES, ARTICLE NO. V10033, FULL PORT, NICKEL PLATED, BSP THREAD SIZE				
	1/2”		4320	1.08	4665.60
	3/4”		4000	1.51	6040.00
	1”		2400	2.30	5520.00
	1-1/4”		1296	3.70	4795.20
	1-1/2”		960	4.90	4704.00
	2”		1152	8.80	10137.60
		TOTAL:	14128		35862.40
SAY TOTAL:	U.S. DOLLARS THIRTY FIVE THOUSAND EIGHT HUNDRED AND SIXTY TWO AND CENTS FORTY ONLY.				
ZHEJIANG DATONG IMPORT AND EXPORT CO., LTD. 桂大同					

【任务 2】制作装箱单

桂小龙根据信用证、货物实际出运信息和已制作的商业发票，制作符合信用证要求的装箱单。

1. 单据名称

根据信用证规定，包装单据名称为 PACKING LIST。

2. 抬头

除非信用证特别要求，否则银行可接受不以开证申请人抬头的装箱单。本业务可以填写 CARK GMBH & CO. KG, DOMSTRASSE 55, D-20095 HAMBURG, GERMANY 或 TO WHOM IT MAY CONCERN。

3. 出单号码和日期

本栏目一般填发票号码和日期。

4. 唛头

本栏目填写发票唛头。

5. 货物描述

装箱单中所表明的货物应为发票中所描述的货物，但可用与其单据无矛盾的统称表示。

6. 数量、包装、净重、毛重和体积

本栏目填写时，注意货物净重和毛重是以千克为单位的，保留整数。货物体积单位是立方米，且保留三位小数。本业务填写黄铜阀门 6 种规格的数量、每箱数量、箱数、每箱毛重、每箱净重、每个托盘的箱数、每个托盘毛重、每个托盘净重、每个托盘体积、总毛重、总净重和总体积。

7. 证明文句

本业务根据信用证“47A”栏目条款：“THE NUMBER AND THE DATE OF THIS CREDIT MUST BE QUOTED ON ALL DOCUMENTS.”，须在装箱单中标出信用证号码 LC-536-089075 和开证日期 MARCH 17，2010。

8. 签署

当信用证没有规定装箱单签名时，可以不盖章签名，当然也可以盖章签名。

以下是制作好的装箱单：

ZHEJIANG DATONG IMPORT AND EXPORT CO., LTD. NO.902 YILE ROAD, HANGZHOU, CHINA TEL: 0086-571-87772409 FAX: 0086-571-87772407			
PACKING LIST			
To:	CARK GMBH & CO. KG DOMSTRASSE 55, D-20095 HAMBURG, GERMANY	Invoice No.:	2010DT00101
		Invoice Date:	APRIL 2, 2010
		S/C No.:	DT1000033
		S/C Date:	MARCH 3, 2010
From:	SHANGHAI, CHINA	To:	HAMBURG, GERMANY
L/C No.:	LC-536-089075	Marks and Numbers	CARK DT1000033 HAMBURG CARTON NO: 1-255
Date of Issue:	MARCH 17, 2010		
Issued By:	BANK OF CHINA, HAMBURG BRANCH		
Description of Goods:	FORGED BRASS BALL VALVES, ARTICLE NO. V10033, FULL PORT, NICKEL PLATED, BSP THREAD		

（续）

SIZE	Quantity	Qty/Ctn	Package	G.W/Ctn	N.W/Ctn	Ctn/Pallet	G.W/Pallet	N.W/Pallet	Meas.
1/2"	4320SETS	160SETS	27CTNS	26.60KGS	25.60KGS	27CTNS	728.20KGS	718.20KGS	0.968M^3
3/4"	4000SETS	100SETS	40CTNS	24.00KGS	23.00KGS	40CTNS	970.00KGS	960.00KGS	0.968M^3
1"	2400SETS	60SETS	40CTNS	22.00KGS	21.00KGS	40CTNS	890.00KGS	880.00KGS	0.968M^3
1-1/4"	1296SETS	36SETS	36CTNS	20.50KGS	19.50KKS	36CTNS	748.00KGS	738.00KGS	0.968M^3
1-1/2"	960SETS	24SETS	40CTNS	18.50KGS	17.50KGS	40CTNS	750.00KGS	740.00KGS	0.968M^3
2"	1152SETS	16SETS	72CTNS	21.50KGS	20.50KGS	36CTNS	784.00KGS	774.00KGS	1.936M^3
TOTAL	14128SETS		255CTNS						6.776M^3
SAY TOTAL:	TWO HUNDRED AND FIFTY FIVE CARTONS ONLY.								

PALLET DIMENSION: 110CM×80CM×110CM=0.968M^3

TOTALLY SEVEN PALLETS.

TOTAL GROSS WEIGHT: 5654.20KGS

TOTAL NET WEIGHT: 5584.20KGS

ZHEJIANG DATONG IMPORT AND EXPORT CO., LTD.

桂大同

知识支撑

一、外贸单证员的制单工作要求

外贸单证员的制单工作要求是“正确、完整、及时、简明、整洁”。

1．正确

正确是外贸单证工作的前提，单证不正确就不能安全收汇。这里所说的正确，包括两方面的内容：

（1）要求各种单证必须做到“四个一致”，即“单证一致、单约一致、单单一致和单货一致”。前面三个一致是针对单证处理而言的。在信用证结算方式下，要求做到单证一致和单单一致；在汇款和托收结算方式下，要求做到单约一致和单单一致。单货一致，使单证代表真实出运的货物，确保正常履约和安全收汇，同时也为企业树立良好的信誉。

（2）要求各种单证必须符合有关国际贸易惯例和进口国的有关法令和规定。信用证结算方式下的单证，要与《跟单信用证统一惯例》（UCP600）和《国际标准银行实务》（ISBP681）条款相一致。托收结算方式下的单证，要与《托收统一规则》（URC522）条款相一致。

2．完整

单证的完整性是构成单证合法性的重要条件之一，是单证成为有价证券的基础。单证的完整一般包括下列几种意义：

（1）单证的种类完整。单证在通过银行议付或托收时，一般都是成套、齐全而不是单一的。遗漏一种单证，就是单证不完整。例如，在 CIF 交易中，出口商向进口商提供的单证至少应有发票、提单和保险单。出口商只有按信用证或合同规定备齐所需单证，银行或进口商才能履行议付或承付的责任。

（2）单证的份数完整。单证的份数完整是指出口商必须按信用证或买卖合同的要求如数交齐各种单证的份数，不能短缺。目前，国外有些地区开来的信用证所列单证条款日趋繁复，所需单证类别甚多，除发票、提单、保险单等主要单据外，还有各种附属证明，如检验证书、产地证、船龄证明、邮政收据、电报副本等。这些单证都需要经过一定手续和事先联系才能取得。因此，在单证制作和审核过程中，必须密切注意，及时催办，防止遗漏和误期，以保证全套单证的完整性。

（3）单证的内容完整。单证内容完整是指每一种单据本身的内容（包括单据本身的格式、项目、文字和签章、背书等）必须完备齐全，否则不能构成有效文件。

3．及时

单证的及时性体现为及时出单和及时交单。

（1）及时出单。及时出单是指各种单证的出单日期必须合理可行，每一种单据的出单日期不能超过信用证规定的有效期限或按商业习惯的合理日期。例如，保险单的出单日期不能迟于提单的签发日期；提单日期不得迟于装运期限等。

（2）及时交单。及时交单是指出口商必须在信用证规定的交单期内向银行交单。过期交单将会遭到拒付。出口业务中，单证工作是一项多环节的综合性工作，单证工作不及时就会严重影响相关部门的工作。如订舱、报检、报关、结汇等工作，都是以单证为纽带，环环相扣，一环脱节，下一环的工作就无法进行，轻则打乱工作秩序，重则发生经济损失。

4．简明

单证的内容应按合同或信用证要求填写，力求简明，切勿加列不必要的内容，以免弄巧成拙。简化单证不仅可以减少工作量和提高工作效率，而且也有利于提高单证的质量和减少单证的差错。

5．整洁

整洁是指单证表面的清洁、美观、大方，单证内容的清楚易认，单证内容简洁明了。要求单证格式的设计和缮制力求标准化和规范化，单证内容的排列要行次整齐、主次有序、重点项目突出醒目、字迹清晰、语法通顺、文句流畅、用词简明扼要、恰如其分。

如果说正确和完整是单证的内在质量，那么整洁则是单证的外观质量。单证的外观质量在一定程度上反映了一个企业的业务水平。单证是否整洁，不但反映出外贸单证员制单的熟练程度和工作态度，而且还会直接影响出单的效果。

二、制单和审单的主要依据

外贸单证员制单和审单的主要依据是外贸合同、信用证、有关货物的原始资料、国际贸易惯例、国内相关规定等。

在信用证结算方式下，外贸单证员制单和审单的主要依据是信用证、有关货物的原始资料、《跟单信用证统一惯例》（UCP600）、《国际标准银行实务》（ISBP681）和国内相关规定。信用证取代外贸合同成为制单和审单的首要依据。

在托收结算方式下，外贸单证员制单和审单的主要依据是外贸合同、有关货物的原始资料、《托收统一规则》（URC522）和国内相关规定。其中外贸合同是制单和审单的首要依据。

在汇款结算方式下，外贸单证员制单和审单的主要依据是外贸合同、有关货物的原始资料和国内相关规定。其中外贸合同是制单和审单的首要依据。

有关货物的原始资料，一般来自生产企业提供的交货单和货物出厂装箱单等单据，包括货物具体的数量、重量、规格、尺码等。

三、商业发票

1. 商业发票的定义

商业发票是出口方向进口方开具的载有交易货物名称、数量、价格等内容的总清单，是装运货物的总说明，是外贸单据中的核心单据。

2. 商业发票的作用

（1）商业发票是最重要的履约证明文件。

（2）商业发票是进出口双方的记账凭证。

（3）商业发票是进出口双方报关和海关征税的依据。

（4）商业发票替代汇票的结算功能。

（5）商业发票是投保、理赔、外汇核销、出口退税等业务的重要凭证。

3. 商业发票份数的常见表示方法

商业发票份数的常见表示方法见表 3-2。

表 3-2 商业发票份数的常见表示方法

一式二份	In Duplicate	2 copies
一式三份	In Triplicate	3 copies
一式四份	In Quadruplicate	4 copies
一式五份	In Quintuplicate	5 copies
一式六份	In Sextuplicate	6 copies
一式七份	In Septuplicate	7 copies
一式八份	In Octuplicate	8 copies
一式九份	In Nonuplicate	9 copies
一式十份	In Decuplicate	10 copies

四、包装单据

包装单据是指一切记载或描述货物包装情况的单据，也是商业发票的补充单据。其主要种类如下：

1. 装箱单

装箱单（Packing List）又称包装单，是表明出口货物的包装形式、包装内容、数量、重量、体积或件数的单据。其主要作用是作为海关验货、公证行和核对进口商提货点数的凭证。装箱单无固定的格式和内容，只能由出口人根据货物的种类和进口商的要求而仿照商业发票的大体格式来制作，但在一般情况下，装箱单除有合同编号、发票号码外，还应包括货物的名称、唛头、装箱编号、包装类型、颜色与尺寸搭配、货物数量、包装数量、重量、体积等内容。若要求提供详细包装单，则必须提供尽可能详细的装箱内容，描述每件包装的细节，包括货物的货号、色号、尺寸搭配、毛重、净重及包装尺码。

2．尺码单

尺码单（Measurement List）又称体积单和码单，是主要记载货物包装的长、宽、高及总体积的清单，供买方及承运人了解货物的尺码，以便合理运输、储存及计算运费。

3．重量单

重量单（Weight List）又称磅码单，是以重量计量、计价的货物清单。一般列明每件包装货物的毛重和净重、整批货物的总毛重和总净重；有的还须增列皮重；按公量计量、计价的货物，则须列明公量及计算公量的有关数据。凡提供重量单的货物，一般不须提供包装单。

实训项目

◆ 实训项目 3-1

上接实训项目 2-1，2010 年 6 月 25 日，浙江曼旎进出口有限公司提出的改证申请得到阿联酋 Emirates Clothes Trader 的同意，修改后的信用证内容如下：

MT 700		ISSUE OF A DOCUMENTARY CREDIT
SENDER		HSBC BANK PLC, DUBAI, UAE
RECEIVER		BANK OF HANGZHOU, HANGZHOU, CHINA
SEQUENCE OF TOTAL	27:	1/1
FORM OF DOC. CREDIT	40A:	IRREVOCABLE
DOC. CREDIT NUMBER	20:	KKK101090
DATE OF ISSUE	31C:	100625
APPLICABLE RULES	40E:	UCP LATEST VERSION
DATE AND PLACE OF EXPIRY	31D:	DATE 100915 PLACE IN CHINA
APPLICANT	50:	EMIRATES CLOTHES TRADER P.O.BOX33, NO.12, SALAHUDDIN ROAD, DUBAI, U.A.E.
BENEFICIARY	59:	ZHEJIANG MANNI IMPORT & EXPORT CORPORATION 99 XUEYUAN SREET, HANGZHOU, P.R.CHINA
AMOUNT	32B:	CURRENCY USD AMOUNT 74000.00
AVAILABLE WITH/BY	41D:	ANY BANK IN CHINA, BY NEGOTIATION
DRAFTS AT ...	42C:	SIGHT
DRAWEE	42A:	HSBC BANK PLC, NEW YORK
PARTIAL SHIPMTS	43P:	PROHIBITED
TRANSSHIPMENT	43T:	ALLOWED
PORT OF LOADING/AIRPORT OF DEPARTURE	44E:	CHINESE MAIN PORT
PORT OF DISCHARGE	44F:	DUBAI, U.A.E.

（续）

SHIPMENT PERIOD	44D:	IN AUGUST, 2010
DESCRIPTION OF GOODS AND/OR SERVICES	45A:	5000PCS BOYS JACKET, SHELL: WOVEN TWILL 100% COTTON, LINING: WOVEN 100% POLYESTER, STYLE NO. SS98, AS PER S/C NO. MN10066 AT USD14.80/PC CIFC5 DUBAI, U.A.E. PACKED IN 20PCS/CTN
DOCUMENTS REQUIRED	46A:	+ COMMERCIAL INVOICE SIGNED IN INK IN TRIPLICATE. ONE ORIGINAL OF WHICH SHOULD BE CERTIFIED BY CHAMBER OF COMMERCE OR CCPIT AND LEGALIZED BY U.A.E. EMBASSY/ CONSULATE IN BENEFICIARY'S COUNTRY. + PACKING LIST IN TRIPLICATE. + CERTIFICATE OF CHINESE ORIGIN CERTIFIED BY CHAMBER OF COMMERCE OR CCPIT AND LEGALIZED BY U.A.E. EMBASSY/ CONSULATE IN SELLER'S COUNTRY. + INSURANCE POLICY/CERTIFICATE IN DUPLICATE ENDORSED IN BLANK FOR 110% INVOICE VALUE, COVERING ALL RISKS AND WAR RISK OF CIC OF PICC (1/1/1981) INCL. WAREHOUSE TO WAREHOUSE AND I.O.P AND SHOWING THE CLAIMING CURRENCY IS THE SAME AS THE CURRENCY OF CREDIT. + FULL SET (3/3) OF CLEAN 'ON BOARD' OCEAN BILLS OF LADING MADE OUT TO ORDER MARKED FREIGHT PREPAID AND NOTIFY APPLICANT. + SHIPPING ADVICE SHOWING THE NAME OF THE CARRYING VESSEL, DATE OF SHIPMENT, MARKS, QUANTITY, NET WEIGHT AND GROSS WEIGHT OF THE SHIPMENT TO APPLICANT WITHIN 3 DAYS AFTER THE DATE OF BILL OF LADING.
ADDITIONAL CONDITION	47A:	+ DOCUMENTS DATED PRIOR TO THE DATE OF THIS CREDIT ARE NOT ACCEPTABLE. + THE COMMISSION WILL BE DEDUCTED FROM THE BILL AMOUNT. + THE NUMBER AND THE DATE OF THIS CREDIT AND THE NAME OF ISSUING BANK MUST BE QUOTED ON ALL DOCUMENTS. + TRANSSHIPMENT ALLOWED AT HONGKONG ONLY. + SHORT FORM/CHARTER PARTY/THIRD PARTY BILL OF LADING IS NOT ACCEPTABLE. + SHIPMENT MUST BE EFFECTED BY 1×20'FULL CONTAINER LOAD. B/L TO SHOW EVIDENCE OF THIS EFFECT IS REQUIRED. + THE GOODS SHIPPED ARE NEITHER ISRAELI ORIGIN NOR DO THEY CONTAIN NEITHER ISRAELI MATERIALS NOR ARE THEY EXPORTED FROM ISRAEL, BENEFICIARY'S CERTIFICATE TO THIS EFFECT IS REQUIRED. + ALL PRESENTATIONS CONTAINING DISCREPANCIES WILL ATTRACT A DISCREPANCY FEE OF GBP40.00 PLUS TELEX COSTS OR OTHER CURRENCY EQUIVALENT. THIS CHARGE WILL BE DEDUCTED FROM THE BILL AMOUNT WHETHER OR NOT WE ELECT TO CONSULT THE APPLICANT FOR A WAIVER.
CHARGES	71B:	ALL CHARGES AND COMMISSIONS OUTSIDE U.A.E. ARE FOR ACCOUNT OF BENEFICIARY INCLUDING REIMBURSING FEE.
PERIOD FOR PRESENTATION	48:	WITHIN 15 DAYS AFTER THE DATE OF SHIPMENT, BUT WITHIN THE VALIDITY OF THIS CREDIT.
CONFIRMATION INSTRUCTION	49:	WITHOUT.
REIMBURSING BANK	53A:	HSBC BANK PLC, NEW YORK.
INFORMATION TO PRESENTING BANK	78:	ALL DOCUMENTS ARE TO BE REMITTED IN ONE LOT BY COURIER TO HSBC BANK PLC, TRADE SERVICES, DUBAI BRANCH, P O BOX 66, HSBC BANK BUILDING 312/45 Al SUQARE ROAD, DUBAI, UAE.

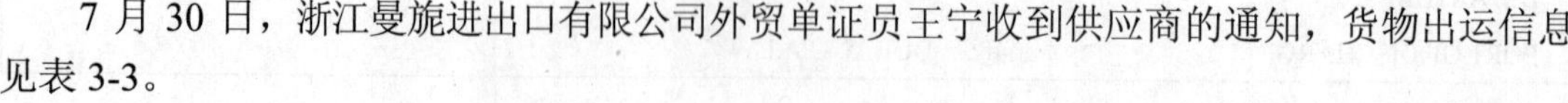

7 月 30 日，浙江曼旎进出口有限公司外贸单证员王宁收到供应商的通知，货物出运信息见表 3-3。

表 3-3　货物出运信息

品　名	男 童 夹 克
数量	5200 件
装箱率	20 件/纸箱
纸箱重量	毛重 10 公斤/箱，净重 9 公斤/箱
纸箱尺寸	57 厘米×40 厘米×40 厘米=0.0912 立方米

【任务 1】制作商业发票

外贸单证员王宁根据信用证和供应商的备货信息制作商业发票。商业发票的号码为 2010MN05015，日期为 2010 年 7 月 30 日。

<table>
<tr><td colspan="6"></td></tr>
<tr><td colspan="6">COMMERCIAL INVOICE</td></tr>
<tr><td rowspan="4">To:</td><td rowspan="4" colspan="2"></td><td colspan="2">Invoice No. :</td><td></td></tr>
<tr><td colspan="2">Invoice Date:</td><td></td></tr>
<tr><td colspan="2">S/C No. :</td><td></td></tr>
<tr><td colspan="2">S/C Date:</td><td></td></tr>
<tr><td>From:</td><td></td><td>To:</td><td colspan="3"></td></tr>
<tr><td>L/C No. .</td><td></td><td rowspan="2">Issued By:</td><td rowspan="2" colspan="3"></td></tr>
<tr><td>Date of Issue:</td><td></td></tr>
<tr><td>Marks and Numbers</td><td>Number and Kind of Package
Description of Goods</td><td>Quantity</td><td>Unit Price</td><td colspan="2">Amount</td></tr>
<tr><td></td><td></td><td></td><td></td><td colspan="2"></td></tr>
<tr><td colspan="2">TOTAL:</td><td></td><td></td><td colspan="2"></td></tr>
<tr><td>SAY TOTAL:</td><td colspan="5"></td></tr>
<tr><td colspan="6"></td></tr>
</table>

【任务 2】制作装箱单

外贸单证员王宁根据信用证和供应商的备货信息制作装箱单。

<table>
<tr><td colspan="7"></td></tr>
<tr><td colspan="7">PACKING LIST</td></tr>
<tr><td rowspan="4">To:</td><td rowspan="4" colspan="2"></td><td colspan="2">Invoice No. :</td><td colspan="2"></td></tr>
<tr><td colspan="2">Invoice Date:</td><td colspan="2"></td></tr>
<tr><td colspan="2">S/C No. :</td><td colspan="2"></td></tr>
<tr><td colspan="2">S/C Date:</td><td colspan="2"></td></tr>
<tr><td>From:</td><td></td><td>To:</td><td colspan="4"></td></tr>
<tr><td>L/C No. :</td><td></td><td rowspan="2">Issued By:</td><td rowspan="2" colspan="4"></td></tr>
<tr><td>Date of Issue:</td><td></td></tr>
<tr><td>Marks and Numbers</td><td>Number and Kind of Package
Description of Goods</td><td>Quantity</td><td>Package</td><td>G.W.</td><td>N.W.</td><td>Meas.</td></tr>
<tr><td></td><td></td><td></td><td></td><td></td><td></td><td></td></tr>
<tr><td colspan="2">TOTAL:</td><td></td><td></td><td></td><td></td><td></td></tr>
<tr><td>SAY TOTAL:</td><td colspan="6"></td></tr>
<tr><td colspan="7"></td></tr>
</table>

◆ **实训项目 3-2**

上接实训项目 2-2，2010 年 9 月 7 日，杭州维丰进出口有限公司提出的改证申请得到意大利 Sri Russa E Johns SPA 的同意，信用证修改书的内容如下：

MT 707	AMENDMENT TO A DOCUMENTARY CREDIT	
SENDER		BANK OF CHINA, MILAN BRANCH, ITALY
RECEIVER		BANK OF CHINA, ZHEJIANG BRANCH
SENDER'S REFERENCE	20:	59340I015228
RECEIVER'S REFERENCE	21:	NON
DATE OF ISSUE	31C:	100907
NUMBER OF AMENDMENT	26E:	01
BENEFICIARY(BEFORE THIS AMENDMENT)	59:	ZHEJIANG WEIFENG IMPORT AND EXPORT CO., LTD. 77 FENGTAN ROAD, HANGZHOU, CHINA
NEW DATE AND PLACE OF EXPIRY	31E:	DATE 101007 PLACE IN CHINA
LATEST DATE OF SHIPMENT	44C:	100930
NARRATIVE	79:	① UNDER FIELD 45A, STYLE NO. AND TRADE TERMS AMEND TO "DE5" AND "CPT" ② UNDER FIELD 71B, THE CHARGE CLAUSE AMENDS TO "ALL CHARGES AND COMMISSIONS OUTSIDE ISSUING BANK ARE FOR ACCOUNT OF BENEFICIARY. " OTHER TERMS AND CONDITIONS REMAIN UNCHANGED. AMENDMENT FEE USD25.00 AND CABLE FEE USD30.00 ARE FOR A/C OF APPLICANT. SUBJECT TO UCPDC (2007 REVISION) ICC PUB. NO.600.

杭州维丰进出口有限公司接受了以上信用证修改。

9 月 20 日，杭州维丰进出口有限公司外贸单证员叶丽收到供应商杭州扬帆皮革制造有限公司的通知，货物出运信息见表 3-4。

表 3-4 货物出运信息

款式号	颜色	数量/件	每箱数量/件	箱数/箱	每箱净重/千克	每箱毛重/千克	每箱体积
DE5	咖啡豆色	1400	10	140	5	6	60 厘米×50 厘米×20 厘米=0.06 立方米

装箱计划（见表 3-5）：

表 3-5 装箱计划

CTN NO.	38	40	42	44	46	48	TOTAL
1～10	100pcs						
11～35		250pcs					
36～65			300pcs				
66～95				300pcs			
96～120					250pcs		
121～140						200pcs	
TOTAL	100pcs	250pcs	300pcs	300pcs	250pcs	200pcs	1 400pcs

【任务 1】制作商业发票

外贸单证员叶丽根据信用证和供应商的备货信息制作商业发票。商业发票的号码为 2010WF02116，日期为 2010 年 9 月 20 日。

COMMERCIAL INVOICE				
To:			Invoice No. :	
			Invoice Date:	
			S/C No. :	
			S/C Date:	
From:		To:		
L/C No. :		Issued By:		
Date of Issue:				
Marks and Numbers	Number and Kind of Package Description of Goods	Quantity	Unit Price	Amount
	TOTAL:			
SAY TOTAL:				

【任务 2】制作装箱单

外贸单证员叶丽根据信用证和供应商的备货信息制作装箱单。

PACKING LIST						
To:			Invoice No. :			
			Invoice Date:			
			S/C No. :			
			S/C Date:			
From:		To:				
L/C No. :		Issued By:				
Date of Issue:						
Marks and Numbers	Number and Kind of Package Description of Goods	Quantity	Package	G.W.	N.W.	Meas.
	TOTAL:					
SAY TOTAL:						

◆ 实训项目 3-3

2010 年 7 月 8 日，浙江大顺进出口有限公司与西班牙 Lina Trading Co.，Ltd.就防弹轮胎出口签订如下出口合同。

SALES CONTRACT

NO.：DS10105　　　　DATE: July 8，2010

THE SELLER: ZHEJIANG DASHUN IMPORT AND EXPORT CO.，LTD.
808 JINGZHOU ROAD，HANGZHOU，P.R.CHINA
TEL: 0086-571-83450998　　FAX: 0086-571-83450999

THE BUYER: LINA TRADING CO.，LTD.
PEZ VOLADOR，33 ESQUINA DR. ESQUERDO，809，02 RETIRO，MADRID，SPAIN
TEL: 0034-902-112609　　FAX: 0034-902-112605

This Contract is made by and between the Buyer and Seller，whereby the Buyer agree to buy and the Seller agree to sell the under-mentioned commodity according to the terms and conditions stipulated below:

Commodity & Specification	Quantity	Unit Price	Amount
Bullet Proofing Tires		FOB Shanghai	
Art. No.205/55R16	180pcs	EUR50.00/pc	EUR9000.00
Art. No.205/60R15	180pcs	EUR50.00/pc	EUR9000.00
TOTAL	360pcs		USD18000.00
TOTAL CONTRACT VALUE: SAY EURO DOLLARS EIGHTEEN THOUSAND ONLY.			

PACKING: one piece per polybag

TIME OF SHIPMENT:
Not later than August 8, 2010.

PORT OF LOADING AND DESTINATION:
From Shanghai, China to Barcelona, Spain.
Transshipment and partial shipment are prohibited.

INSURANCE: To be covered by the Buyer.

TERMS OF PAYMENT: By D/P at sight.

DOCUMENTS:
+ Invoice in triplicate.
+ Packing List in triplicate.
+ Full set of clean on board ocean Bill of Lading made out to order blank endorsed marked “freight collect” notifying the applicant and marked the contact telephone no. and fax no.
+GSP Certificate of Origin FORM A.
+ Seller’s Certified Copy of Fax dispatched to the Buyer within three days after shipment advising name of vessel and voyage no, and date of shipment, shipping marks, quantity, gross weight, net weight of goods, number of packages.

OTHER CONDITIONS: Omitted.

This contract is made in four original copies and becomes valid after signature, two copies to be held by each party.

Signed by:

THE SELLER:	**THE BUYER**:
ZHEJIANG DASHUN IMPORT AND EXPORT CO., LTD.	COCA TRADING CO., LTD.
李劲松	Andy Raul

7 月 26 日，江苏致远轮胎厂通知浙江大顺进出口有限公司预计在 7 月 31 日能顺利完成全部防弹轮胎的生产。具体备货情况见表 3-6：

表 3-6 备货情况

款 式 号	数 量/条	塑料袋数量/袋	每袋净重/千克	每袋毛重/千克	每袋体积/立方米
205/55R16	180	180	11.73	11.79	0.0807
205/60R15	180	180	11.73	11.79	0.0807
合计	360	360			

【任务 1】制作商业发票

浙江大顺进出口有限公司外贸单证员朱丽娅根据出口合同和供应商的备货信息制作商业发票。商业发票的号码为 2010DS07012，日期为 2010 年 7 月 26 日。

<table>
<tr><td colspan="6"> </td></tr>
<tr><td colspan="6">COMMERCIAL INVOICE</td></tr>
<tr><td rowspan="4">To:</td><td colspan="2" rowspan="4"></td><td colspan="2">Invoice No. :</td><td></td></tr>
<tr><td colspan="2">Invoice Date:</td><td></td></tr>
<tr><td colspan="2">S/C No. :</td><td></td></tr>
<tr><td colspan="2">S/C Date:</td><td></td></tr>
<tr><td>From:</td><td></td><td>To:</td><td colspan="3"></td></tr>
<tr><td>L/C No. :</td><td></td><td rowspan="2">Issued By:</td><td colspan="3" rowspan="2"></td></tr>
<tr><td>Date of Issue:</td><td></td></tr>
<tr><td>Marks and Numbers</td><td>Number and Kind of Package
Description of Goods</td><td>Quantity</td><td>Unit Price</td><td colspan="2">Amount</td></tr>
<tr><td></td><td></td><td></td><td></td><td colspan="2"></td></tr>
<tr><td colspan="2">TOTAL:</td><td></td><td></td><td colspan="2"></td></tr>
<tr><td>SAY TOTAL:</td><td colspan="5"></td></tr>
<tr><td colspan="6"> </td></tr>
</table>

【任务 2】制作装箱单

浙江大顺进出口有限公司外贸单证员朱丽娅根据出口合同和供应商的备货信息制作装箱单。

<table>
<tr><td colspan="7"></td></tr>
<tr><td colspan="7">PACKING LIST</td></tr>
<tr><td rowspan="4">To:</td><td colspan="2" rowspan="4"></td><td>Invoice No. :</td><td colspan="3"></td></tr>
<tr><td>Invoice Date:</td><td colspan="3"></td></tr>
<tr><td>S/C No. :</td><td colspan="3"></td></tr>
<tr><td>S/C Date:</td><td colspan="3"></td></tr>
<tr><td>From:</td><td></td><td>To:</td><td colspan="4"></td></tr>
<tr><td>L/C No. :</td><td></td><td rowspan="2">Issued By:</td><td colspan="4" rowspan="2"></td></tr>
<tr><td>Date of Issue:</td><td></td></tr>
<tr><td>Marks and Numbers</td><td>Number and Kind of Package
Description of Goods</td><td>Quantity</td><td>Package</td><td>G.W.</td><td>N.W.</td><td>Meas.</td></tr>
<tr><td></td><td></td><td></td><td></td><td></td><td></td><td></td></tr>
<tr><td colspan="2">TOTAL:</td><td></td><td></td><td></td><td></td><td></td></tr>
<tr><td>SAY TOTAL:</td><td colspan="6"></td></tr>
<tr><td colspan="7"></td></tr>
</table>

项目四

制作订舱委托书和办理订舱操作

能力目标

能准确填制订舱委托书并办理订舱。

知识目标

熟悉托运操作流程、集装箱的装箱方式，了解托运的注意事项。

上接项目三的导入项目。

【任务1】制作订舱委托书

2010年4月2日，浙江大同进出口有限公司外贸单证员根据LC-536-089075信用证、商业发票、装箱单、浙江玉环金山阀门有限公司提供的货物出货信息，制作订舱委托书。

订舱委托书

年　月　日

托运人		合同号	
		发票号	
		信用证号	
		运输方式	
收货人		启运港	
		目的港	
		装运期	
通知人		可否转运	
		可否分批	
		运费支付方式	
		正本提单	

（续）

唛　头	货　名	包装件数	总毛重	总体积

<table>
<tr><td>注
意
事
项</td><td colspan="3"></td><td colspan="4"></td></tr>
<tr><td colspan="4">受托人：</td><td colspan="4">委托人：</td></tr>
<tr><td colspan="4"></td><td colspan="4"></td></tr>
<tr><td>电　话：</td><td></td><td>传　真：</td><td></td><td>电　话：</td><td></td><td>传　真：</td><td></td></tr>
<tr><td>联系人：</td><td colspan="3"></td><td>联系人：</td><td colspan="3"></td></tr>
</table>

【任务 2】办理订舱手续

外贸单证员桂小龙根据订舱委托书，委托浙江双马国际货运有限公司办理订舱手续。

示范操作

【任务 1】制作订舱委托书

第一步：外贸单证员桂小龙或指示外贸单证员上网查找船期和比较运价，选择一家国际货运代理公司。

2010 年 4 月 2 日，外贸单证员桂小龙登陆中国国际海运网（http://www. shippingchina.com）。

（1）进入船期查询，输入上海装运港、汉堡目的港和中国—欧洲航线，查到若干家国际货代公司的船期。

（2）点击各国际货代公司网站或进行电话联系，获得上海港至汉堡港的运价表。

（3）通过比较，选择浙江双马国际货运有限公司代理中海集装箱运输股份有限公司 2010 年 4 月 12 日的船期，船名为 XIN YA ZHOU，航次为 0023W，报价为 USD10/立方米。预计货物将于 5 月 6 日到达汉堡港。

第二步：制作符合要求的订舱委托书。

1．托运人

该栏目填写受益人或出口商的名称和地址。

2．收货人

该栏目根据信用证或合同的规定，填写收货人的名称和地址。收货人也称为提单抬头，包括记名抬头、不记名抬头和指示抬头等类型。采用记名抬头时，如规定 Consigned to KKK Company，则收货人栏目填写特定的收货人名称 KKK Company，相应的提单不能流通转让，因此很少使用；采用不记名抬头时，则收货人栏目空着不填或填写 To bearer，相应的提单无需背书即可流通转让，风险很大，因此也很少使用；实务中使用最多的是指示抬头，收货人栏目填写 To order，To order of shipper，To order of applicant，To order of issuing bank，To order of negotiating bank 等。

本业务根据信用证规定，填写 TO ORDER。

3．通知人

通知人是船公司在货物到达目的港时发送到货通知的收件人。通知人接到承运人的到货通知后，通知收货人去办理换单提货手续。本业务根据信用证规定，填写开证申请人的名称、地址、联系电话、传真。

4．运输方式

本业务填写 BY SEA。

5．启运港和目的港

本栏目根据合同或信用证规定填写启运港和目的港名称。

6．转运和分批装运

若合同或信用证规定了转运港，则要标出转运港，否则只要标注是否允许转运即可；若信用证没有规定是否允许转运，则根据 UCP600 规定，允许转运。关于分批装运，只要标注是否允许分批装运即可；若信用证没有规定是否允许分批装运，则根据 UCP600 规定，允许分批装运。

7．运费支付方式

在 FOB 和 FCA 贸易术语下，运费到付 Freight collect。在 CFR、CPT、CIF、CIP 贸易术语下，运费预付 Freight prepaid。根据信用证规定，本业务填写 FREIGHT PREPAID。

8．正本提单份数

若信用证未规定正本提单份数，一般要求 2～3 份正本。根据 UCP600 第 20 条规定，1 份正本海运提单也是允许的。根据信用证规定，本业务填写 THREE。

9．唛头

该栏目内容与商业发票的内容相同。

10．货物名称

该栏目根据信用证要求填写，也可以填写统称。

11．总毛重和总体积

该栏目内容与装箱单的内容相同。

12．装运期限和预订船期

该栏目按照合同或信用证规定填写装运期限，但同时要结合实际备货情况在“注意事项”栏目写明预订船期。本业务填写 NOT LATER THAN APRIL 17, 2010。预订船期为 2010 年 4 月 12 日，要求拼箱。

13．参考业务编号

该栏目填写合同号、发票号和信用证号等参考业务编号。

14．特殊条款

该栏目往往填写提单的特殊条款，对集装箱的冷冻、熏蒸等特殊要求。

本业务根据信用证要求，提单上要显示以下内容：

L/C NO.：LC-536-089075

L/C DATE：MARCH 17, 2010

15．委托人

委托人进行盖章签名，写上联系人名称、电话号码和传真号码。

本业务的填写：

委托人：ZHEJIANG DATONG IMPORT AND EXPORT CO., LTD.

联系人：桂小龙

电　话：0571-87772409

传　真：0571-87772407

以下是制作好的订舱委托书：

订舱委托书

2010年4月2日

<table>
<tr><td rowspan="4">托运人</td><td colspan="3" rowspan="4">ZHEJIANG DATONG IMPORT AND EXPORT CO., LTD.
NO.902 YILE ROAD, HANGZHOU, CHINA</td><td>合同号</td><td>DT1000033</td></tr>
<tr><td>发票号</td><td>2010DT00101</td></tr>
<tr><td>信用证号</td><td>LC-536-089075</td></tr>
<tr><td>运输方式</td><td>BY SEA</td></tr>
<tr><td rowspan="3">收货人</td><td colspan="3" rowspan="3">TO ORDER</td><td>启运港</td><td>SHANGHAI</td></tr>
<tr><td>目的港</td><td>HAMBURG</td></tr>
<tr><td>装运期</td><td>NOT LATER THAN APRIL 17, 2010</td></tr>
<tr><td rowspan="4">通知人</td><td colspan="3" rowspan="4">CARK GMBH & CO. KG
DOMSTRASSE 55, D-20095 HAMBURG, GERMANY
TEL：0049-40-3410967
FAX：0049-40-3410966</td><td>可否转运</td><td>NO</td></tr>
<tr><td>可否分批</td><td>NO</td></tr>
<tr><td>运费支付方式</td><td>PREPAID</td></tr>
<tr><td>正本提单</td><td>THREE</td></tr>
<tr><td colspan="2">唛头</td><td>货物名称</td><td>包装件数</td><td>总毛重</td><td>总体积</td></tr>
<tr><td colspan="2">CARK
DT1000033
HAMBURG
CARTON NO：1-255</td><td>FORGED BRASS BALL VALVES</td><td>7 PALLETS
（255CTNS）</td><td>5654.20KGS</td><td>6.776M³</td></tr>
<tr><td>注意事项</td><td colspan="5">1．请订2010年4月12日船期，拼箱；
2．提单上要显示以下内容：
（1）L/C NO.：LC-536-089075
（2）L/C DATE：MARCH 17, 2010</td></tr>
<tr><td colspan="3">受托人：</td><td colspan="3">委托人：
ZHEJIANG DATONG IMPORT AND EXPORT CO., LTD.</td></tr>
<tr><td>电　话：</td><td></td><td>传　真：</td><td>电　话：0571-87772409</td><td colspan="2">传　真：0571-87772407</td></tr>
<tr><td>联系人：</td><td colspan="2"></td><td colspan="3">联系人：桂小龙</td></tr>
</table>

【任务2】办理订舱手续

外贸单证员桂小龙把订舱委托书传真给浙江双马国际货运有限公司，指示其代理向中海集装箱运输股份有限公司订2010年4月12日船期，船名为XIN YA ZHOU，航次为0023W的拼箱。

知识支撑

一、选择货运代理公司

外贸企业在选择国际货运代理公司委托订舱时，主要权衡货运代理公司的海运报价、货代服务及公司实力等主要因素。托运化工产品、冷冻产品、食品、危险品和液态物品等特殊货物时，还应了解国际货运代理公司是否有能力办理这些特殊货物的出口托运业务，是否能提供相应的冷冻柜、干冻柜、平板柜、开顶柜等特殊服务。

二、出口托运操作流程

出口货物运输包括租船与班轮两种形式，班轮运输包括件杂货与集装箱两类，由于绝大部分货物是集装箱班轮运输，因此下面重点介绍集装箱班轮的托运操作流程。

（1）外贸企业填制订舱委托书，委托国际货运代理公司办理货物运输相关手续；

（2）国际货运代理公司接受外贸企业的委托，填制托运单，向船公司提出订舱申请；

（3）船公司同意承运后，将装货单、配舱回单等退还给国际货运代理公司，要求外贸企业（托运人）将货物按规定时间送达指定码头仓库；

（4）国际货运代理公司通知外贸企业已订舱；

（5）外贸企业或其国际货运代理公司自船公司的空箱堆场按订舱规定的数量提取空箱装箱，装箱方式可以分为门到门、内装箱及自拉自送三种；

（6）外贸企业将货物按规定时间交至码头仓库，交至理货公司，完成货物集港任务；

（7）码头堆场接收指定货物后签发场站收据给国际货运代理公司；

（8）外贸企业准备好报关单据后寄送国际货运代理公司，由其委托报关行向海关报关，海关审查合格后，在装货单上盖放行章，货物报关完成；

（9）待运货物按要求装上指定载货船舶；

（10）国际货运代理公司进入船舶代理公司系统打印海运提单确认书，传真给外贸企业确认。经外贸企业确认后，国际货运代理公司在海运提单申领单上盖章后，凭此到船舶代理公司处领取正本海运提单，再寄给外贸企业。

三、集装箱的装箱方式

集装箱整箱运输中货物的装箱方式可以分为门到门、内装箱和自拉自送三种方式。

门到门是指国际货运代理公司为客户提供货物运输的门到门服务，即国际货运代理公司从承运人处提取空箱，送至客户所在地将货物装箱、封铅，再由国际货运代理公司将重箱自客户所在地运至港区集港，安排货物装船运输至目的地，由国际货运代理公司在进口地的代理或分支机构负责将货物送至进口商仓库或进口商指定的其他地方，实现货物运输的门到门方式。

内装箱是指国际货运代理公司将空箱提回自己的货运站，向客户发出“发货通知书”或

"进仓通知书"，要求客户在指定期限内将指定货物送至指定货运站，在货运站内完成货物装箱，并封铅，然后向客户出具"货物进仓接受单"或"入库单"，再由货运代理公司安排装箱送至港区的方式。

自拉自送是指国际货运代理公司完成订舱，并向承运人提出用箱申请后，由客户自己派车队提取空箱，送至客户货物存储地，并在货物装箱后，由客户将货物按港区要求集港。

四、出口托运的注意事项

出口货物托运流程中，需要注意以下几方面事项。

（1）关于托运要求。出口商在出口货物备妥出运前，应严格遵照外贸合同的规定向国际货运代理公司提出货物托运要求，注意明确货物运输时间、运输方式、装运地、目的地、是否分批转运等要素。

（2）关于托运责任人。有义务完成货物订舱、运输的当事人依贸易术语不同而不同。在FOB术语下，买方有义务与承运人签订运输合同，所以，此时出口商需要密切关注指定船舶到港时间，做好船货衔接的准备，否则，一旦出现由于出口商的原因造成船货脱节，则出口商需要承担因此产生的滞期费、空舱费等费用。在CIF或CFR术语下，则需要出口商负责租船订舱，安排货物运输，在这种情况下，外贸单证员要认真遵照外贸合同规定，向船公司提出托运申请，在指定时间、指定装运港至目的港之间安排货物的运输，并且应该做好货物装船前的一切准备工作，包括货物检验、领证、报关、装箱等环节。

（3）关于托运单据。作为外贸单证员，在委托国际货运代理公司代理租船订舱的情况下，要明确托运单上托运人、收货人、通知人、货物信息等相关内容，这是国际货运代理公司向船公司订舱时的依据，其内容应该与装船后签发的提单上相关的内容一致。

（4）关于装船时间。装船时间是托运业务中重要的内容，是外贸单证员特别关注的要素。

1）装船时间必须符合外贸合同与信用证的相关规定，否则，将构成出口商违约并可能导致进口商拒付货款。

2）外贸单证员依据合同或信用证的规定订舱后，需要有足够的时间完成货物的商检、报关等手续。

3）订舱完成后，外贸单证员在接到国际货运代理公司货物进仓通知后，要保证货物在规定时间内到达港区，交给指定的仓库。

（5）承运人责任起讫：根据《中华人民共和国海关法》的相关规定，承运人的责任期间因运输货物属件杂货或集装箱货物不同而不同。件杂货运输中，承运人的责任起讫期间为"船至船"，即承运人自货物装上船至卸下船止；而集装箱运输中，承运人的责任起讫期间为自接收货物时起至交付货物时止。所以，在出口商在码头堆场将货物交付承运人时起，承运人开始承担货物运输责任。

实训项目

◆ **实训项目 4-1**

上接实训项目 3-1。

【任务 1】制作订舱委托书

2010 年 7 月 30 日，浙江曼旎进出口有限公司外贸单证员王宁根据信用证、商业发票、装箱单和以下信息，制作订舱委托书。

（1）要求订 8 月 7 日马士基航运的 Columbine Maersk 船，V.1007。

（2）仓库地址：浙江省绍兴市解放路 158 号绍兴力美服装有限公司

联系人：刘美

电　话：0575-66368911

订舱委托书

年　月　日

<table>
<tr><td rowspan="4">托运人</td><td colspan="4" rowspan="4"></td><td>合同号</td><td colspan="2"></td></tr>
<tr><td>发票号</td><td colspan="2"></td></tr>
<tr><td>信用证号</td><td colspan="2"></td></tr>
<tr><td>运输方式</td><td colspan="2"></td></tr>
<tr><td rowspan="3">收货人</td><td colspan="4" rowspan="3"></td><td>启运港</td><td colspan="2"></td></tr>
<tr><td>目的港</td><td colspan="2"></td></tr>
<tr><td>装运期</td><td colspan="2"></td></tr>
<tr><td rowspan="4">通知人</td><td colspan="4" rowspan="4"></td><td>可否转运</td><td colspan="2"></td></tr>
<tr><td>可否分批</td><td colspan="2"></td></tr>
<tr><td>运费支付方式</td><td colspan="2"></td></tr>
<tr><td>正本提单</td><td colspan="2"></td></tr>
<tr><td colspan="2">唛　头</td><td colspan="2">货　名</td><td>包装件数</td><td>总毛重</td><td colspan="2">总体积</td></tr>
<tr><td colspan="2"></td><td colspan="2"></td><td></td><td></td><td colspan="2"></td></tr>
<tr><td>注意事项</td><td colspan="7"></td></tr>
<tr><td colspan="4">受托人：</td><td colspan="4">委托人：</td></tr>
<tr><td colspan="4"></td><td colspan="4"></td></tr>
<tr><td>电　话：</td><td></td><td>传　真：</td><td></td><td>电　话：</td><td></td><td>传　真：</td><td></td></tr>
<tr><td>联系人：</td><td colspan="3"></td><td>联系人：</td><td colspan="3"></td></tr>
</table>

【任务 2】办理订舱手续

外贸单证员王宁根据订舱委托书，委托浙江双马国际货运有限公司办理订舱手续。

◆　**实训项目 4-2**

上接实训项目 3-2。

【任务 1】制作订舱委托书

2010 年 9 月 20 日，杭州维丰进出口有限公司外贸单证员叶丽根据信用证、商业发票、装箱单，制作订舱委托书。要求订国航 9 月 27 日的 CA2304/CA1069 航班。

订舱委托书

年　月　日

<table>
<tr><td rowspan="4">托运人</td><td colspan="4" rowspan="4"></td><td>合同号</td><td></td></tr>
<tr><td>发票号</td><td></td></tr>
<tr><td>信用证号</td><td></td></tr>
<tr><td>运输方式</td><td></td></tr>
<tr><td rowspan="3">收货人</td><td colspan="4" rowspan="3"></td><td>启运港</td><td></td></tr>
<tr><td>目的港</td><td></td></tr>
<tr><td>装运期</td><td></td></tr>
<tr><td rowspan="4">通知人</td><td colspan="4" rowspan="4"></td><td>可否转运</td><td></td></tr>
<tr><td>可否分批</td><td></td></tr>
<tr><td>运费支付方式</td><td></td></tr>
<tr><td>正本提单</td><td></td></tr>
<tr><td colspan="2">唛　头</td><td colspan="2">货　名</td><td>包 装 件 数</td><td>总 毛 重</td><td>总 体 积</td></tr>
<tr><td colspan="2"></td><td colspan="2"></td><td></td><td></td><td></td></tr>
<tr><td>注意事项</td><td colspan="6"></td></tr>
<tr><td colspan="4">受托人：</td><td colspan="3">委托人：</td></tr>
<tr><td colspan="4"></td><td colspan="3"></td></tr>
<tr><td>电　话：</td><td></td><td>传　真：</td><td></td><td>电　话：</td><td>传　真：</td><td></td></tr>
<tr><td>联系人：</td><td colspan="3"></td><td>联系人：</td><td colspan="2"></td></tr>
</table>

【任务 2】办理订舱手续

外贸单证员叶丽根据订舱委托书，委托浙江双马国际货运有限公司办理订舱手续。

◆ **实训项目 4-3**

上接实训项目 3-3。

【任务 1】制作订舱委托书

2010 年 7 月 26 日，浙江大顺进出口有限公司外贸单证员朱丽娅根据出口合同、商业发票、装箱单，制作订舱委托书。计划通过 Lina Trading Co., Ltd.指定的国际货运代理公司——德莎国际货运代理（上海）有限公司，订 8 月 2 日马士基的 Marit Maersk 船，航次为 1004，1 个 20 英尺的集装箱。

订舱委托书

年　月　日

托运人		合同号	
		发票号	
		信用证号	
		运输方式	
收货人		启运港	
		目的港	
		装运期	
通知人		可否转运	
		可否分批	
		运费支付方式	
		正本提单	

唛　头	货　名	包装件数	总毛重	总体积

注意事项	

受托人：				委托人：			
电　话：		传　真：		电　话：		传　真：	
联系人：				联系人：			

【任务 2】办理订舱手续

外贸单证员朱丽娅根据订舱委托书，委托德莎国际货运代理（上海）有限公司办理订舱手续。

项目五

制作出境货物报检单和办理报检操作

能力目标

能根据信用证条款和/或外贸合同条款、货物实际出运信息和订舱委托书填制出境货物报检单和报检委托书。

知识目标

掌握报检的依据、条件、时限、地点，报检所需提供的单证，法定报检的含义、范围和方式；熟悉商检机构的种类，预报检，重新报检和出口货物检验检疫的一般流程；了解电子转单、电子通关和检验检疫证书。

上接项目四的导入项目。2010 年 4 月 5 日，浙江大同进出口有限公司外贸单证员桂小龙收到浙江双马国际货运有限公司的通知，已按要求订妥舱位：2010 年 4 月 12 日的船期，船名为 XIN YA ZHOU，航次为 0023W 的拼箱。

【任务 1】制作报检委托书

因为黄铜球阀 H.S.编码为 8481801090，监管证件代码是 B，即出境货物通关单，属于法定检验货物，所以浙江大同进出口有限公司外贸单证员桂小龙在 2010 年 4 月 6 日，根据商业发票、装箱单和以下信息制作报检委托书，委托浙江玉环金山阀门有限公司向浙江省出入境检验检验局台州分局报检。

（1）浙江大同进出口有限公司，属私营有限责任公司，邮政编码是 310016；

（2）浙江玉环金山阀门有限公司的登记号为 3800708358，属私营有限责任公司，法人代表是瞿金山，联系人是周斌，邮政编码是 317600，联系电话为 0576-86578908。

报检委托书

__________出入境检验检疫局：

本委托人声明，保证遵守《中华人民共和国进出口商品检验法》、《中华人民共和国进出境动植物检疫法》、《中华人民共和国国境卫生检疫法》、《中华人民共和国食品卫生法》等有关法律、法规的规定和检验检疫机构制定的各项规章制度。如有违法行为，自愿接受检验检疫机构的处罚并负法律责任。本委托人所委托受委托人向检验检疫机构提交的“报检单”和随附各种单据所列内容是真实无讹的。具体委托情况如下：

本单位将于______年____月间出口如下货物：

品　名：		数（重）量：	
合　同　号：		信 用 证 号：	

特委托________________（地址：______________________________）代表本公司办理本批货物所有的检验检疫事宜，请贵局按有关法律规定予以办理。

委托单位名称（签章）：	受委托单位名称（签章）：
单 位 地 址：	单 位 地 址：
邮 政 编 码：	邮 政 编 码：
法 人 代 表：	法 人 代 表：
本批货物业务联系人：	本批货物业务联系人：
联系电话（手机）：	联系电话（手机）：
企 业 性 质：	企 业 性 质：
日　　期：　　年　月　日	日　　期：　　年　月　日
本委托书有效期至　　年　月　日	

【任务 2】制作出境货物报检单

4 月 7 日，浙江玉环金山阀门有限公司外贸单证员周斌在收到浙江大同进出口有限公司的报检委托书和随附单据后，制作出境货物报检单，向浙江省出入境检验检疫局台州分局办理报检。

中华人民共和国出入境检验检疫

出境货物报检单

报检单位（加盖公章）：　　　　　　　　　　＊编号　380400210025679

报检单位登记号：　　　联系人：　　　电话：　　　报检日期：　年　月　日

发货人	（中文）				
	（外文）				
收货人	（中文）				
	（外文）				
货物名称（中/外文）	H.S.编码	产地	数量/重量	货物总值	包装种类及数量

运输工具名称号码		贸易方式		货物存放地点	
合同号		信用证号		用途	
发货日期	年　月　日	输往国家（地区）		许可证 / 审批号	
启运地		到达口岸		生产单位注册号	

（续）

<table>
<tr><td colspan="2">集装箱规格、数量及号码</td><td colspan="4"></td></tr>
<tr><td colspan="2">合同、信用证订立的检验检疫条款或特殊要求</td><td colspan="2">标 记 及 号 码</td><td colspan="2">随附单据（划“✓”或补填）</td></tr>
<tr><td colspan="2"></td><td colspan="2"></td><td colspan="2">□合同 □装箱单
□信用证 □厂检单
□发票 □包装性能结果单
□换证凭单 □许可/审批文件</td></tr>
<tr><td colspan="4">需要证单名称（划“✓”或补填）</td><td colspan="2">*检验检疫费</td></tr>
<tr><td colspan="2" rowspan="3">□品质证书 __正__副
□重量证书 __正__副
□数量证书 __正__副
□兽医卫生证书 __正__副
□健康证书 __正__副</td><td colspan="2" rowspan="3">□卫生证书 __正__副
□动物卫生证书 __正__副
□植物检疫证书 __正__副
□熏蒸/消毒证书 __正__副
□出境货物换证凭单 _1_正__副</td><td>总金额
（人民币元）</td><td></td></tr>
<tr><td>计费人</td><td></td></tr>
<tr><td>收费人</td><td></td></tr>
<tr><td colspan="4" rowspan="3">报检人郑重声明：
1．本人被授权报检。
2．上列填写内容正确属实，货物无伪造或冒用他人的厂名、标志、认证标志，并承担货物质量责任。
签名：</td><td colspan="2">领取证单</td></tr>
<tr><td>日 期</td><td></td></tr>
<tr><td>签 名</td><td></td></tr>
</table>

注：有“*”号栏由出入境检验检疫机关填写

◆ 国家出入境检验检疫局制

[1-2（2000.1.1）]

示范操作

【任务 1】制作报检委托书

由于本业务中，出口货物的产地在台州，因此浙江大同进出口有限公司外贸单证员桂小龙须委托浙江玉环金山阀门有限公司向浙江省出入境检验检疫局台州分局报检。为此，制作如下报检委托书：

<table>
<tr><td colspan="4">报 检 委 托 书

台州市出入境检验检疫局：
本委托人声明，保证遵守《中华人民共和国进出口商品检验法》、《中华人民共和国进出境动植物检疫法》、《中华人民共和国国境卫生检疫法》、《中华人民共和国食品卫生法》等有关法律、法规的规定和检验检疫机构制定的各项规章制度。如有违法行为，自愿接受检验检疫机构的处罚并负法律责任。本委托人所委托受委托人向检验检疫机构提交的“报检单”和随附各种单据所列内容是真实无讹的。具体委托情况如下：
本单位将于_2010_年_4_月间出口如下货物：</td></tr>
<tr><td>品 名：</td><td>黄铜球阀</td><td>数（重）量：</td><td>14128 套</td></tr>
<tr><td>合 同 号：</td><td>DT1000033</td><td>信 用 证 号：</td><td>LC-536-089075</td></tr>
<tr><td colspan="4">特委托浙江玉环金山阀门有限公司（地址：浙江省玉环市利民路 11 号）代表本公司办理本批货物所有的检验检疫事宜，请贵局按有关法律规定予以办理。
委托单位名称（签章）：浙江大同进出口有限公司　　受委托单位名称（签章）：浙江玉环金山阀门有限公司</td></tr>
</table>

（续）

单 位 地 址：	浙江省杭州市益乐路 902 号	单 位 地 址：	浙江省玉环市利民路 11 号
邮 政 编 码：	310016	邮 政 编 码：	317600
法 人 代 表：	季大同	法 人 代 表：	瞿金山
本批货物业务联系人：	桂小龙	本批货物业务联系人：	周斌
联系电话 （手机）：	0571-87772409	联系电话 （手机）：	0576-86578908
企 业 性 质：	私营有限责任公司	企 业 性 质：	私营有限责任公司
日　　期：	2010 年 4 月 6 日	日　　期：	2010 年 4 月 6 日
本委托书有效期至	2010 年 7 月 6 日		

外贸单证员桂小龙把制作的报检委托书、商业发票、装箱单、信用证和外贸合同等单据寄给浙江玉环金山阀门有限公司委托代为报检。

【任务 2】制作出境货物报检单

第一步：制作出境货物报检单。

浙江玉环金山阀门有限公司外贸单证员周斌通过九城软件或榕基软件登录电子报检系统填制出境货物报检单如下各栏目内容：

1. 编号

该编号是由系统在正式受理报检时自动生成 15 位数的报检号。

2. 报检单位

报检单位是指经国家质量监督检验检疫总局审核，获得许可、登记，并取得国家质检总局颁发的《自理报检单位备案登记证明书》或《代理报检单位备案登记证明书》的企业。本业务盖报检单位浙江玉环金山阀门有限公司的公章。

3. 报检单位登记号

本业务填 3800708678，联系人填周斌，电话填 05766578908。

4. 报验日期

本业务填报检日期 2010 年 4 月 7 日。

5. 发货人

本栏分行填写发货人浙江大同进出口有限公司的中、英文名称。

6. 收货人

本业务填写收货人英文名称 CARK GMBH & CO. KG，中文名称可不填。

7. 货物名称（中/英文）

本栏应按外贸合同、信用证、商业发票中所列货物名称的中、英文填写。

8. H. S. 编码

本栏填写 8481801090。

9. 产地

本栏填报出境货物生产地的省、市、县的中文名称。

10. 数/重量

本栏按实际申请检验检疫的数量/重量填写，重量还须列明毛/净/皮重。本业务填写14128套。

11. 货物总值

本栏应按合同、发票或报关单上所列货物总值一致。本业务填写35862.40美元。

12. 包装种类及数量

本栏应按照实际运输外包装的种类及对应数量填报。本业务填写255个纸箱。

13. 运输工具名称号码

本栏填制实际出境运输工具的名称及编号，如船舶名称及航次等。实际报检申请时，若未定运输工具的名称及编号时，可以笼统填制运输方式总称。如填报“船舶”或“飞机”等。本业务填写XIN YA ZHOU/0023W。

14. 合同号

本业务填写DT1000033。

15. 贸易方式

本栏填报与实际情况一致的海关规范贸易方式。常见的贸易方式有：“一般贸易”、“进料加工贸易”、“来料加工贸易”、“易货贸易”、“补偿贸易”等九十多种贸易方式。本业务填写一般贸易。

16. 货物存放地点

货物存放地点是指出口货物的生产企业存放出口货物的地点。本业务填写浙江省玉环市利民路11号。

17. 发货日期

本栏目按实际开船日或起飞日等，填报发货日期，以年、月、日的方式填报。本业务填写2010年4月12日。

18. 输往国家（地区）

本栏填出口货物直接运抵的国家（地区），即货物的最终销售国。本业务填写德国。

19. 许可证号/审批号

本栏应填报有关许可证号或审批号。无需许可证或审批文件的出境货物本栏免报。

20. 生产单位注册号

本栏填报出入境检验检疫机构签发给生产单位的卫生注册证书号或加工厂的注册号码等。本业务填写无。

21. 起运地

本栏填报出境货物最后离境的口岸或所在地的中文名称。本业务填写上海。

22. 到达口岸

最终目的港可预知的，本栏按实际到达口岸的中文名称填报；最终到达口岸不可预知的，可按尽可能预知的到达口岸填报。本业务填写汉堡。

23. 集装箱规格/数量及号码

集装箱规格是指国际标准的集装箱规格尺寸。常见的四种箱型有A型、B 型、C型和D

型。它们的尺寸有十多种，主要有 20'C 型、40'A 型等。集装箱的数量是指实际集装箱数量，而不是作为换算标准箱。集装箱号码是指国际集装箱的识别号码。拼箱时无须填写。

24. 合同、信用证订立的检验检疫条款或特殊要求

在合同中订阅的有关检验检疫的特殊条款及其他要求应填入此栏。本业务填写无。

25. 标记和号码

货物的标记号码，又称为货物的唛头。本栏内容与发票相同。

26. 用途

本栏目用途包括 9 种：①种用或繁殖；②食用；③奶用；④观赏或演艺；⑤伴侣动物；⑥试验；⑦药用；⑧饲用；⑨其他。

本业务填写其他。

27. 随附单据（划“√”或补填）

按照实际随附的单据种类划“√”或补充填报随附单据。

本业务在合同、信用证、商业发票、装箱单、厂检单和包装性能结果单前划“√”。

28. 签名

本栏由持有《报检员证》的报检员手签。

29. 检验检疫费用

本栏由检验检疫机构计费人员核定费用后填写，如熏蒸费和消毒费等。

30. 领取证单

报检人在领取证单时填写领证日期和领证人签名。

填制好的出境货物报检单如下。

中华人民共和国出入境检验检疫
出境货物报检单

报检单位（加盖公章）：　浙江玉环金山阀门有限公司　　*编号　380400210025679

报检单位登记号：3800708358　联系人：周斌　电话：0576-6578908　报检日期：2010 年 4 月 7 日

发货人	（中文）	浙江大同进出口有限公司					
	（外文）	ZHEJIANG DATONG IMPORT AND EXPORT CO., LTD.					
收货人	（中文）						
	（外文）	CARK GMBH & CO. KG					
货物名称（中/外文）		H.S.编码	产地	数/重量	货物总值	包装种类及数量	
黄铜球阀 FORGED BRASS BALL VALVES		8481801090	浙江玉环	14128 套	35862.40 美元	255 个纸箱	
运输工具名称号码	XIN YA ZHOU/0023W	贸易方式	一般贸易	货物存放地点	浙江省玉环市利民路 11 号		
合同号	DT1000033	信用证号		LC-536-089075	用途	其他	
发货日期	2010 年 4 月 12 日	输往国家（地区）		德国	许可证 / 审批号	无	
启运地	上海	到达口岸		汉堡	生产单位注册号	无	
集装箱规格、数量及号码							
合同、信用证订立的检验检疫条款或特殊要求		标 记 及 号 码		随附单据（划“✓”或补填）			

（续）

	CARK DT1000033 HAMBURG CARTON NO：1-255	☑合同 ☑信用证 ☑发票 ☐换证凭单	☑装箱单 ☑厂检单 ☑包装性能结果单 ☐许可/审批文件

需要证单名称（划“✓”或补填）				*检验检疫费	
☐品质证书	__正__副	☐卫生证书	__正__副	总金额（人民币元）	
☐重量证书	__正__副	☐动物卫生证书	__正__副		
☐数量证书	__正__副	☐植物检疫证书	__正__副	计费人	
☐兽医卫生证书	__正__副	☐熏蒸/消毒证书	__正__副	收费人	
☐健康证书	__正__副	☑出境货物换证凭单	1 正__副		

报检人郑重声明：	领取证单	
1. 本人被授权报检。	日 期	
2. 上列填写内容正确属实，货物无伪造或冒用他人的厂名、标志、认证标志，并承担货物质量责任。 签名：周斌	签 名	

注：有“*”号栏由出入境检验检疫机关填写

◆国家出入境检验检疫局制

[1-2（2000.1.1）]

填写出境货物报检单并保存发送后，会得到系统“收到”的回执，表明已通过机审，但尚未正确受理。此时系统会产生15位数+E的预录入号。当检验检疫机构正式受理时，会由检务人员进行审单，审单结束后，企业会得到系统“正确”或“错误”的回执。回执显示“错误”表示系统审查有误退回或检务审核有误退回，回执显示“正确”表示检务已正式受理报检，产生正式报检号为15位数。然后，外贸单证员即可打印出境货物报检单，完成报检工作。

第二步，办理报检。

浙江玉环金山阀门有限公司凭出境货物报检单、厂检单、包装性能结果单和浙江大同进出口有限公司寄来的报检委托书、商业发票、装箱单、信用证、外贸合同向台州出入境检验检疫局报检。2010年4月9日，货物检验通过后，台州出入境检验检疫局发给浙江玉环金山阀门有限公司一张换证凭条。

转单号	380400210007898T		报检号	380400210025679	
报检单位	浙江玉环金山阀门有限公司				
品名	黄铜球阀				
合同号	DT1000033		H.S.编码	8481801090	
数（重）量	14128套	包装件数	255个纸箱	金额	35862.40美元
评定意见： 贵单位报检的该批货物，经我局检验检疫，已合格。请执此单到上海局本部办理出境验证业务。本单有效期截止于 2010年6月8日。 台州局本部 2010年4月9日					

知识支撑

（一）出入境检验检疫含义

出入境检验检疫是指作为政府的一个行政部门，以保护国家整体利益和社会效益为衡量标准，以法律、行政法规、国际惯例或进口国法规要求为准则，对出入境货物、交通运输工具、人员及其事项等进行检验检疫、管理及认证，并提供官方检验检疫证明、居间检验检疫公证和鉴定证明的全部活动。

（二）商检机构的种类

1. 我国的货物检验机构

中华人民共和国国家质量监督检验检疫总局，简称国家质检总局，于 2001 年 4 月成立。它行使原国家技术监督局和原国家出入境检验检疫局的职能。国家质检总局设在全国各地的直属检验检疫局、商检机构和办事处管理所辖地区出入境检验检疫工作。国家质检总局下设的主要事业单位有，中国国家认证认可监督管理委员会、中国国家标准化管理委员会和中国进出口货物检验总公司。其中中国进出口货物检验总公司（China National Import and Export Commodities Inspection Corporation，简称 CCIC）是非政府的综合性进出口货物检验机构，按照国际惯例运作，以第三者的地位，独立、公正、科学的态度，开展进出口货物的检验和鉴定业务服务。国家质检总局在出入境检验检疫方面包括进出口货物检验、进出境动植物检疫、进口货物认证管理、进口废物原料装运前检验、出口货物质量许可、食品卫生监督检验、出口货物运输包装检验、外商投资财产鉴定、货物装载和残损鉴定、卫生检疫与处理等业务。

2. 国外著名的货物检验机构

在国际上，常被世界广泛认可的检验机构很多。除了政府设立的官方货物检验机构外，由商会、协会、同业公会或私人设立的半官方或非官方货物检验机构，担负着很多检验和鉴定工作，并取得了很高的信誉。以下是部分国外著名的货物检验机构：

（1）瑞士通用公证行（SGS）。瑞士通用公证行是当今世界上最大的检验鉴定公司，总部设在日内瓦，是专门从事检验、实验、质量保证和质量认证的国际性检验鉴定公司。

（2）英国英之杰检验集团（IITS）。英国英之杰检验集团是一个国际性的货物检验组织，集团主要成员有英国嘉碧集团、中国香港天祥公证行、英特泰克国际服务有限公司、英之杰劳埃德代理公司等。英之杰检验集团与中国商检机构建立了业务合作往来关系，并签订了委托检验协议。

（3）日本海事鉴定协会（NKKK）。日本海事鉴定协会是日本最大的综合性货物检验鉴定机构。NKKK 与中国商检机构签订了长期的委托检验协议，多年来相互之间有着密切的合作关系与业务往来，并共同组建了日中货物检查株式会社从事检验鉴定业务，以及进行经常性的技术交流。

（4）美国安全实验所（UL）。美国安全实验所，又称为美国保险人实验室，其宗旨是采用科学测试方法来研究确定各种材料、装置、产品、建筑等对生命财产有无危害和危害的程度，确定编写、发行相应的标准和资料，从而确保安全的可靠性。UL 在中国的业务由中国进出口货物检验总公司（CCIC）承办。

（三）报检

1．报检的含义

进出口货物报检是指进出口货物的收发货人或其代理人根据《商检法》及其实施条例等有关法律、行政法规的规定，在检验检疫机构规定的地点和期限内向出入境检验检疫机构申请对其进出口货物实施法定检验的程序。

2．报检的依据

（1）《中华人民共和国进出口商品检验法》（简称《商检法》）及其实施条例；

（2）《中华人民共和国进出境动植物检疫法》及其实施条例；

（3）《中华人民共和国国境卫生检疫法》及其实施细则；

（4）《中华人民共和国食品卫生法》；

（5）其他与出入境检验检疫相关的法规。

3．报检单位

出入境检验检疫报检单位包括自理报检单位和代理报检单位。

（1）自理报检单位。自理报检单位是指经报检单位工商注册所在地辖区出入境检验检疫机构审查合格，办理过备案登记手续并取得报检单位代码后，自行办理相关的报检/申报手续的境内企业法人或其他报检单位。

（2）代理报检单位。代理报检单位是指经国家质检总局注册登记，受出口货物生产企业的委托或受进出口货物发货人、收货人的委托，或受对外贸易关系人等的委托依法代为办理出入境检验检疫报检/申请事宜的，在工商行政管理部门注册登记的境内企业法人。

4．报检条件

（1）已经生产加工完毕并完成包装、刷唛、准备发运的整批出口货物；

（2）已经经过生产企业检验合格，并出具厂检合格单的出口货物；

（3）对于执行质量许可制度的出口货物，必须具有商检机构颁发的质量许可证或卫生注册登记证；

（4）必须备齐各种相互吻合的单证。

上述四个条件必须同时具备。

5．报检范围

（1）国家法律、行政法规规定必须由出入境检验检疫机构实施检验检疫的；

（2）对外贸易合同约定须凭检验检疫机构签发的证书进行结算的；

（3）有关国家条约规定必须经检验检疫的。

6．报检时限和地点

（1）出入货物最迟应在出口报关或装运前 7 天报检，对于个别检验检疫周期较长的货物，应留有相应的检验检疫时间。

（2）需隔离检疫的出境动物在出境前 60 天预报，隔离前 7 天报检。

（3）法定检验检疫货物，除活动物需由出境口岸检验检疫机构检验检疫外，原则上应坚持产地检验检疫。

7．出境货物预报检

为了方便对外贸易，检验检疫机构对某些经常出口的、非易腐烂变质、非易燃易爆的货物予以接受预先报检，这样既有利于检验检疫工作的开展，又有利于防止内地的不合格货物运抵口岸。需要申请办理预报检的范围：

（1）整批出口的货物。对于已生产的整批出口货物，生产厂已检验合格及经营单位已验收合格，货已全部备齐，堆存于仓库，但尚未签订外贸合同或虽已签订合同，但信用证尚未到达，不能确定出运数量、运输工具、唛头的，为了使货物在信用证达到后及时出运，可以办理预报检。

（2）分批出口的货物。需要分批装运出口的货物，整批货物可办理预先报检。出口货物经检验检疫合格后，检验检疫机构签发《出境货物换证凭单》。正式装运出口时，可在检验检疫有效期内逐批向检验检疫机构申请办理放行手续。放行时，检验检疫机构查验合格后，在《出境货物换证凭单》的登记栏内对货物的数量予以登记核销。

8．重新报检

报检人在向检验检疫机构办理了报检手续，并领取了检验检疫证单后，凡有下列情况之一的应重新报检：①超过检验检疫有效期限的；②变更输入国家或地区，并有不同检验检疫要求的；③改换包装或重新拼装的；④已撤销报检的。

重新报检时，要求按规定填写《出境货物报检单》，交附有关函电等证明单据；交还原证书或证单，不能交还的应按有关规定办理。

9．报检时应提供的单证

货物出境时，应填制和提供《出境货物报检单》，并提供外贸合同、销售确认书或订单，信用证或有关函电，生产单位出具的厂检结果单原件，检验检疫机构签发的《出境货物运输包装性能检验结果单》正本。下列情况报检时应按要求提供相关物品和材料。

（1）凭样品成交的，还须提供样品。

（2）经预检的货物，在向检验检疫机构办理换证放行手续时，应提供该检验检疫机构签发的《出境货物换证凭单》正本。

（3）产地与报关地不一致的出境货物，在向报关地检验检疫机构申请《出境货物通关单》时，应提交产地检验检疫机构签发的《出境货物换证凭单》正本或《出境货物换证凭条》。

（4）按照国家法律、行政法规的规定实行卫生注册和质量许可的出境货物，必须提供经检验检疫机构批准的注册编号或许可证编号。

（5）危险货物出境时，必须提供《出境货物运输包装性能检验结果单》正本和《出境危险货物运输包装使用鉴定结果单》正本。

（6）特殊货物出境时，根据法律法规规定应提供的有关审批文件。

（四）法定检验

1．法定检验的含义

法定检验，又称强制性检验，是指为了保护人类健康和安全、保护动物或者植物的生命和健康、保护环境、防止欺诈行为、维护国家安全，由国家行政执法机构依照国家法律和行政法规规定的程序，对与国计民生关系重大的，必须实施检验的进出口货物实施强制性检验。

2．法定检验的范围

按照《商检法》及实施条例和我国其他有关法律法规规定，商检机构实施的法定检验的范围如下：

（1）对列入《法检目录》的进出口货物的检验，这是法定检验的主要范围。

（2）对进出口食品的卫生检验。

（3）对出口危险货物包装容器的性能鉴定和使用鉴定以及法定检验货物的一般运输包装鉴定。

（4）对装运出口易腐烂变质食品和冷冻品的船舱、集装箱等运载工具的适载检验。

（5）对有关国际条约规定须经商检机构检验的进出口货物的检验。

（6）对其他法律、行政法规规定须经商检机构检验的进出口货物的检验。

（7）商检机构对《法检目录》以外的进出口货物实施的抽查检验和监督管理。

3．法定检验的方式

（1）自检，指商检人员亲自实施检验，直接抽取样品检测，使用检验检疫机构自己的检测设备对样品进行检测，或使用报检单位的检测设备进行检测。

（2）"共同检验"或"组织检验"，指由商检人员与报验单位的检验技术人员共同实施的检验，或由商检人员组织指导报检单位的检验人员检验。

（3）认可检验，指由检验机构培训出口产品生产企业或供货单位的检验人员，对合格者发给认可证件，由报检单位的认可检验员自行检验其进出口货物。国家检验检疫机构对报检单位和认可检验员实施监督管理，认可其检验结果，必要时可凭其检验报告，核发检验证书。

（4）免检，根据《中华人民共和国进出口商品检验法》及其实施条例的有关规定，具备质量长期稳定等免验条件的进出口货物收货人、发货人，可以申请对其进出口的法定检验货物予以免验，经国家商检部门组织专家审查考核合格，发给免验证书，可以批准免予检验。

（五）出口货物检验检疫的一般程序

（1）法定检验检疫的出境货物，在报关时必须提供出入境检验检疫机构签发的《出境货物通关单》，海关凭报关地出入境检验检疫机构出具的《出境货物通关单》验放。

（2）出境货物的检验检疫工作程序是先检验检疫，后放行通关，即法定检验检疫的出境货物的发货人或其代理人向检验检疫机构报检，检验检疫机构受理报检和计收费。

（3）转检验或检疫部门实施检验检疫。

（4）对产地和报关地相一致的出境货物，经检验检疫合格的，出具《出境货物通关单》；对产地和报关地不一致的出境货物，出具《出境货物换证凭单》或《出境货物换证凭条》，由报关地检验检疫机构换发《出境货物通关单》；出境货物经检验检疫不合格的出具《出境货物不合格通知单》。

（六）电子转单

"电子转单"指通过系统网络，将产地检验检疫机构和口岸检验检疫机构的相关信息相互连通，对出境货物产地检验检疫机构将已经检验检疫合格的相关电子信息传输到出境口岸检验检疫机构，对入境货物入境口岸检验机构将已经签发的《入境货物通关单》相关电子信息传输到目的地检验检疫机构实施检验检疫的监管模式。与传统的报检验程序相比，电子转单具有数据信息共享、简化操作程序、降低外贸成本、提高通关速度的功能。

（七）电子通关

国家质检总局和海关总署联合开发了电子通关联网核查系统，并于 2003 年 1 月 1 日在主要口岸的检验检疫机构和海关推广使用。该系统采用网络信息技术，将检验检疫机构签发的出入境通关单的电子数据传输到海关计算机作业系统，海关将报检报关数据比对确认，相符合的，予以放行。

在目前阶段，检验检疫机构和海关联合采取的单联网核查系统还需要同时校验纸质的通关单据，这是将来实现无纸化通关的一个过渡阶段。这种通关方式相比原来的传统通关方式已经有了一个飞跃发展。它具有数据信息共享、简化操作程序、降低外贸成本、提高通关速度的功能，还有效控制了报检数据与报关数据不符合的问题和不法分子伪造、编造通关单证的不法行为。

（八）检验检疫证书

1. 含义

检验检疫证书（Inpection Certificate）是由政府机构或公证机构对进出口货物检验检疫或鉴定后，根据不同的检验结果或鉴定项目出具并且签署的书面声明，证明货物已检验达标并评述检验结果的书面单证。

2. 种类

根据进出境货物不同的检验检疫要求、鉴定项目和不同作用，我国检验检疫机构签发不同的检验检疫证书，包括品质证书、数量检验证书、植物检疫证书、动物检疫证书、卫生证书、熏蒸/消毒证书、出境货物运输包装性能检验结果单、残损鉴定证书、包装检验证书、温度检验证书等。

实训项目

◆ 实训项目 5-1

上接实训项目 4-1。2010 年 7 月 30 日，浙江曼旎进出口有限公司外贸单证员王宁收到浙江双马国际货运有限公司的通知，已按要求订妥舱位：2010 年 8 月 7 日的船期，船名为 Columbine Maersk，航次为 1007。

【任务 1】制作报检委托书

因为男童夹克的监管证件代码是 B，即出境货物通关单，属于法定检验商品，所以浙江曼旎进出口有限公司外贸单证员王宁在 7 月 30 日，根据商业发票、装箱单和以下信息制作报检委托书，委托绍兴力美服装有限公司向浙江省出入境检验检验局绍兴分局报检。

（1）浙江曼旎进出口有限公司，属私营有限责任公司，邮政编码是 310016。

（2）绍兴力美服装有限公司的登记号为 3800708358，属私营有限责任公司，法人代表是汪力美，联系人是刘美，邮政编码是 317601，联系电话为 0575-66368911。

报检委托书

__________出入境检验检疫局：

本委托人声明，保证遵守《中华人民共和国进出口商品检验法》、《中华人民共和国进出境动植物检疫法》、《中华人民共和国国境卫生检疫法》、《中华人民共和国食品卫生法》等有关法律、法规的规定和检验检疫机构制定的各项规章制度。如有违法行为，自愿接受检验检疫机构的处罚并负法律责任。本委托人所委托受委托人向检验检疫机构提交的“报检单”和随附各种单据所列内容是真实无讹的。具体委托情况如下：

本单位将于______年_____月间出口如下货物：

品　名：		数（重）量：	
合　同　号：		信用证号：	

特委托________________（地址：______________________）代表本公司办理本批货物所有的检验检疫事宜，请贵局按有关法律规定予以办理。

委托单位名称（签章）：	受委托单位名称（签章）：
单位地址：	单位地址：
邮政编码：	邮政编码：
法人代表：	法人代表：
本批货物业务联系人：	本批货物业务联系人：
联系电话（手机）：	联系电话（手机）：
企业性质：	企业性质：
日　　期：　　年　月　日	日　　期：　　年　月　日
本委托书有效期至　　年　月　日	

【任务 2】制作出境货物报检单

8 月 2 日，绍兴力美服装有限公司外贸单证员刘美在收到浙江曼旎进出口有限公司的报检委托书和随附单据后，制作出境货物报检单，向浙江省出入境检验检验局绍兴分局办理报检。

CIQ

中华人民共和国出入境检验检疫
出境货物报检单

报检单位（加盖公章）：　　　　* 编号　380400210025679

报检单位登记号：　　联系人：　　电话：　　报检日期：　年　月　日

发货人	（中文）				
	（外文）				
收货人	（中文）				
	（外文）				
货物名称（中/外文）	H.S.编码	产地	数/重量	货物总值	包装种类及数量
运输工具名称号码		贸易方式		货物存放地点	
合同号		信用证号		用途	

（续）

发货日期	年　月　日	输往国家（地区）		许可证/审批号	
启运地		到达口岸		生产单位注册号	
集装箱规格、数量及号码					

合同、信用证订立的检验检疫条款或特殊要求	标 记 及 号 码	随附单据（划“✓”或补填）	
		□合同 □信用证 □发票 □换证凭单	□装箱单 □厂检单 □包装性能结果单 □许可/审批文件

需要证单名称（划“✓”或补填）				*检验检疫费	
□品质证书	__正__副	□卫生证书	__正__副	总金额（人民币元）	
□重量证书	__正__副	□动物卫生证书	__正__副		
□数量证书	__正__副	□植物检疫证书	__正__副	计费人	
□兽医卫生证书	__正__副	□熏蒸/消毒证书	__正__副	收费人	
□健康证书	__正__副	□出境货物换证凭单	1 正__副		

报检人郑重声明：	领 取 证 单	
1. 本人被授权报检。 2. 上列填写内容正确属实，货物无伪造或冒用他人的厂名、标志、认证标志，并承担货物质量责任。	日　期	
签名：	签　名	

注：有“*”号栏由出入境检验检疫机关填写

◆国家出入境检验检疫局制

[1-2（2000.1.1）]

◆ 实训项目 5-2

上接实训项目 4-2。2010 年 9 月 21 日，杭州维丰进出口有限公司外贸单证员叶丽收到浙江双马国际货运有限公司的通知，已按要求订妥舱位：国航 9 月 27 日的 CA2304/CA1069 航班。

【任务 1】制作出境货物报检单

因为腊感绵羊皮女上衣 4203100090 的监管证件代码是 B，即出境货物通关单，属于法定检验商品，所以杭州维丰进出口有限公司外贸单证员叶丽在 9 月 21 日，根据商业发票、装箱单制作出境货物报检单。杭州维丰进出口有限公司的报检登记号为 3800708302。供应商杭州扬帆皮革制造有限公司的地址为：杭州市黄龙路 1001 号。

CIQ

中华人民共和国出入境检验检疫

出境货物报检单

报检单位（加盖公章）：　　　　* 编号　380400210025803

报检单位登记号：　　联系人：　　电话：　　报检日期：　年　月　日

发货人	（中文）	
	（外文）	
收货人	（中文）	
	（外文）	

货物名称（中/外文）	H.S.编码	产地	数/重量	货物总值	包装种类及数量

（续）

<table>
<tr><td>运输工具名称号码</td><td></td><td>贸易方式</td><td></td><td>货物存放地点</td><td colspan="2"></td></tr>
<tr><td>合同号</td><td></td><td>信用证号</td><td></td><td>用途</td><td colspan="2"></td></tr>
<tr><td>发货日期</td><td>年　月　日</td><td>输往国家（地区）</td><td></td><td>许可证/审批号</td><td colspan="2"></td></tr>
<tr><td>启运地</td><td></td><td>到达口岸</td><td></td><td>生产单位注册号</td><td colspan="2"></td></tr>
<tr><td colspan="2">集装箱规格、数量及号码</td><td colspan="5"></td></tr>
<tr><td colspan="2">合同、信用证订立的检验检疫条款或特殊要求</td><td colspan="2">标 记 及 号 码</td><td colspan="3">随附单据（划“✓”或补填）</td></tr>
<tr><td colspan="2"></td><td colspan="2"></td><td colspan="3">□合同　□装箱单
□信用证　□厂检单
□发票　□包装性能结果单
□换证凭单　□许可/审批文件</td></tr>
<tr><td colspan="4">需要证单名称（划“✓”或补填）</td><td colspan="3">*检验检疫费</td></tr>
<tr><td colspan="2" rowspan="3">□品质证书　__正__副
□重量证书　__正__副
□数量证书　__正__副
□兽医卫生证书　__正__副
□健康证书　__正__副</td><td colspan="2" rowspan="3">□卫生证书　__正__副
□动物卫生证书　__正__副
□植物检疫证书　__正__副
□熏蒸/消毒证书　__正__副
□出境货物换证凭单　1 正__副</td><td>总金额
（人民币元）</td><td colspan="2"></td></tr>
<tr><td>计费人</td><td colspan="2"></td></tr>
<tr><td>收费人</td><td colspan="2"></td></tr>
<tr><td colspan="4" rowspan="3">报检人郑重声明：
1. 本人被授权报检。
2. 上列填写内容正确属实，货物无伪造或冒用他人的厂名、标志、认证标志，并承担货物质量责任。
签名：</td><td colspan="3">领 取 证 单</td></tr>
<tr><td>日　期</td><td colspan="2"></td></tr>
<tr><td>签　名</td><td colspan="2"></td></tr>
</table>

注：有“*”号栏由出入境检验检疫机关填写

◆国家出入境检验检疫局制

[1-2（2000.1.1）]

【任务 2】办理报检

杭州维丰进出口有限公司外贸单证员叶丽制作好出境货物报检单后，向浙江省出入境检验检验局杭州分局办理报检。

◆ 实训项目 5-3

上接实训项目 4-3。2010 年 7 月 26 日，浙江大顺进出口有限公司外贸单证员朱丽娅收到德莎国际货运代理（上海）有限公司的通知，已按要求订妥舱位。

【任务 1】制作报检委托书

因为防弹轮胎的 H.S.编码为 4011100010，监管证件代码是 B，即出境货物通关单，属于法定检验商品，所以浙江大顺进出口有限公司外贸单证员朱丽娅在 7 月 26 日，根据出口合同、商业发票、装箱单和以下信息制作报检委托书，委托江苏致远轮胎厂向苏州市出入境检验检验局报检。

（1）浙江大顺进出口有限公司，属私营有限责任公司，邮政编码是 310012。

（2）江苏致远轮胎厂的登记号为 3800709900，属私营有限责任公司，地址为苏州市建设路 33 号，法人代表是刘致远，联系人是萧何，邮政编码是 215001，联系电话为 0512-69220077。

报检委托书

__________出入境检验检疫局：

本委托人声明，保证遵守《中华人民共和国进出口货物检验法》、《中华人民共和国进出境动植物检疫法》、《中华人民共和国国境卫生检疫法》、《中华人民共和国食品卫生法》等有关法律、法规的规定和检验检疫机构制定的各项规章制度。如有违法行为，自愿接受检验检疫机构的处罚并负法律责任。本委托人所委托受委托人向检验检疫机构提交的“报检单”和随附各种单据所列内容是真实无讹的。具体委托情况如下：

本单位将于______年_____月间出口如下货物：

品　名：		数（重）量：	
合 同 号：		信 用 证 号：	

特委托__________________（地址：____________________________）代表本公司办理本批货物所有的检验检疫事宜，请贵局按有关法律规定予以办理。

委托单位名称（签章）：		受委托单位名称　（签章）：	
单 位 地 址：		单 位 地 址：	
邮 政 编 码：		邮 政 编 码：	
法 人 代 表：		法 人 代 表：	
本批货物业务联系人：		本批货物业务联系人：	
联系电话　（手机）：		联系电话　（手机）：	
企 业 性 质：		企 业 性 质：	
日　　期：	年　月　日	日　　期：	年　月　日
本委托书有效期至	年　月　日		

【任务 2】制作出境货物报检单

7 月 27 日，江苏致远轮胎厂外贸单证员萧何在收到浙江大顺进出口有限公司的报检委托书和随附单据后，制作出境货物报检单，向苏州市出入境检验检验局办理报检。

中华人民共和国出入境检验检疫
出境货物报检单

报检单位（加盖公章）：　　　　　　　　　　　　* 编号　380400210028866

报检单位登记号：　　　　联系人：　　　　电话：　　　　报检日期：　　年　月　日

发货人	（中文）					
	（外文）					
收货人	（中文）					
	（外文）					
货物名称（中/外文）		H.S.编码	产地	数/重量	货物总值	包装种类及数量

（续）

运输工具名称号码		贸易方式		货物存放地点	
合同号		信用证号		用途	
发货日期	年 月 日	输往国家（地区）		许可证／审批号	
启运地		到达口岸		生产单位注册号	
集装箱规格、数量及号码					

合同、信用证订立的检验检疫条款或特殊要求	标 记 及 号 码	随附单据（划“✓”或补填）	
		□合同	□装箱单
		□信用证	□厂检单
		□发票	□包装性能结果单
		□换证凭单	□许可/审批文件

需要证单名称（划“✓”或补填）				*检验检疫费	
□品质证书	__正__副	□卫生证书	__正__副	总金额（人民币元）	
□重量证书	__正__副	□动物卫生证书	__正__副		
□数量证书	__正__副	□植物检疫证书	__正__副	计费人	
□兽医卫生证书	__正__副	□熏蒸/消毒证书	__正__副	收费人	
□健康证书	__正__副	□出境货物换证凭单	1 正__副		

报检人郑重声明：	领 取 证 单	
1. 本人被授权报检。 2. 上列填写内容正确属实，货物无伪造或冒用他人的厂名、标志、认证标志，并承担货物质量责任。	日 期	
签名：	签 名	

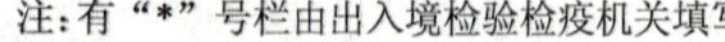

注：有“*”号栏由出入境检验检疫机关填写

◆国家出入境检验检疫局制

[1-2（2000.1.1）]

项目六

制作和申领原产地证操作

学习目标

能力目标

能根据信用证或外贸合同条款中关于原产地证条款、商业发票和装箱单，制作和办理一般原产地证；能制作和办理普惠制产地证。

知识目标

熟悉原产地证的含义、作用和种类。

导入项目

上接项目五的导入项目。

【任务 1】制作普惠制产地证

2010 年 4 月 7 日，浙江大同进出口有限公司外贸单证员桂小龙根据信用证的规定“GSP CERTIFICATE OF ORIGIN FORM A FROM PEOPLES'S REPUBLIC OF CHINA IN 1 COPY, IN THE SECOND COLUMN OF FORM A, GOODS CONSIGNED TO APPLICANT, THE THIRD PARTY'S FORM A IS ACCEPTABLE.”，以及商业发票、装箱单，制作格式 A 普惠制产地证。

ORIGINAL

1. Goods consigned from (Exporter's business name, address, country)	Reference No.	
	GENERALIZED SYSTEM OF PREFERENCES **CERTIFICATE OF ORIGIN** (Combined declaration and certificate)	

（续）

<table>
<tr><td colspan="3">2. Goods consigned to (Consignee's name, address, country)</td><td colspan="3">FORM A
Issued in THE PEOPLE'S REPUBLIC OF CHINA
(country)
See Notes overleaf</td></tr>
<tr><td colspan="3">3. Means of transport and route (as far as known)</td><td colspan="3">4. For official use</td></tr>
<tr><td>5. Item number</td><td>6. Marks and numbers of packages</td><td>7. Number and kind of packages; description of goods</td><td>8. Origin criterion (see Notes overleaf)</td><td>9. Gross weight or other quantity</td><td>10. Number and date of invoices</td></tr>
<tr><td></td><td></td><td></td><td></td><td></td><td></td></tr>
<tr><td colspan="3">11. Certification
It is hereby certified, on the basis of control carried out, that the declaration by the exporter is correct.</td><td colspan="3">12. Declaration by the exporter
The undersigned hereby declares that the above details and statements are correct, that all the goods were
produced in CHINA
(country)
and that they comply with the origin requirements specified for those goods in the Generalized System of Preferences for goods exported to____________________</td></tr>
<tr><td colspan="3">--
Place and date, signature and stamp of certifying authority</td><td colspan="3">--
Place and date, signature and stamp of authorized signatory</td></tr>
</table>

【任务 2】办理普惠制产地证

外贸单证员桂小龙制作好格式 A 普惠制产地证后，向浙江省出入境检验检疫局申领格式 A 普惠制产地证。

【任务 1】制作普惠制产地证

浙江大同进出口有限公司外贸单证员桂小龙通过九城软件或榕基软件登录浙江省出入境检验检疫局的网页填写普惠制产地证的各栏目内容。

1．出口方

本栏填写出口方的名称、详细地址。本业务根据信用证的“59”栏目内容填写。

2. 收货方

应填写最终收货方的名称、详细地址及国家（地区），通常是外贸合同中的买方或信用证上规定的提单通知人。本业务根据信用证的“50”栏目内容填写。

3. 运输方式和路线

一般应填装货地点、到货地点（始运港、目的港）及运输方式（如海运、陆运、空运）。转运货物应加上转运港，如 VIA HONGKONG。本业务填写 SHIPPED FROM SHANGHAI，CHINA TO HAMBURG，GERMANY BY SEA。

4. 签证机构用栏

此栏为签证机构在签发后发证书、补发证书或加注其他声明时使用。证书申领单位应将此栏留空。

5. 货物顺序号

如同批出口货物有不同品种，则按不同品种、发票号等分列“1”、“2”、“3”……，以此类推。本业务填“1”。

6. 唛头及包装号

所填唛头应与货物外包装上的唛头及发票上的唛头一致；应按照出口发票上所列唛头填写完整图案、文字标记及包装号码，不可简单地填写“按照发票（AS PER INVOICE NO. ...）”或“按照提单（AS PER B/L NO. ...）”；唛头不得出现中国以外的地区或国家制造的字样（如 MADE IN INDIA 等）；如货物无唛头应填“无唛头”，即“N/M”或“NO MARK”。如唛头过多，此栏不够填，可填打在第 7、8、9、10 栏截止线以下的空白处。如还不够，此栏打上“SEE THE ATTACHMENT”，用附页填打所有唛头（附页的纸张要与原证书一般大小），在右上角打上证书号，并由申请单位和签证当局授权签字人分别在附页末页的右下角和左下角手签、盖印。附页手签的笔迹、地点、日期均与证书第 11、12 栏相一致。

本业务填写发票中的唛头。

7. 包装件数量及种类，货物的名称

包装件数量必须用英文和阿拉伯数字同时表示；货物名称必须具体填明，其详细程度应可在 H.S.CODE 的 8 位数字中准确归类，不能笼统填“MACHINE”、“GARMENT”等；货物名称等项填完后，应在下一行加上“***”，即表示结束的符号，以防止加填伪造内容；国外信用证有时要求填具合同、信用证号码等，可加填在此栏空白处。

8. 原产地标准

此栏用字最少，但却是国外海关审核的核心项目。对含有进口成分的货物，因情况复杂，国外要求严格，极易弄错而造成退证查询，应认真审核、慎重填写。现将填写该栏原产地标准符号的一般规定说明如下：

（1）完全原产品，不含任何进口成分，出口到所有给惠国，填“P”。

（2）含有进口成分的产品，出口到欧盟、挪威、瑞士和日本，填“W”，其后加上出口产品的 H.S.税目号，如“W”42.02。条件：①产品列入了上述给惠国的“加工清单”符合其加工条件；②产品未列入“加工清单”，但产品生产过程中使用的进口原材料和零部件要经过充分的加工，产品的 H.S.税目号不同于所用的原材料或零部件的 H.S.税目号。

（3）含有进口成分的产品，出口到加拿大，填“F”。条件：进口成分的价值未超过产品出厂价的 40%。

（4）含有进口成分的产品，出口到波兰，填“W”，其后加上出口产品的 H.S.税目号，如“W”42.02。条件：进口成分的价值未超过产品离岸价的 50%。

（5）含有进口成分的产品，出口到俄罗斯、乌克兰、白俄罗斯、哈萨克斯坦、捷克、斯洛伐克六国，填“Y”，其后加上进口成分价值占该产品离岸价格的百分比，如“Y”38%。条件：进口成分的价值未超过产品离岸价的 50%。

（6）输往澳大利亚、新西兰的货物，此栏可以留空。

本业务填“P”。

9. 毛重或其他数量

此栏应以货物的正常计量单位填，如“只”、“件”、“双”、“台”、“打”等。以重量计算的则填毛重，只有净重的，填净重亦可，但要标上 N.W.。

本业务同时填写毛重和数量 5654.20KGS/14128SETS。

10. 发票号码及日期

此栏的日期必须按照商业发票填写，发票日期不得迟于出货日期。

11. 签证当局的证明

检验检疫局签证人经审核后在此栏〈正本〉签名，盖签证印章。此栏日期不得早于发票日期（第 10 栏）和申报日期 （第 12 栏），而且应早于货物的出运日期（第 3 栏）。

12. 栏目出口商的申明

在生产国横线上填英文的“中国”（CHINA）。进口国横线上填最终进口国，进口国必须与第三栏目的港的国别一致，本业务填“德国”。另外，申请单位应授权专人在此栏手签，标上申报地点、日期，并加盖申请单位中英文印章。此栏日期不得早于发票日期。

ORIGINAL

1. Goods consigned from (Exporter's business name, address, country)			Reference No.		
ZHEJIANG DATONG IMPORT AND EXPORT CO., LTD. NO.902 YILE ROAD, HANGZHOU, CHINA			GENERALIZED SYSTEM OF PREFERENCES **CERTIFICATE OF ORIGIN** **FORM A** (Combined declaration and certificate)		
2. Goods consigned to (Consignee's name, address, country)					
CARK GMBH & CO. KG DOMSTRASSE 55, D-20095 HAMBURG, GERMANY			Issued in **THE PEOPLE'S REPUBLIC OF CHINA** (country) See Notes overleaf		
3. Means of transport and route (as far as known)			4. For official use		
SHIPPED FROM SHANGHAI, CHINA TO HAMBURG, GERMANY BY SEA.					
5. Item no.	6. Marks and no. of packages	7. Number and kind of packages; description of goods	8. Origin criterion (see Notes overleaf)	9. Gross weight or other quantity	10. Number and date of invoices
1	CARK DT1000033 HAMBURG CARTON NO：1-255	TWO HUNDRED AND FIFTY FIVE (255) CARTONS OF FORGED BRASS BALL VALVES. ************************** L/C NO.: LC-536-089075 DATE: MARCH 17, 2010	P	5654.20KGS/ 14128SETS	2010DT00101 APRIL 2, 2010

（续）

11. Certification It is hereby certified, on the basis of control carried out, that the declaration by the exporter is correct.	12. Declaration by the exporter The undersigned hereby declares that the above details and statements are correct, that all the goods were produced in　**CHINA** (country) and that they comply with the origin requirements specified for those goods in the Generalized System of Preferences for goods exported to　**GERMANY** ZHEJIANG DATONG IMPORT AND EXPORT CO., LTD. 桂大同
HANGZHOU, APRIL 7, 2010 ------------------------------------ Place and date, signature and stamp of certifying authority	HANGZHOU, APRIL 7, 2010 ------------------------------------ Place and date, signature and stamp of authorized signatory

【任务 2】办理普惠制产地证

外贸单证员桂小龙网上审核通过后，向浙江省出入境检验检疫局申领普惠制产地证。浙江省出入境检验检疫局工作人员审核通过后，在一般普惠制产地证上盖章后生效。

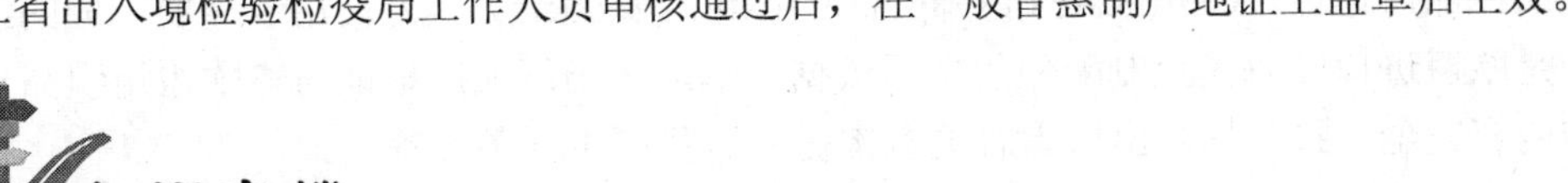

（一）原产地证的含义和作用

1．含义

原产地证是证明产品真实来源地的商业文书，简称产地证。

2．作用

（1）证明出口货物产地的书面文件。

（2）进口国海关作为实施差别关税、进口限制、不同进口配额和不同税率的依据。

（3）进出口通关和贸易统计的重要依据。

（二）原产地证的种类

原产地证主要包括以下四类：

1．一般原产地证

一般原产地证（Certificate of Origin，简称 C/O）是出口国根据一定原产地规则签发的证明货物原产地的证明文书。一般原产地证一般是由检验检疫机构、贸促会、出口商、生产厂家等出具。

2．普惠制产地证

普惠制是发达国家给予发展中国家出口制成品和半制成品（包括某些初级产品）普遍的、非歧视性的、非互惠的一种关税优惠制度。普惠制产地证（Generalized System of Preferences/Certificate of Origin，简称 GSP　C/O）是一种受惠国有关机构就本国出口商向给惠国出口受惠货物签发的用以证明原产地的文件。在我国普惠制产地证是由检验检疫机构签发的。

目前 38 个国家给予我国普惠制待遇，分别是欧盟 27 国（比利时、丹麦、英国、德国、法国、爱尔兰、意大利、卢森堡、荷兰、希腊、葡萄牙、西班牙、奥地利、芬兰、瑞典、波兰、捷克、斯洛伐克、拉脱维亚、爱沙尼亚、立陶宛、匈牙利、马耳他、塞浦路斯、斯洛文尼亚、罗马尼亚、保加利亚)、挪威、瑞士、土耳其、俄罗斯、白俄罗斯、乌克兰、哈萨克斯坦、日本、加拿大、澳大利亚和新西兰。

普惠制产地证格式包括格式 A、格式 59A 和格式 APR，其中格式 A（FORM A）使用范围最广。

3．对美国出口的原产地声明书

若向美国出口纺织品，出口商必须向进口商提供对美国出口的原产地声明书（Declaration of Country Origin），作为进口商进口报关的单据之一，其格式包括：

（1）格式 A。单一国家产地声明书，一般适用于本国原料并由本国生产的产品。

（2）格式 B。多国产地声明书，一般适用于来料加工、来件装配的产品，由多国生产。

（3）格式 C。非多种纤维纺织品声明书，一般适用于纺织品的主要价值或主要重量属于麻或丝的原料或含羊毛量不超过 17%。

4．输欧盟纺织品产地证

输欧盟纺织品产地证（Certificate of Origin of Textile Products）是专门用于需要配额的纺织类产品，是欧盟进口国海关控制配额的主要依据。输欧盟纺织品产地证与输欧盟纺织品出口许可证的内容完全一致，均由出口国有关机构提供。我国由商务部签发。

实训项目

◆ **实训项目 6-1**

上接实训项目 5-1。

【任务 1】制作一般原产地证

2010 年 8 月 5 日，浙江曼旋进出口有限公司外贸单证员王宁根据信用证以及商业发票、装箱单的要求，制作一般原产地证。

ORIGINAL

<table>
<tr><td colspan="2">1. Exporter</td><td colspan="3">Certificate No.</td></tr>
<tr><td colspan="2"></td><td colspan="3" rowspan="3">CERTIFICATE OF ORIGIN
OF
THE PEOPLE'S REPUBLIC OF CHINA</td></tr>
<tr><td colspan="2">2. Consignee</td></tr>
<tr><td colspan="2"></td></tr>
<tr><td colspan="2">3. Means of transport and route</td><td colspan="3">5. For certifying authority use only</td></tr>
<tr><td colspan="2"></td><td colspan="3" rowspan="3"></td></tr>
<tr><td colspan="2">4. Country / region of destination</td></tr>
<tr><td colspan="2"></td></tr>
<tr><td>6. Marks and numbers</td><td>7. Number and kind of packages; description of goods</td><td>8. H.S.Code</td><td>9. Quantity</td><td>10. Number and date Of invoices</td></tr>
<tr><td></td><td></td><td></td><td></td><td></td></tr>
</table>

（续）

11. Declaration by the exporter The undersigned hereby declares that the above details and statements are correct, that all the goods were produced in China and that they comply with the Rules of Origin of the People's Republic of China.	12. Certification It is hereby certified that the declaration by the exporter is correct.
Place and date, signature and stamp of authorized signatory	Place and date, signature and stamp of certifying authority

【任务 2】办理一般原产地证

外贸单证员王宁制作好一般原产地证后，向浙江省贸促会申领一般原产地证。

◆ **实训项目 6-2**

上接实训项目 5-2。

【任务 1】制作普惠制原产地证

2010 年 9 月 21 日，杭州维丰进出口有限公司外贸单证员叶丽根据信用证以及商业发票、装箱单的要求，制作普惠制原产地证。

ORIGINAL

1. Goods consigned from (Exporter's business name, address, country)	Reference No.	
	GENERALIZED SYSTEM OF PREFERENCES **CERTIFICATE OF ORIGIN** (Combined declaration and certificate)	
2. Goods consigned to (Consignee's name, address, country)	**FORM A**	
	Issued in	**THE PEOPLE'S REPUBLIC OF CHINA**
		(country)
	See Notes overleaf	
3. Means of transport and route (as far as known)	4. For official use	

（续）

5. Item number	6. Marks and numbers of packages	7. Number and kind of packages; description of goods	8. Origin criterion (see Notes overleaf)	9. Gross weight or other quantity	10. Number and date of invoices

11. Certification	12. Declaration by the exporter
It is hereby certified, on the basis of control carried out, that the declaration by the exporter is correct.	The undersigned hereby declares that the above details and statements are correct, that all the goods were produced in CHINA (country) and that they comply with the origin requirements specified for those goods in the Generalized System of Preferences for goods exported to __________
------------------------------ Place and date, signature and stamp of certifying authority	------------------------------ Place and date, signature and stamp of authorized signatory

【任务 2】办理普惠制原产地证

外贸单证员叶丽制作好格式 A 普惠制产地证后，向浙江省出入境检验检疫局申领格式 A 普惠制产地证。

◆ **实训项目 6-3**

上接实训项目 5-3。

【任务 1】制作普惠制原产地证

2010 年 7 月 27 日，浙江大顺进出口有限公司外贸单证员朱丽娅根据出口合同以及商业发票、装箱单的要求，制作普惠制原产地证。

ORIGINAL

1. Goods consigned from (Exporter's business name, address, country)	Reference No.
	GENERALIZED SYSTEM OF PREFERENCES **CERTIFICATE OF ORIGIN** (Combined declaration and certificate)

（续）

2. Goods consigned to (Consignee's name, address, country)	FORM A Issued in THE PEOPLE'S REPUBLIC OF CHINA (country) See Notes overleaf
3. Means of transport and route (as far as known)	4. For official use

5. Item number	6. Marks and numbers of packages	7. Number and kind of packages; description of goods	8. Origin criterion (see Notes overleaf)	9. Gross weight or other quantity	10. Number and date of invoices

11. Certification It is hereby certified, on the basis of control carried out, that the declaration by the exporter is correct.	12. Declaration by the exporter The undersigned hereby declares that the above details and statements are correct, that all the goods were produced in CHINA (country) and that they comply with the origin requirements specified for those goods in the Generalized System of Preferences for goods exported to__________________
-- Place and date, signature and stamp of certifying authority	-- Place and date, signature and stamp of authorized signatory

【任务 2】办理普惠制原产地证

浙江大顺进出口有限公司外贸单证员朱丽娅制作好格式 A 普惠制产地证后，向浙江省出入境检验检疫局申领格式 A 普惠制产地证。

项目七

制作和办理报关单证操作

能力目标

能根据信用证或外贸合同条款、商业发票、装箱单和其他相关信息，填制出口收汇核销单、报关委托书、出口货物报关单及其他随附单据。

知识目标

熟悉报关的期限和流程、报关单的填制要求，了解报关流程和报关单位。

上接项目六的导入项目。2010 年 4 月 8 日，外贸单证员桂小龙收到浙江双马国际货运有限公司如下进仓通知单通知后，马上通知浙江玉环金山阀门有限公司。

浙江双马国际货运有限公司

货物进仓通知单

TO：浙江大同进出口有限公司

进仓编号：	SM10E00130897	客户编号：	DT10C00789
货名：	FORGED BRASS BALL VALVES	件数：	255 CARTONS
毛重：	5654.20KGS	体积：	6.776M^3
起运港：	SHANGHAI	目的港：	HAMBURG
开航日期：	2010-04-12		

货物请务必于 4 月 10 日 12 时前进仓。

唛头：

如有问题，请与我司联系：李红玲，电话：0571-82379057

进仓要求：

1．进仓截止时间为报关前一天中午 12：00，遇节假日则向前顺延。

2．凭本通知在规定时间内将有关单据及货物送至我司仓库。如不能在规定时间内送达，我们将不能保证货物如期运出。

3．所送货物需按规定货号分票理清进仓，否则将被收取分票费。

4．对于受潮受湿和外包装损坏的货物，仓库将不予受理，特殊情况，货代出保函。

5．从 2007 年 8 月 1 日起，仓库对所有进仓货物将收取进仓费：一般货物 5 元/立方吨，特殊货物 10 元/立方吨，托盘 10 元/托盘。现金付清。

仓库名称：	上海飞杰储运有限公司	仓库地址：	上海浦东五洲大道 79 号
联系人：	冯小姐	电话：	021-50401828

【任务1】申领并制作出口收汇核销单

4 月 8 日，浙江大同进出口有限公司外贸单证员桂小龙根据商业发票、装箱单和相关信息申领和制作出口收汇核销单。浙江大同进出口有限公司的组织机构代码是 3101003826。

出口收汇核销单 存根

（浙）编号：

出口企业：
单位代码：
出口币种总价：
收汇方式：
预计收款日期：
报关日期：
备注：
此单报关有效期截止到

（出口单位盖章）

出口收汇核销单

（浙）编号：

出口企业				
单位代码				
银行签注栏	类别	币种金额	日期	盖章
海关签注栏：				
外管局签注栏： 年　月　日（盖章）				

（出口单位盖章）

（海关盖章）

出口收汇核销单 出口退税专用

（浙）编号：

出口企业		
单位代码		
货物名称	数量	币种总价
报关单编号：		
外管局签注栏： 年　月　日（盖章）		

未经核销此联不得撕开

【任务2】制作出口货物报关单和报关委托书

4 月 8 日，浙江大同进出口有限公司外贸单证员桂小龙根据商业发票、装箱单和相关信息出口货物报关单和报关委托书。保险费率为 1‰。

中华人民共和国海关出口货物报关单

预录入编号：　　　　　　　　　　　　　　　　海关编号：

出口口岸		备案号	出口日期	申报日期
经营单位		运输方式	运输工具	提运单号
发货单位		贸易方式	征免性质	结汇方式
许可证号		运抵国（地区）	指运港	境内货源地
批准文号	成交方式	运费	保费	杂费
合同协议号	件数	包装种类	毛重（公斤）	净重（公斤）
集装箱号		随附单据		生产厂家
标记唛码及备注				

（续）

项号	货物编码	货物名称、规格型号	数量及单位	最终目的国（地区）	单价	总价	币制	征免
税费征税情况								

录入员　录入单位	兹声明以上申报无讹并承担法律责任	海关审单批注及放行日期（签章） 审单　审价
报关员	申报单位（签章）	征税　统计
单位地址 邮编　电话	填制日期	查验　放行

【任务 3】整理报关单据并办理委托报关

4 月 8 日，浙江大同进出口有限公司外贸单证员桂小龙制作和办理好相关报关单证后，同时与报检委托书、出境货物换证凭条一起寄给浙江双马国际货运有限公司，委托其办理报检和报关手续。

示范操作

【任务 1】申领并制作出口收汇核销单

外贸单证员桂小龙去外汇管理局领取核销单前，应当根据业务实际需要先通过“中国电子口岸出口收汇系统”向外汇管理局提出领取核销单申请，然后持“中国电子口岸”操作员 IC 卡到外管局领取核销单，并进行填制。

1．编号

该栏目是事先印制好的。本业务的编号是 338667889。

2．出口企业

该栏目填写出口企业的中文名称。

3．单位代码

该栏目填写出口企业的十位组织机构代码。本业务填写 3101003826。

4．货物名称、数量和币种总价

在出口退税专用联中，货物名称填写出口货物名称；数量填写外包装件数；币种总价，填写货币符号及总金额。在存根联中，只填写出口币种总价。

5．收汇方式

该栏目填写出口收汇方式。本业务填写 L/C AT SIGHT。

6．预计收款日期

该栏目一般情况下不填。只有当收汇日期超过报关日期后 180 天需要办理远期备案时，该栏目内容才由外汇局进行变更。

7．报关日期

该栏目一般由货代公司代理填写。

8．备注

该栏目填写商业发票的号码。

9．出口收汇核销单报关有效期

该栏目填写出口收汇核销单报关有效期截止日，一般不填。

10．出口单位盖章

该栏目由出口单位在存根联与正联之间盖章，以及在正联与出口退税专用联之间盖章。

出口收汇核销单
存根

（浙）编号：　338667889

出口企业：浙江大同进出口有限公司
单位代码：　3101003826
出口币种总价：　USD35862.40
收汇方式：　L/C AT SIGHT
预计收款日期：
报关日期：
备注：合同号为：DT10000[illegible]
此单报关有效期截止到

（出口单位盖章）

出口收汇核销单

（浙）编号：　338667889

出口企业　浙江大同进出口有限公司				
单位代码　3101003826				
银行签注	类别	币种金额	日期	盖章
海关签注栏：				
外管局签注栏： 年　月　日（盖章）				

（海关盖章）

出口收汇核销单
出口退税专用

（浙）编号：　338667889

出口企业　浙江大同进出口有限公司		
单位代码　3101003826		
货物名称	数量	币种总价
黄铜球阀	255 箱	USD35862.40
报关单编号：		
外管局签注栏： 年　月　日（盖章）		

未经核销此联不得撕开

【任务 2】制作出口货物报关单和报关委托书

第一步，制作出口货物报关单。

由于这批货物共有 6 种规格，因此分两张出口货物报关单填报。

1．预录入编号

该栏目是申报单位或预录入单位对该单位填制录入的报关单的编号，用于该单位与海关之间引用其申报后尚未批准放行的报关单。报关单录入凭单的编号规则由申报单位自行决定。

预录入报关单及EDI报关单的预录入编号由接受申报的海关决定编号规则，计算机自动打印。

2．海关编号

该栏目是海关接受申报时给予报关单的编号。海关编号由各海关接受申报的环节确定，应标志在报关单的每一联上。报关单海关编号为18位数码，由各直属海关统一管理。各直属海关对进口报关和出口报关单应分别编号，并确保在同一公历年度内，能按进口和出口唯一地标志本关区的每一份报关单。

3．进口口岸/出口口岸

该栏目是货物实际进（出）口我国关境口岸海关的名称。该栏目应根据货物实际进（出）口的口岸海关选择填报《关区代码表》中相应的口岸海关名称及代码。在不同出口加工区之间转让的货物，填报对方出口加工区海关名称及代码。无法确定进（出）口口岸以及无实际进出口报关单的，填报接受申报的海关名称及代码。本业务填写上海海关。

4．备案号

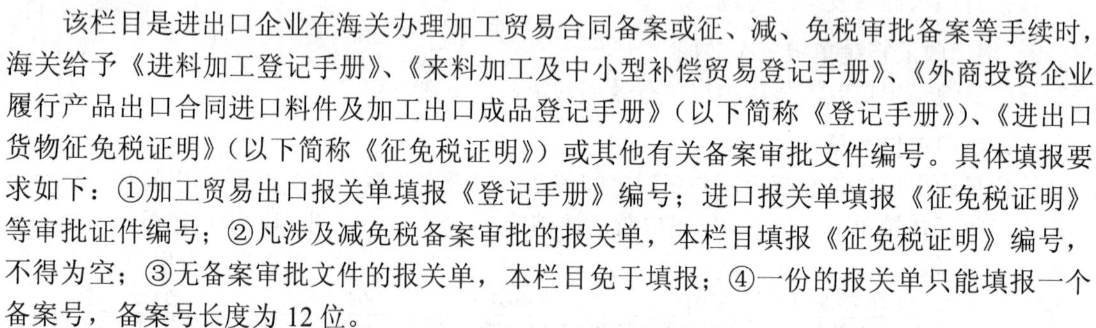

该栏目是进出口企业在海关办理加工贸易合同备案或征、减、免税审批备案等手续时，海关给予《进料加工登记手册》、《来料加工及中小型补偿贸易登记手册》、《外商投资企业履行产品出口合同进口料件及加工出口成品登记手册》（以下简称《登记手册》）、《进出口货物征免税证明》（以下简称《征免税证明》）或其他有关备案审批文件编号。具体填报要求如下：①加工贸易出口报关单填报《登记手册》编号；进口报关单填报《征免税证明》等审批证件编号；②凡涉及减免税备案审批的报关单，本栏目填报《征免税证明》编号，不得为空；③无备案审批文件的报关单，本栏目免于填报；④一份的报关单只能填报一个备案号，备案号长度为12位。

5．进口日期/出口日期

进口日期是运载所申报货物的运输工具申报进境的日期，必须与相应的运输工具申报进境日期一致。出口日期是运载所申报货物的运输工具办结出境手续的日期。该栏目供海关打印报关单证明联用，预录入报关单及EDI报关单均免于填报。无实际进出口的报关单填报办理申报手续的日期。本栏目为6位数，顺序为年、月、日各2位。

6．申报日期

该栏目是海关接受进（出）口货物的收、发货人或代理人申请办理货物进（出）口手续的日期。预录入及EDI报关单填报向海关申报的日期，与实际情况不符时，由审单人员按实际日期修改批注。本栏目为6位数，顺序为年、月、日各2位。

7．经营单位

该栏目是对外签订并执行进出口贸易合同的中国境内企业或单位，应填报经营单位名称及经营单位编码。经营单位编码是进出口企业在所在地主管海关办理注册登记手续时，海关给企业设置的注册登记编码。本业务填写浙江大同进出口有限公司（3101003826）。

8．运输方式

该栏目是载运货物进出关境所使用的运输工具的分类。该栏目应根据实际运输方式按海关规定的《运输方式代码表》选择填报相应的运输方式。特殊情况下运输方式的填报原则如下：①非邮政方式进出口的快递货物，按实际运输方式填报；②进出境旅客随身携带货物，按旅客所乘运输工具填报；③进口转关运输货物根据载运货物抵达进境地的运输工具填报，出口转关运输货物根据载运货物驶离出境地的运输工具填报；④无实际进出口的，根据实际情况选择填报《运输方式代码表》中的运输方式；⑤出口加工区与区外之间进出口的货物，填报“Z”；同一出口加工区内或不同出口加工区的企业之间相互结转（调拨）的货物，填报“9”（其他运输）。

本业务填写水陆运输。

9. 运输工具名称

该栏目是载运货物进出境的运输工具的名称或运输工具编号。一份报关单只能填写一个运输工具名称。本栏目填制内容应与运输部门向海关申报的载货清单一致。具体填报要求如下：①江海运输填报船名及航次或载货清单编号（按受理申报海关要求选填）；②汽车运输填报该跨境运输车辆的国内行驶车牌号码；③铁路运输填报车次或车厢号，以及进出境日期；④航空运输填报分运单号，无分运单的，本栏目为空；⑤邮政运输填报邮政包裹单号。本业务填写 XIN YA ZHOU/VOY. NO. 0023W。

10. 提/运单号

该栏目是进出口货物提单或运单的编号，应与运输部门向海关申报的载货清单所列内容一致。一票货物对应多个提运单时，应按接受申报的海关规定，分单填报。具体填报要求如下：①运输填报进口提单号或出口运单号；②铁路运输填报运单号；③汽车运输免于填报；④航空运输填报总运单号；⑤邮政运输填报邮政包裹单号；⑥无实际进出口的，本栏目为空；⑦转关运输货物免于填报。

11. 收货单位/发货单位

收货单位是进口货物在境内的最终消费和使用单位，包括自行从境外进口货物的单位和委托有外贸进出口经营权的企业进口货物的单位。发货单位是出口货物在境内的生产或销售单位，包括自行出口货物的单位和委托有进出口经营资格的企业出口货物的单位。该栏目应填报收、发货单位的中文名称或其海关注册编码。加工贸易中，报关单的收发货单位应与《登记手册》的“货主单位”一致。本业务同发货单位的填写内容。

12. 贸易方式

该栏目应根据实际情况按海关规定的《贸易方式代码表》选择填报相应的贸易方式简称或代码。一份报关单只允许填报一种贸易方式。出口加工区内企业填制的《出口加工区进（出）境货物备案清单》应选择填报适用于出口加工区货物的监管方式简称或代码。本业务填写一般贸易。

13. 征免性质

该栏目是海关对进出口货物实施征、减、免税管理的性质类别，应按照海关核发的《征免税证明》中批注的征免性质填报，或根据实际情况按海关规定的《征免性质代码表》选择填报相应的征免性质简称或代码。一份报关单只允许填报一种征免性质。加工贸易中，报关单栏目应按照海关核发的《登记手册》中批注的征免性质填报相应的征免性质简称或代码。特殊情况下填报的具体要求如下：①保税工厂经营的加工贸易，根据《登记手册》填报“进料加工”或“来料加工”；②三资企业按内外销比例为加工内销产品而进口料件，填报“一般征税”，或其他相应的征免性质；③加工贸易转内销的货物，按实际应享受的征免性质填报；

④料件退运出口、成品退运进口货物填报“其他法定”；⑤加工贸易结转货物本栏为空。本业务填写一般征税。

14. 结汇方式

该栏目是出口货物的发货人或其代理人收结外汇的方式，应按海关规定的《结汇方式代码表》选择填报相应的结汇方式名称或代码。本业务填写信用证。

15. 许可证号

该栏目用于应申领进（出）口许可证的货物。此类货物必须填报商务部及其授权发证机关签发的进（出）口货物许可证的编号，不得为空。一份报关单只允许填报一个许可证号。

16. 起运国（地区）/运抵国（地区）

起运国（地区）是进口货物起始发出的国家（地区）。运抵国（地区）是出口货物直接运抵的国家（地区）。该栏目应按海关规定的《国别（地区）代码表》选择填报相应的起运国（地区）或运抵国（地区）中文名称或代码。无实际进出口的，该栏目填报“中国”（代码“142”）。对运输中发生中转的货物，如中转地未发生任何商业性交易，则起运地、运抵地不变，如中转地发生商业性交易，则以中转地作为起运/运抵国（地区）填报。本业务填写德国。

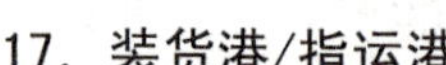

17. 装货港/指运港

装货港是进口货物入境前的最后一个境外装运港。指运港是出口货物运往境外的最终目的港；最终目的港不可预知的，可按尽可能预知的目的港填报。该栏目应根据实际情况按海关规定的《港口航线代码表》选择填报相应的港口中文名称或代码。无实际进出口的，本栏目填报“中国境内”。本业务填写汉堡。

18. 境内目的地/境内货源地

境内目的地是进口货物在国内的消费、使用地或最终运抵地。境内货源地是出口货物在国内的产地或原始发货地。该栏目应根据进口货物的收货单位、出口货物生产厂家或发货单位所属地区，按海关规定的《国内地区代码表》选择填报相应的国内地区名称或代码。本业务填写浙江玉环。

19. 批准文号

该栏目用于填报进口《付汇核销单》编号。出口报关单栏目用于填《出口收汇核销单》编号。本业务填写338667889。

20. 成交方式

该栏目应根据实际成交价格条款按海关规定的《成交方式代码表》选择填报相应的成交方式代码。无实际进出口的，进口填报CIF价，出口填报FOB价。本业务填写CIF。

21. 运费

该栏目用于成交价格中不包含运费的进口货物或成交价格中含有运费的出口货物，应填报该份报关单所含全部货物的国际运输费用。可按运费单价、总价或运费率三种方式之一填报，同时注明运费标记，并按海关规定的《货币代码表》选择填报相应的币种代码。运保费合并计算的，运保费填报在本栏目。运费标记“1”表示运费率，“2”表示每吨货物的运费单价，“3”表示运费总价。例如，6%的运费率填报为6/1。本业务填写USD67.76。

22．保费

该栏目用于成交价格不包含保险费的进口货物或成交价格中含有保险费的出口货物，应填报该份报关单所含全部货物国际运输的保险费用。可按保险费总价或保险费率两种方式之一填报，同时注明保险费标记，并按海关规定的《货币代码表》选择填报相应的币种代码。运保费合并计算的，运保费填报在运费栏目中。保险费标记“1”表示保险费率，“3”表示保险费总价。例如：1‰的保险费填报为 0.1/1；200 港元保险费总价填报为 110/200/3。本业务填写 USD39.45。

23．杂费

该栏目是成交价格以外的应计入完税价格或应从完税价格中扣除的费用，如手续费、佣金、回扣等。可按杂费总价或杂费率两种方式之一填报，同时注明杂费标记，并按海关规定的《货币代码表》选择填报相应的币种代码。应计入完税价格的杂费填报为正值或正率，应从完税价格中扣除的杂费填报为负值或负率。杂费标记“1”表示杂费率，“3”表示杂费总价。例如：应计入完税价格的 1.5%的杂费率填报为 1.5/1；应从完税价格中扣除的 1%的回扣率填报为 –1/1；应计入完税价格的 500 英镑杂费总价填报为 303/500/3。

24．合同协议号

该栏目应填报进（出）口货物合同（协议）的全部字头和号码。本业务填写 DT1000033。

25．件数

该栏目应填报有外包装的进（出）口货物的实际件数。特殊情况下填报要求如下：①舱单件数为集装箱的，填报集装箱个数；②舱单件数为托盘的，填报托盘数；③本栏目不得填报为零，裸装货物填报为 1。本业务填写 255。

26．包装种类

该栏目应填报进（出）口货物的实际外包装种类，如集装箱（container）、托盘（pallet）、木箱（wooden case）、纸箱（carton）、散装（bulk）等。本业务填写纸箱。

27．毛重（公斤）

该栏目填报进（出）口货物实际毛重，计量单位为公斤，不足 1 公斤填报为“1”。本业务填写 5654.20。

28．净重（公斤）

该栏目填报进（出）口货物的实际净重，计量单位为公斤，不足 1 公斤填报为“1”。本业务填写 5584.20。

29．集装箱号

该栏目是装载货物进出境的集装箱两侧标志的全球唯一的编号，填报装载进（出）口货物的集装箱编号，集装箱数量比照标准箱四舍五入填报整数，非集装箱货物填报为“0”。一票货物多集装箱装载的，填报其中之一，其余集装箱编号在备注栏填报或随附清单。本业务暂时不填。

30．随附单据

该栏目填写随进（出）口货物报关单一并向海关递交的单证或文件。合同、发票、装箱单、许可证等必备的随附单证不在本栏目填报。该栏目应按海关规定的《监管证件名称代码表》选择填报相应证件的代码，并填报每种证件的编号（编号打印在备注栏下半部分），由代理报关行填写。本业务该栏目不填。

31．用途/生产厂家

进口货物填报用途，应根据进口货物的实际用途按海关规定的《用途代码表》选择填报相应的用途名称或代码。生产厂家指出口货物的境内生产企业。本栏目供必要时手工填写。本业务填写浙江玉环金山阀门有限公司。

32．标记唛码与备注

该栏目下部供打印随附单据栏中监管证件的编号，上部用于选报以下内容：①受外商投资企业委托代理其进口投资设备、物品的外贸企业名称；②一票货物多个集装箱的，在本栏目填报其余的集装箱号；③一票货物多个提运单的，在本栏目填报其余的提运单号；④标记的唛码等其他申报时必须说明的事项。

此外，凡申报采用协定税率的货物，必须在报关单本栏目填报原产地证明标记，具体填报方法为：在一对"＜＞"内以"协"字开头，依次填入该份报关单内企业能提供原产地证明的申报货物项号，各货物项号之间以"，"隔开；如果货物项号是连续的，则填报"起始货物项号"+"—"+"终止货物项号"。例如：某份报关单的第2、5、16项货物，企业能够提供原产地证明，则填报"＜协2，5，16＞"；某份报关单的第4、9、10、11、12、17项货物，企业能够提供原产地证明，则填报"＜协4，9—12，17＞"。

本业务填写与商业发票相同的唛头。

33．项号

该栏目分两行填报及打印。第一行打印报关单中的货物排列序号。第二行专用于加工贸易等已备案的货物，填报和打印该项货物在《登记手册》中的项号。

34．商品编码

该栏目是按海关规定的货物分类编码规则确定的进（出）口货物的货物编号。本业务填写8481801090。

35．商品名称、规格型号

该栏目分两行填报及打印。第一行打印进（出）口货物规范的中文货物名称，第二行打印规格型号。必要时加注原文。具体填报要求如下：①货物名称及规格型号应据实填报，并与所提供的商业发票相符；②货物名称应当规范，规格型号应当足够详细，以能满足海关归类、审价以及许可证管理要求为准；③加工贸易等已备案的货物，本栏目填报录入的内容必须与备案登记中同项号下货物的名称与规格型号一致。

36．数量及单位

该栏目填写进（出）口货物的实际成交数量及计量单位。本栏目分三行填报及打印。具体填报要求如下：①进出口货物必须按法定计量单位填报。法定第一计量单位及数量打印在本栏目第一行。②凡海关列明第二计量单位的，必须报明该货物第二计量单位及数量，打印在本栏目第二行。无统计第二计量单位的，本栏目第二行为空。③成交计量单位与海关统计计量单位不一致时，还需填报成交计量单位及数量，打印在本栏目第三行，成交计量单位与海关统计法定计量单位一致时，本栏目第三行为空。④加工贸易等已备案的货物，成交计量单位必须与备案登记中同项号下货物的计量单位一致，不相同时必须修改备案或转换一致后填报。

37．原产国（地区）/最终目的国（地区）

原产国（地区）是进口货物的生产、开采或加工制造国家（地区）。最终目的国（地区）是出口货物的最终实际消费、使用或进一步加工制造国家（地区）。该栏目应按海关规定的《国别（地区）代码表》选择填报相应的国家（地区）名称或代码。例如：日本（116）。本业务填写德国。

38．单价

该栏目应填报同一项号下进（出）口货物实际成交的货物单位价格。无实际成交价格的，本栏目填报货值。

39．总价

该栏目应填报同一项号下进（出）口货物实际成交的货物总价。无实际成交价格的，本栏目填报货值。

40．币制

该栏目填写进（出）口货物实际成交价格的币种，应根据实际成交情况按海关规定的《货币代码表》选择填报相应的货币名称或代码，例如“美元（502）”或“USD（502）”。如《货币代码表》中无实际成交币种，需转换后填报。

41．征免

该栏目填写海关对进（出）口货物进行征税、减税、免税或特案处理的实际操作方式，应按照海关核发的《征免税证明》或有关政策规定，对报关单所列每项货物选择填报海关规定的《征免税方式代码表》中相应的征减免税方式。本业务填写照章征税。

42．税费征收情况

该栏目供海关批注进（出）口货物税费征收及减免情况。

43．录入员

该栏目用于预录入和EDI报关单，打印录入人员的姓名。

44．录入单位

该栏目用于预录入和EDI报关单，打印录入单位名称。

45．申报单位

申报单位是对申报内容的真实性直接向海关负责的企业或单位。自理报关的，应填报进（出）口货物的经营单位名称及代码；委托代理报关的，应填报经海关批准的专业或代理报关企业名称及代码，本栏目内应加盖申报单位有效印章。该栏目指报关单左下方用于填报申报单位有关情况的总栏目。本栏目还包括报关员姓名、单位地址、邮编和电话等分项目，由申报单位的报关员填报。本业务由浙江大同进出口有限公司盖章和签名。

46．填制日期

该栏目填写报关单的填制日期、预录入和EDI报关单，由计算机自动打印。本栏目为6位数，顺序为年、月、日各2位。

47．海关审单批注栏

该栏目指供海关内部作业时签注的总栏目，由海关关员手工填写在预录入报关单上，其中“放行”栏填写海关对接受申报的进出口货物作出放行决定的日期。

填制好的出口货物报关单如下：

中华人民共和国海关出口货物报关单（1）

预录入编号：　　　　　　　　　　　　　　　　　　　　　　海关编号：

出口口岸：上海海关	备案号	出口日期	申报日期：2010-04-08
经营单位：浙江大同进出口有限公司（3101003826）	运输方式：水陆运输	运输工具：XIN YA ZHOU/ VOY. NO. 0023W	提运单号：
发货单位：浙江大同进出口有限公司（3101003826）	贸易方式：一般贸易	征免性质：一般征税	结汇方式：信用证
许可证号：	运抵国（地区）：德国	指运港：汉堡	境内货源地：浙江玉环
批准文号：338667889　成交方式：CIF	运费：USD67.76	保费：USD39.45	杂费：
合同协议号：DT1000033　件数：255	包装种类：纸箱	毛重（公斤）：5654.20	净重（公斤）：5584.20
集装箱号：	随附单据：	生产厂家：浙江玉环金山阀门有限公司	
标记唛码及备注：CARK DT1000033 HAMBURG CARTON NO：1-255			

项号	商品编码	商品名称、规格型号	数量及单位	最终目的国（地区）	单价	总价	币制	征免
01	8481801090	黄铜阀门 1/2 英寸	4320 套 691.20 千克	德国	1.08	4665.60	美元	照章征税（0）
02	8481801090	黄铜阀门 3/4 英寸	4000 套 920.00 千克	德国	1.51	6040.00	美元	照章征税（0）
03	8481801090	黄铜阀门 1 英寸	2400 套 840.00 千克	德国	2.30	5520.00	美元	照章征税（0）
04	8481801090	黄铜阀门 1-1/4 英寸	1296 套 699.84 千克	德国	3.70	4795.20	美元	照章征税（0）
05	8481801090	黄铜阀门 1-1/2 英寸	960 套 700.80 千克	德国	4.90	4704.00	美元	照章征税（0）

税费征收情况		
录入员　　录入单位	兹声明以上申报无讹并承担法律责任	海关审单批注及放行日期（签章）
报关员 单位地址： 浙江省杭州市益乐路 902 号 邮编：310016　电话：87772409	浙江大同进出口有限公司 报关专用章 申报单位（签章） 填制日期：2010-04-08	审单　审价 征税　统计 查验　放行

中华人民共和国海关出口货物报关单（2）

预录入编号：　　　　　　　　　　　　　　　　　　　　　　海关编号：

出口口岸：上海海关	备案号	出口日期	申报日期：2010-04-08
经营单位：浙江大同进出口有限公司（3101003826）	运输方式：水陆运输	运输工具：XIN YA ZHOU/ VOY. NO. 0023W	提运单号：
发货单位：浙江大同进出口有限公司（3101003826）	贸易方式：一般贸易	征免性质：一般征税	结汇方式：信用证
许可证号：	运抵国（地区）：德国	指运港：汉堡	境内货源地：浙江玉环
批准文号：338667889　成交方式：CIF	运费：USD67.76	保费：USD39.45	杂费：
合同协议号：DT1000033　件数：255	包装种类：纸箱	毛重（公斤）：5654.20	净重（公斤）：5584.20
集装箱号：	随附单据：	生产厂家：浙江玉环金山阀门有限公司	
标记唛码及备注：CARK DT1000033 HAMBURG CARTON NO：1-255			

（续）

项号	商品编码	商品名称、规格型号	数量及单位	最终目的国（地区）	单价	总价	币制	征免
06	8481801090	黄铜阀门 2英寸	1152套 1474.56千克	德国	8.80	10137.60	美元	照章征税（0）

税费征税情况		
录入员 录入单位	兹声明以上申报无讹并承担法律责任	海关审单批注及放行日期（签章）
报关员 单位地址： 浙江省杭州市益乐路902号 邮编：310016 电话：87772409	申报单位（签章）（浙江大同进出口有限公司 报关专用章） 填制日期：2010-04-08	审单 审价 征税 统计 查验 放行

第二步：制作报关委托书。

在实务中，考虑实际装运时货物数量可变动，外贸单证员一般只在报关委托书上盖章，而不填写详细内容，详细内容由报关员报关时填写。报关委托书正反两面都印有内容。

正面：

代理报关委托书

编号：00082827061

我单位现（A逐票、B长期）委托贵公司代理等通关事宜。（A、填单申报 B、辅助查验 C、垫缴税款 D、办理海关证明联 E、审批手册 F、核销手册 G、申办减免税手续 H、其他）详见《委托报关协议》。

我单位保证遵守《海关法》和国家有关法规，保证所提供的情况真实、完整、单货相符。否则，愿承担相关法律责任。

本委托数自签字之日起至 年 月 日止。

委托方（盖章）：

法定代表人或其授权签署《代理报关委托书》的人（签字）

年 月 日

委托报关协议

为明确委托报关具体事项和各自责任，双方经平等协商签订协议如下：

委托方		被委托方		
主要货物名称		*报关单编码	No.	
H.S.编码		收到单证日期	年 月 日	
货物总价		收到单证情况	合同□	发票□
进出口日期	年 月 日		装箱清单□	提（运）单□
提单号			加工贸易手册□	许可证件□
贸易方式			其他	
原产地/货源地		报关收费	人民币： 元	
其他要求：		承诺说明：		
背面所列通用条款是本协议不可分割的一部分，对本协议的签署构成了对背面通用条款的同意。		背面所列通用条款是本协议不可分割的一部分，对本协议的签署构成了对背面通用条款的同意。		
委托方业务签章： 经办人签章： 联系电话： 年 月 日		被委托方业务签章： 经办报关员签章： 联系电话： 年 月 日		

CCB/L （白联：海关留存；黄联：被委托方留存；红联：委托方留存） 中国报关协会监制

背面

委托报关协议通用条款

委托方责任 委托方应及时提供报关报检所需的全部单证，并对单证的真实性、准确性和完整性负责。

委托方负责在报关企业办结海关手续后，及时、履约支付代理报关费用，支付垫支费用，以及因委托方责任产生的滞报金、滞纳金和海关等执法单位依法处以的各种罚款。

负责按照海关要求将货物运抵指定场所。

负责与被委托方报关员一同协助海关进行查验，回答海关的询问，配合相关调查，并承担产生的相关费用。

在被委托方无法做到报关前提取货样的情况下，承担单货相符的责任。

被委托方责任 负责解答委托方有关向海关申报的疑问。

负责对委托方提供的货物情况和单证的真实性、完整性进行“合理审查”，审查内容包括：（一）证明进出口货物实际情况的资料，包括进出口货物的品名、规格、用途、产地、贸易方式等；（二）有关进出口货物的合同、发票、运输单据、装箱单等商业单据；（三）进出口所需的许可证件及随附单证；（四）海关要求的加工贸易手册（纸质或电子数据的）及其他进出口单证。

因确定货物的品名、归类等原因，海关批准，可以看货或提取货样。

在接到委托方交付齐备的随附单证后，负责依据委托方提供的单证，按照《中华人民共和国海关进出口报关单填制规范》认真填制报关单，承担“单单相符”的责任，在海关规定和本委托报关协议中约定的时间内报关，办理海关手续。

负责及时通知委托方共同协助海关进行查验，并配合海关开展相关调查。

负责支付因报关企业的责任给委托方造成的直接经济损失，所产生的滞报金、滞纳金和海关等执法单位依法处以的各种罚款。

负责在本委托书约定的时间内将办结海关手续的有关委托内容的单证、文件交还委托方或其指定的人员（详见《委托报关协议》“其他要求”栏）。

赔偿原则 被委托方不承担因不可抗力给委托方造成损失的责任。因其他过失造成的损失，由双方自行约定或按国家有关法律法规的规定办理。由此造成的风险，委托方可以投保方式自行规避。

不承担的责任 签约双方各自不承担因另一方原因造成的直接经济损失，以及滞报金、滞纳金和相关罚款。

收费原则 一般货物报关收费原则上按当地《报关行业收费指导价格》规定执行。特殊货物可由双方另行商定。

法律强制 本《委托报关协议》的任一条款与《海关法》及有关法律、法规不一致时，应以法律、法规为准。但不影响《委托报关协议》其他条款的有效。

协商解决事项 变更、中止本协议或双方发生争议时，按照《中华人民共和国合同法》有关规定及程序处理。因签约双方以外的原因产生的问题或报关业务需要修改协议条款，应写协商订立补充协议。双方可以在法律、行政法规准许的范围内另行签署补充条款，但补充条款不得与本协议的内容相抵触。

【任务 3】整理报关单据并办理委托报关

4 月 8 日，外贸单证员桂小龙整理报关单据，然后把出口货物报关单、报关委托书、出口收汇核销单、商业发票、装箱单、换证凭条寄给浙江双马国际货运有限公司，委托其代理向商检局上海分局换取出境货物通关单和代理报关。

4 月 9 日，浙江双马国际货运有限公司从商检局上海分局换取出境货物通关单如下：

中华人民共和国出入境检验检疫

出境货物通关单

<table>
<tr><td colspan="3">1. 发货人：
浙江大同进出口有限公司</td><td colspan="2" rowspan="3">5. 标记及号码
CARK
DT1000033
HAMBURG
CARTON NO：1-255</td></tr>
<tr><td colspan="3">2. 收货人：
CARK GMBH & CO. KG</td></tr>
<tr><td colspan="2">3. 合同/信用证号：
DT1000033/LC-536-089075</td><td>4. 输往国家或地区：
德国</td></tr>
<tr><td colspan="2">6. 运输工具及名称：
船舶</td><td>7. 发货日期：
2010.4.12</td><td colspan="2">8. 集装箱规格及数量</td></tr>
<tr><td>9. 货物名称及规格
黄铜球阀</td><td>10. H.S.编码
8481801090</td><td>11. 申报总值
35862.40 美元</td><td colspan="2">12. 数/重量、包装及种类
14128 套/255 个纸箱</td></tr>
<tr><td colspan="5">13. 证明
上述货物业经检验检疫，请海关予以放行。
本通关单有效期至二〇一〇年七月八日。
签字： （盖章） 2010 年 4 月 9 日</td></tr>
</table>

一、报关的含义及期限

报关是指进出口贸易的有关当事人或其代理人、进出境运输工具负责人，进出境物品的所有人在规定的有效期内向海关办理有关货物、运输工具、物品进出境手续的全过程。按照《中华人民共和国海关法》的规定，所有进出境的货物和运输工具必须通过设有海关的地方进境或出境，并接受海关的监督。只有经过海关查验放行后，货物才能提取或装运出口。

货物必须在规定的期限内报关，具体规定为：

（1）进口货物的收货人或其代理人应当自运输工具申报进境之日起 14 日内向海关申报。第 14 日遇法定节假日的，则顺延至其后第一个工作日，逾期则按日以进口货物完税价格的 0.5‰征收滞报金。

（2）出口货物的发货人或其代理人应当在货物运抵海关监管区后、装货的 24 小时以前向海关申报。企业出口报关时，出口货物必须实际运抵海关监管或海关指定的监管地点。否则，海关不接受出口报关。

二、报关单位

报关单位分为报关企业和进出口收发货人，报关企业分为报关公司和货运代理公司。

三、报关员

报关员是指取得资格证书，按规定程序在海关注册，向海关办理进出口货物报关业务的人员。我国海关规定进出口货物的报关必须由经海关批准的专业人员代表收发货人或者报关企业向海关办理。这些专业人员就是报关员。

四、进出口货物报关流程

为了确保进出口货物合法进出境，海关根据国家有关法律法规的不同要求，对进出口货物的报关规定了一系列特定的手续和步骤。遵守这些规定的程序是报关人的法定义务，否则将承担相应的法律责任。根据时间的先后顺序和海关管理要求的不同，报关可分为前期报关程序、进出境报关程序和后续报关程序。

（1）前期报关程序是指进出口货物在实际进出境之前，进出口货物收发货人或其代理人向海关说明进出口货物的情况，申请适用特定的报关程序。

（2）进出境报关程序是指进出口货物在进出境环节需向海关履行的手续。进出境报关程序是任何进出口货物通关时都必须履行经过的环节。一般进出口货物的报关只需履行进出境报关程序即可，主要包括进出口申报、陪同查验、缴纳税费、提取或装运货物等。

（3）后续报关程序则主要指进出口货物实际进出境以后，进出口货物收发货人或其代理人根据海关管理的要求向海关办理的旨在证明有关进出口货物合法进出口、在境内合规使用并已经完成有关海关监管义务的手续。

五、进出口货物报关单

进出口货物报关单是由海关总署规定统一格式和填制规范，由进出口货物收、发货人或其代理人填制并向海关提交的申报货物状况的法律文书，是海关依法监管货物进出口，征收关税及其他税费，编制海关统计以及处理其他海关业务的重要凭证。

一切进口货物的收货人、出口货物的发货人或他们的委托代理人都必须在货物进出口时填写《进口货物报关单》或《出口货物报关单》，向海关申报。电子数据报关单与纸质报关单具有同等法律效力。报关单填写的质量如何，直接关系到报关的效率、企业的经济利益和海关的征税、减免税和查验、发行等工作。

1. 报关单的填制要求

（1）报关单的填报必须真实，不能伪报、瞒报及虚报，要做到两个相符：①单证相符，即报关单与合同、批文、发票、装箱单等相符；②单货相符，即报关单中所报内容与实际进出口货物情况相符。

（2）不同合同、运输工具名称、征免性质、许可证号及贸易方式的货物，不能填在同一份报关单上。一张报关单上最多不能超过五项海关统计货物编号的货物。

（3）报关单填写要准确、齐全，字迹工整。若有更改，必须在更改项目上加盖校对章。

2. 报关单的份数及颜色

一般进出口贸易需填写一式三份，使用电子数据报关的填写一份录入即可。

报关单有不同的颜色，并有不同的要求：进料加工进出口货物报关时，填写粉红色的报关单；来料加工装配和补偿贸易进出口货物驳岸时，填写浅绿色的报关单；外商投资企业进出口货物报关时，填写浅蓝色的报关单；需国内退税的出口货物，另增填浅黄色专用报关单一份；一般贸易和其余贸易方式进出口货物报关时，所使用的进出口收付汇专用报关单联，均填写白色的报关单。

◆ 实训项目 7-1

上接实训项目 6-1。

2010 年 8 月 4 日，浙江曼旎进出口有限公司外贸单证员王宁收到浙江双马国际货运有限公司如下进仓通知单通知后，马上转通知绍兴帝浩服装有限公司做好装箱准备的通知，要求货物务必于 8 月 5 日 12 时前进仓，8 月 7 日装运。

浙江双马国际货运有限公司

货物进仓通知单

TO：浙江曼旎进出口有限公司

进仓编号：	SM10E00130080	客户编号：	JY10C00709
货名：	BOYS JACKET	件数：	5200PCS
毛重：	2600KGS	体积：	23.712M^3

（续）

起运港：	NINGBO	目的港：	DUBAI
开航日期：	2010-08-07		
货物请务必于 8 月 5 日 12 时前进仓。 唛头： 如有问题，请与我司联系：李红玲，电话：0571-82379057 进仓要求： 1. 进仓截止时间为报关前一天中午 12：00，遇节假日则向前顺延。 2. 凭本通知在规定时间内将有关单据及货物送至我司仓库。如不能在规定时间内送达，我们将不能保证货物如期运出。 3. 所送货物需按规定货号分票理清进仓，否则将被收取分票费。 4. 对于受潮受湿和外包装损坏的货物，仓库将不予受理，特殊情况，货代出保函。 5. 从 2007 年 8 月 1 日起，仓库对所有进仓货物将收取进仓费：一般货物 5 元/立方吨，特殊货物 10 元/立方吨，托盘 10 元/托盘。现金付清。			
仓库名称：	宁波市雄业仓储有限公司	仓库地址：	宁波市北仑区大港工业城渤海路 638 号
联系人：	张小姐	电话：	0574 -27686311

【任务 1】申领并制作出口收汇核销单

8 月 4 日，浙江曼旋进出口有限公司外贸单证员王宁根据商业发票、装箱单和相关信息申领和制作出口收汇核销单。浙江曼旋进出口有限公司的组织机构代码是 3101003855。

出口收汇核销单 存根

（浙）编号：

出口企业：
单位代码：
出口币种总价：
收汇方式：
预计收款日期：
报关日期：
备注：
此单报关有效期截止到

（出口单位盖章）

出口收汇核销单

（浙）编号：

出口企业				
单位代码				
银行签注栏	类别	币种金额	日期	盖章
海关签注栏：				
外管局签注栏： 年 月 日（盖章）				

（出口单位盖章）

（海关盖章）

出口收汇核销单 出口退税专用

（浙）编号：

出口企业		
单位代码		
货物名称	数量	币种总价
报关单编号：		
外管局签注栏： 年 月 日（盖章）		

未经核销此联不得撕开

【任务 2】制作出口货物报关单和报关委托书

8 月 4 日，浙江曼旋进出口有限公司外贸单证员王宁根据商业发票、装箱单和相关信息制作出口货物报关单和报关委托书（略）。运费为 900 美元/20 英尺柜，保险费率为 1.5‰。

中华人民共和国海关出口货物报关单

预录入编号：　　　　　　　　　　　　　　　　　　　　海关编号：

出口口岸		备案号	出口日期	申报日期
经营单位		运输方式	运输工具	提运单号
发货单位		贸易方式	征免性质	结汇方式
许可证号		运抵国（地区）	指运港	境内货源地
批准文号	成交方式	运费	保费	杂费
合同协议号	件数	包装种类	毛重（公斤）	净重（公斤）
集装箱号		随附单据		生产厂家
标记唛码及备注				

项号	货物编码	货物名称、规格型号	数量及单位	最终目的国（地区）	单价	总价	币制	征免

税费征税情况		
录入员　录入单位	兹声明以上申报无讹并承担法律责任	海关审单批注及放行日期（签章） 审单　审价
报关员	申报单位（签章）	征税　统计
单位地址 邮编　电话	填制日期	查验　放行

【任务 3】整理报关单据并办理委托报关

8 月 4 日，浙江曼旎进出口有限公司外贸单证员王宁制作和办理好相关报关单证后，同时与报检委托书、出境货物换证凭条一起寄给浙江双马国际货运有限公司，委托其办理报检和报关手续。

◆ **实训项目 7-2**

上接实训项目 6-2。

2010 年 9 月 24 日，杭州维丰进出口有限公司外贸单证员叶丽收到浙江双马国际货运有限公司杭州分公司如下进仓通知单通知后，马上转通知供应商。

浙江双马国际货运有限公司

货物进仓通知单

TO：杭州维丰进出口有限公司

贵司委托我司出运的 140 件货至 米兰机场 ，现预配 CA2304/CA1069 航班，

进仓编号： SM10F00900234 ，货物请于 2010-09-25 前送至以下仓库：

仓库地址：杭州萧山国际机场 5 号路航空货站 B 区 7 号门

联系人：顾先生：13065717361，吴先生：15868166436

进舱时间：周一至周五 8:30-16:30，双休日需进舱请提前与工作人员联系

如有任何问题，请即致电：

TEL：0571-88390710

FAX：0571-88390120

ATTN：叶慧

【任务 1】申领并制作出口收汇核销单

9 月 24 日，杭州维丰进出口有限公司外贸单证员叶丽根据商业发票、装箱单和相关信息申领和制作出口收汇核销单。杭州维丰进出口有限公司的组织机构代码是 3101003811。

出口收汇核销单
存根

（浙）编号：

出口企业：
单位代码：
出口币种总价：
收汇方式：
预计收款日期：
报关日期：
备注：
此单报关有效期截止到

（出口单位盖章）

出口收汇核销单

（浙）编号：

出口企业				
单位代码				
银行签注栏	类别	币种金额	日期	盖章
海关签注栏：				
外管局签注栏： 年 月 日（盖章）				

（出口单位盖章）

（海关盖章）

出口收汇核销单
出口退税专用

（浙）编号：

出口企业		
单位代码		
货物名称	数量	币种总价
报关单编号：		
外管局签注栏： 年 月 日（盖章）		

未经核销此联不得撕开

【任务 2】制作出口货物报关单和报关委托书

9 月 24 日，杭州维丰进出口有限公司外贸单证员叶丽根据商业发票、装箱单和相关信息制作出口货物报关单和报关委托书（略）。由中国杭州机场至意大利米兰机场的空运费为 42

元/千克，按照 W/M 计价。

中华人民共和国海关出口货物报关单

预录入编号：　　　　　　　　　　　　　　　　　　　　　海关编号：

<table>
<tr><td colspan="2">出口口岸</td><td>备案号</td><td>出口日期</td><td>申报日期</td></tr>
<tr><td colspan="2">经营单位</td><td>运输方式</td><td>运输工具</td><td>提运单号</td></tr>
<tr><td colspan="2">发货单位</td><td>贸易方式</td><td>征免性质</td><td>结汇方式</td></tr>
<tr><td colspan="2">许可证号</td><td>运抵国（地区）</td><td>指运港</td><td>境内货源地</td></tr>
<tr><td>批准文号</td><td>成交方式</td><td>运费</td><td>保费</td><td>杂费</td></tr>
<tr><td>合同协议号</td><td>件数</td><td>包装种类</td><td>毛重（公斤）</td><td>净重（公斤）</td></tr>
<tr><td colspan="2">集装箱号</td><td colspan="2">随附单据</td><td>生产厂家</td></tr>
<tr><td colspan="5">标记唛码及备注</td></tr>
<tr><td colspan="5">项号　货物编码　货物名称、规格型号　数量及单位　最终目的国（地区）　单价　总价　币制　征免</td></tr>
<tr><td colspan="5"></td></tr>
<tr><td colspan="5">税费征税情况</td></tr>
<tr><td colspan="3">录入员　录入单位　　兹声明以上申报无讹并承担法律责任

报关员

申报单位（签章）

单位地址

邮编　　电话　　填制日期</td><td colspan="2">海关审单批注及放行日期（签章）

审单　　审价

征税　　统计

查验　　放行</td></tr>
</table>

【任务 3】整理报关单据并办理委托报关

9 月 24 日，杭州维丰进出口有限公司外贸单证员叶丽制作和办理好相关报关单证后，寄给浙江双马国际货运有限公司，委托其办理报关手续。

◆ **实训项目 7-3**

上接实训项目 6-3。

2010 年 7 月 29 日，商检通过后，苏州市出入境检验检疫局发给江苏致远轮胎厂以下换证凭条，江苏致远轮胎厂立即把换证凭条传真给浙江大顺进出口有限公司。

转单号：	380400305119912T		报检号：	380400515066609	
报检单位：	江苏致远轮胎厂				
品名：	防弹轮胎	合同号：	DS10105	H.S.编码：	4011100010
数（重）量	360 条	包装件数	360 袋	金额	18000.00 欧元
评定意见： 贵单位报检的该批货物，经我局检验检疫，已合格。请执此单到上海局本部办理出境验证业务。本单有效期截止于 2010 年 9 月 28 日。 苏州局本部 2010 年 7 月 29 日					

【任务 1】申领并制作出口收汇核销单

7 月 29 日，浙江大顺进出口有限公司外贸单证员朱丽娅根据商业发票、装箱单和相关信息申领和制作出口收汇核销单。浙江大顺进出口有限公司的组织机构代码是 3101005566。

出口收汇核销单
存根

（浙）编号：

出口企业：
单位代码：
出口币种总价：
收汇方式：
预计收款日期：
报关日期：
备注：
此单报关有效期截止到

（出口单位盖章）

出口收汇核销单

（浙）编号：

出口企业				
单位代码				
银行签注栏	类别	币种金额	日期	盖章
海关签注栏：				
外管局签注栏： 年　月　日（盖章）				

（出口单位盖章）

（海关盖章）

出口收汇核销单
出口退税专用

（浙）编号：

出口企业		
单位代码		
货物名称	数量	币种总价
报关单编号：		
外管局签注栏： 年　月　日（盖章）		

未经核销此联不得撕开

【任务 2】制作出口货物报关单和报关委托书

7 月 29 日，浙江大顺进出口有限公司外贸单证员朱丽娅根据商业发票、装箱单和相关信息制作出口货物报关单和报关委托书（略）。

中华人民共和国海关出口货物报关单

预录入编号： 海关编号：

出口口岸		备案号	出口日期	申报日期
经营单位		运输方式	运输工具	提运单号
发货单位		贸易方式	征免性质	结汇方式
许可证号		运抵国（地区）	指运港	境内货源地
批准文号	成交方式	运费	保费	杂费
合同协议号	件数	包装种类	毛重（公斤）	净重（公斤）
集装箱号		随附单据		生产厂家
标记唛码及备注				

项号	货物编码	货物名称、规格型号	数量及单位	最终目的国（地区）	单价	总价	币制	征免

税费征税情况

录入员 录入单位	兹声明以上申报无讹并承担法律责任	海关审单批注及放行日期（签章）
报关员	申报单位（签章）	审单 审价
		征税 统计
单位地址		查验 放行
邮编 电话 填制日期		

【任务 3】整理报关单据并办理委托报关

7 月 29 日，浙江大顺进出口有限公司外贸单证员朱丽娅制作和办理好相关报关单证后，寄给德莎国际货运代理（上海）有限公司，委托其办理报关手续。

项目八

制作投保单和办理保险操作

能力目标

能根据信用证或外贸合同的保险相关条款和托运情况制作投保单，并能办理保险操作。

知识目标

掌握平安险、水渍险和一切险等中国保险条款海运货物保险、UCP600 的保险相关条款，熟悉中国保险条款海运货物保险、航空货物运输保险、保险除外责任和责任起讫、保险金额和保费的计算、保险单的种类，了解中国保险条款的一般附加险和特别附加险、协会保险条款。

上接项目七的导入项目。

【任务 1】制作投保单

2010 年 4 月 9 日，在完成托运手续确认船期后，浙江大同进出口有限公司外贸单证员桂小龙根据信用证中保险单条款“INSURANCE POLICY/CERTIFICATE IN DUPLICATE ENDORSED IN BLANK FOR 110% INVOICE VALUE, COVERING ALL RISKS OF CIC OF PICC (1/1/1981).”和“THE NUMBER AND THE DATE OF THIS CREDIT MUST BE QUOTED ON ALL DOCUMENTS.”等其他相关条款，以及商业发票和装箱单制作投保单。

货物运输保险投保单

APPLICATION FORM FOR CARGO TRANSPORTATION INSURANCE

投保单号：

被保险人：

INSURED: ____________________

（续）

发票号（INVOICE NO.）

合同号（CONTRACT NO.）

信用证号（L/C NO.）

发票金额（INVOICE AMOUNT）________________投保加成（PLUS）_____%

兹有下列物品向中国大地财产保险股份有限公司投保（INSURANCE IS REQUIRED ON THE FOLLOWING COMMODITIES：）

标记 MARKS & NO.S	包装及数量 QUANTITY	保险货物项目 DESCRIPTION OF GOODS	保险金额 AMOUNT INSURED

启运日期：　　　　　　　　　　装载工具

DATE OF COMMENCEMENT________________PER CONVEYANCE ________________

自　　　　　　经　　　　　　至

FORM________________VIA________________TO________________

提单号：　　　　　　　　　　赔款偿付地点：

B/L NO.________________CLAIM PAYABLE AT________________

投保险别：（PLEASE INDICATE THE CONDITIONS &/OR SPECIAL COVERAGES）

请如实告知下列情况：（如“是”在（　）打“×”）IF ANY, PLEASE MARK“×”：

1．货物种类　袋装（　）　散装（　）　冷藏（　）　液体（　）　活动物（　）　机器/汽车（　）　危险品等级（　）

GOODS　BAG/JUMBO　BULK　　LIQUID　LIVE ANIMAL　MACHINE/AUTO　DANGEROUS CLASS

2．集装箱种类　普通（　）　开顶（　）　框架（　）　平板（　）　冷藏（　）

CONTAINER　ORDINARY　OPEN　FRAME　FLAT　REFRIGERATOR

3．转运工具　海轮（　）　飞机（　）　驳船（　）　火车（　）　汽车（　）

BY TRANSIT　SHIP　PLANE　BARGE　TRAIN　TRUCK

4．船舶资料　　船籍（　）　　船龄（　）

PARTICULAR OF SHIP　REGISTRY________________AGE________________

备件：被保险人确认本保险合同条款和内容已经完全了解　　投保人（签名盖章）APPLICANT’S SIGNATURE

THE ASSURED CONFIRMS HEREWITH THE TERMS AND CONDITIONS OF THESE INSURANCE CONTRACT FULLY UNDERSTOOD

电话（TEL）

投保日期（DATE）________________　　地址（ADD）________________

本公司自用（FOR OFFICE USE ONLY）

费率　　　　保费　　　　备注：

RATE＿AS ARRANGED＿　PREMIUM＿AS ARRANGED＿

经办人 BY________　核保人________________　负责人________________

总公司地址：上海市浦东南路 855 号　电话：021-58369588　邮政编码：200120　网址：www.ccic-net.com.cn

【任务 2】向保险公司办理保险

外贸单证员桂小龙制作好投保单后，向中国大地财产保险股份有限公司浙江省分公司办理保险。

【任务 1】制作投保单

1．被保险人（Insured）

被保险人有以下几种填法：

（1）L/C 无特殊要求或要求“Endorsed in blank”一般应填 L/C 受益人名称，可不填详细地址，且出口公司应在保险单背面背书。

（2）若来证指定以××公司为被保险人，则应在此栏填×× CO.。出口公司不要背书。

（3）若来证规定以某银行为抬头，如“to the order of ××× bank”，则在此栏先填上受益人名称，再填上“held to the order of ×× bank”。

本业务填写：ZHEJIANG DATONG IMPORT AND EXPORT CO., LTD.。

2．发票号、合同号和信用证号（Invoice no., Contract no. and L/C no.）

本栏目要根据商业发票以及合同、信用证信息进行填写。

3．商业发票金额和投保加成

本栏目根据商业发票和信用证的要求填写。如果信用证没有规定投保加成比例，则根据 UCP600 规定，应至少在 CIF 或 CIP 的基础上加成 10%进行投保。

本业务填写：发票金额（INVOICE AMOUNT）USD35862.40 投保加成（PLUS）10 %。

4．唛头（Marks & Nos.）

保险单上标记应与发票提单上一致。若来证无特殊规定，一般可简单填成“as per Invoice No.×××.”。

5．包装及数量（Quantity）

有包装的填写最大包装件数；裸装货物要注明本身件数；煤炭、石油等散装货注明净重；有包装但以重量计价的，应把包装重量与计价重量都注上。

本业务填写：255CTNS。

6．货物名称（Description of goods）

允许用统称，但不同类别的多种货物应注明不同类别的各自总称。这里与提单此栏目的填写一致。

本业务填写：FORGED BRASS BALL VALVES。

7．保险金额（Amount Insured ）

保险金额填写时，保险货币应与信用证一致，大小写应该一致；保险金额的加成百分比应严格按信用证或合同规定掌握。如未规定，应按 CIF 或 CIP 发票价格的 110%投保；保险金额不要小数，出现小数时无论多少一律向上进位。

本业务填写：USD39449.00。

8．装载运输工具（Per Conveyance S.S）

海运方式下填写船名，最好再加航次。若整个运输由两次完成时，应分别填写一程船名及二程船名，中间用"/"隔开。铁路运输加填运输方式为"By railway"，最好再加车号；航空运输为"By air"，邮包运输为"By parcel post"。

本业务填写：XIN YA ZHOU，VOY. NO. 0023W。

9．开航日期（Slg on or abt.）

应按 B/L 中的签发日期填，还可以简单地填作"AS PER B/L"。

10．装运港和目的港（From…to…）

本业务填写：From SHANGHAI, CHINA to HAMBURG, GERMANY。

11．承保险别（Conditions）

出口公司在制单时，先在投保单上填写这一栏的内容，当全部保险单填好交给保险公司审核确认时，才由保险公司把承保险别的详细内容加注在正本保单上。

本业务填写：COVERING ALL RISKS OF CIC OF PICC (1/1/1981)。

12．赔款偿付地点（Claim payable at）

严格按照信用证规定打制；若来证未规定，则应打目的港。如信用证规定不止一个目的港或赔付地，则应全部照打。

本业务填写：HAMBURG, GERMANY。

13．投保日期（Date）

保险手续要求货物离开出口仓库前办理。投保日期填写应至少早于提单签发日、发运日或接受监管日。

本业务填写：APRIL 9, 2010。

14．其他

根据信用证中关于保险单的特殊要求条款，投保时应在投保单上注明。如"所有单据注明信用证号码、开证日期和开证行名称"、"保险单上显示保险公司在目的地的保险代理名称、地址和联系方式"等。

本业务填写：INSURANCE POLICY MUST SHOW:

THE NUMBER OF L/C: LC-536-089075

THE DATE OF L/C: MARCH 17, 2010

15．签字（signature）

投保人进行盖章签字。

制作好的投保单如下：

中国大地财产保险股份有限公司
China Continent Property&Casualty Insurance Company Ltd.
货物运输保险投保单
APPLICATION FORM FOR CARGO TRANSPORTATION INSURANCE

投保单号：

被保险人：
INSURED: ZHEJIANG DATONG IMPORT AND EXPORT CO., LTD.
发票号（INVOICE NO.） 2010DT00101
合同号（CONTRACT NO.） DT1000033
信用证号（L/C NO.） LC-536-089075
发票金额（INVOICE AMOUNT） USD35862.40 投保加成（PLUS） 10 %
兹有下列物品向中国大地财产保险股份有限公司投保（INSURANCE IS REQUIRED ON THE FOLLOWING COMMODITIES:）

标记 MARKS & NOS	包装及数量 QUANTITY	保险货物项目 DESCRIPTION OF GOODS	保险金额 AMOUNT INSURED
AS PER INVOICE NO. 2010DT00101	255CTNS	FORGED BRASS BALL VALVES	USD39449.00

启运日期： 装载工具
DATE OF COMMENCEMENT AS PER B/L PER CONVEYANCE XIN YA ZHOU， VOY. NO. 0023W
自 经 至
FORM SHANGHAI, CHINA VIA *** TO HAMBURG, GERMANY
提单号： 赔款偿付地点：
B/L NO.______ CLAIM PAYABLE AT HAMBURG, GERMANY

投保险别：（PLEASE INDICATE THE CONDITIONS &/OR SPECIAL COVERAGES）
COVERING ALL RISKS OF CIC OF PICC (1/1/1981)
INSURANCE POLICY MUST SHOW:
THE NUMBER OF L/C: LC-536-089075
THE DATE OF L/C: MARCH 17, 2010

请如实告知下列情况：（如“是”在（ ）打“×”）IF ANY, PLEASE MARK “×”:
1. 货物种类 GOODS　袋装（×）BAG/JUMBO　散装（ ）BULK　冷藏（ ）　液体（ ）LIQUID　活动物（ ）LIVE ANIMAL　机器/汽车（ ）MACHINE/AUTO　危险品等级（ ）DANGEROUS CLASS
2. 集装箱种类 CONTAINER　普通（×）ORDINARY　开顶（ ）OPEN　框架（ ）FRAME　平板（ ）FLAT　冷藏（ ）REFRIGERATOR
3. 转运工具 BY TRANSIT　海轮（×）SHIP　飞机（ ）PLANE　驳船（ ）BARGE　火车（ ）TRAIN　汽车（ ）TRUCK
4. 船舶资料 PARTICULAR OF SHIP　船籍（ ）REGISTRY______　船龄（ ）AGE______

备件：被保险人确认本保险合同条款和内容已经完全了解
THE ASSURED CONFIRMS HEREWITH THE TERMS AND CONDITIONS OF THESE INSURANCE CONTRACT FULLY UNDERSTOOD.
投保日期（DATE） APRIL 9, 2010

投保人（签名盖章）APPLICANT'S SIGNATURE
ZHEJIANG DATONG IMPORT AND EXPORT CO., LTD.
电话（TEL） 0571-87772409
地址（ADD） 0571-87772407

本公司自用（FOR OFFICE USE ONLY）
费率 RATE AS ARRANGED　保费 PREMIUM AS ARRANGED　备注：
经办人 BY______ 核保人______ 负责人______
总公司地址：上海市浦东南路 855 号 电话：021-58369588 邮政编码：200120 网址： www.ccic-net.com.cn

【任务 2】向保险公司办理保险

外贸单证员桂小龙制作好投保单后，向中国大地财产保险股份有限公司浙江省分公司办

理保险。中国大地财产保险股份有限公司浙江省分公司接受投保，并出具如下保险单。

中国大地财产保险股份有限公司

China Continent Property&Casualty Insurance Company Ltd.

货物运输保险单

CARGO TRANSPORTATION INSURANCE POLICY

发票号（INVOICE NO.） 2010DT00101 保单号次 POLICY NO. BJ123990

合同号（CONTRACT NO.） DT1000033

信用证号（L/C NO.） LC-536-089075

被保险人：INSURED: ZHEJIANG DATONG IMPORT AND EXPORT CO., LTD.

中国大地财产保险股份有限公司（以下简称本公司）根据被保险人的要求，由被保险人向本公司缴付约定的保险费，按照本保险单承保险别和背面所载条款与下列特款承保下述货物运输保险，特立本保险单。

THIS POLICY OF INSURANCE WITNESSES THAT CHINA CONTINENT PROPERTY & CASUALLY INSURANCE COMPANY LTD. (HEREINAFTER CALLED "THE COMPANY") AT THE REQUEST OF THE INSURED AND IN CONSIDERATION OF THE AGREED PREMIUM PAID TO THE COMPANY BY THE INSURED, UNDERTAKES TO INSURE THE UNDERMENTIONED GOODS IN TRANSPORTATION SUBJECT TO THE CONDITIONS OF THIS OF THIS POLICY AS PER THE CLAUSES PRINTED OVERLEAF AND OTHER SPECIAL CLAUSES ATTACHED HEREON.

标记 MARKS&NOS	包装及数量 QUANTITY	保险货物项目 DESCRIPTION OF GOODS	保险金额 AMOUNT INSURED
AS PER INVOICE NO. 2010DT00101	255CTNS	FORGED BRASS BALL VALVES	USD39449.00

总保险金额

TOTAL AMOUNT INSURED: SAY U.S. DOLLARS THIRTY NINE THOUSAND FOUR HUNDRED FORTY NINE ONLY

保费： 启运日期 装载运输工具：

PERMIUM: AS ARRANGED DATE OF COMMENCEMENT: AS PER B/L PER CONVEYANCE: XIN YA ZHOU, VOY. NO. 0023W

自 经 至

FROM: SHANGHAI, CHINA VIA *** TO HAMBURG, GERMANY

承保险别：

CONDITIONS:

COVERING ALL RISKS OF CIC OF PICC (1/1/1981)

THE DATE OF L/C: MARCH 17, 2010

所保货物，如发生保险单项下可能引起索赔的损失或损坏，应立即通知本公司下述代理人查勘。如有索赔，应向本公司提交保单正本（本保险单共有 2 份正本）及有关文件。如一份正本已用于索赔，其余正本自动失效。

IN THE EVENT OF LOSS OR DAMAGE WITCH MAY RESULT IN A CLAIM UNDER THIS POLICY, IMMEDIATE NOTICE MUST BE GIVEN TO THE COMPANY'S AGENT AS MENTIONED HEREUNDER. CLAIMS, IF ANY, ONE OF THE ORIGINAL POLICY WHICH HAS BEEN ISSUED IN **TWO** ORIGINAL(S) TOGETHER WITH THE RELEVANT DOCUMENTS SHALL BE SURRENDERED TO THE COMPANY. IF ONE OF THE ORIGINAL POLICY HAS BEEN ACCOMPLISHED. THE OTHERS TO BE VOID.

中国大地财产保险股份有限公司

China Continent Property & Casualty Insurance Company Ltd.

杨菲

赔款偿付地点

CLAIM PAYABLE AT HAMBURG IN USD

出单日期

ISSUING DATE APR.12, 2010

（Authorized Signature）

知识支撑

一、协会货物保险条款

英国伦敦保险业协会的《协会货物条款》已沿用 200 余年，在国际保险界处于垄断地位。

它是世界上通用的保险条款，尽管许多保险公司有自己的保险条款，但基本上都以其为母本，内容也与ICC基本相同。它包括：

（1）协会货物保险条款（Institute Cargo Clause（A）、（B）、（C）（1/1/1982），I.C.C.）。

（2）协会散装油条款 Institute Bulk Oil Clauses（1/2/1983）

（3）协会货物战争险条款 Institute War Clauses（Cargo）

（4）协会货物罢工险条款 Institute Strike Clauses（Cargo）。

（5）恶意损害险条款 Malicious Damage Clauses。

二、中国保险条款

中国保险条款（China Insurance Clause，简称CIC）是中国人民保险公司参照国际通常做法结合我国实际情况拟订的，经过几十年来的应用与实践，已被国际贸易、航运、保险界广泛接受。

中国保险条款按运输方式来分，有海洋、陆上、航空和邮包运输保险条款四大类。其中以海运险为主要险种，陆运险、空运险和邮包险是在海运险基础上发展起来的，在一些基本内容上，与海运险是相似的，下面着重介绍海运险和空运险。

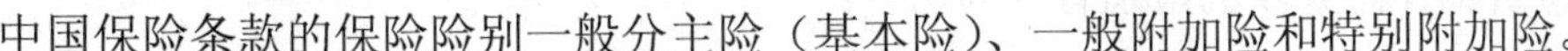

中国保险条款的保险险别一般分主险（基本险）、一般附加险和特别附加险。

1．主险

主险包括海洋运输货物保险条款、海洋运输冷藏货物保险条款、海洋运输散装桐油保险条款、陆上运输货物保险条款、陆上运输冷藏货物保险条款、航空运输货物保险条款、邮包险条款、活牲畜和家禽的海上、陆上、航空运输保险条款等。

2．一般附加险

一般附加险包括偷窃提货不着险条款、淡水雨淋险条款、短量险条款、混杂沾污险条款、渗漏险条款、碰损破碎险条款、串味险条款、受潮受热险条款、钩损险条款、包装破裂险条款、锈损险条款等。

3．特别附加险

特别附加险包括进口关税条款、舱面货物条款、拒收险条款、黄曲霉素险条款、易腐货物条款、交货不到条款、出口货物到港澳存仓火险责任扩展条款、海关检验条款、码头检验条款、战争险条款、战争险的附加费用、罢工险条款等。

三、中国保险条款海运货物保险

1．平安险（Free From Particular Average, F.P.A.）

平安险的责任范围是海运险中最狭小的，主要包括以下责任：

（1）被保险货物在运输中因恶劣气候、雷电、海啸、地震、洪水自然灾害造成整批货物的全损或推定全损，当被保险人要求按推定全损赔付时，须将受损物及权利委付给保险公司。

（2）由于运输工具遭受搁浅、触礁、沉没、互撞、与流冰或其他物体碰撞以及失火、爆炸意外事故造成货物的全部或部分损失。

（3）在运输工具已经发生搁浅、触礁、沉没、焚毁意外事故的情况下，货物在此前后又在海上遭受恶劣气候、雷电、海啸等自然灾害所造成的部分损失。

（4）在装卸或转运时由于一件或数件货物落海造成的全部或部分损失。

（5）被保险人对遭受承保责任内危险的货物采取抢救，防止或减少货损的措施而支付的合理费用，但以不超过这批被救货物的保险金额为限。

（6）运输工具遭遇海难后，在避难港由于卸货所引起的损失，以及在中途港、避难港由于卸货、存仓以及运送货物所产生的特别费用。

（7）共同海损的牺牲、分摊和救助费用。

（8）运输契约订有“船舶互撞责任”条款，根据该条款规定应由货方偿还船方的损失。

2．水渍险（With Particular Average, W.A.或 W.P.A.）

水渍险的责任范围包括平安险的全部责任和上述列举的自然灾害造成的部分损失。

3．一切险（All Risks）

一切险的责任范围包括负责平安险和水渍险的全部责任以及因各种外来原因所造成的保险货物的损失。这里所指的“各种外来原因”，是指以上所有一般附加险所涵盖的风险。

四、航空货物运输保险

航空运输货物保险条款的险别有下列两种：

1．航空运输险（Air Transportation Risks）

对被保险货物在运输途中遭受雷电、火灾、爆炸或由于飞机遭受恶劣气候或其他危难事故而被抛弃，或由于飞机遭受碰撞、倾覆、坠落或失踪等意外事故所造成的全部或部分损失负责赔偿。

2．航空运输一切险（Air Transportation All Risks）

除包括航空运输险责任外，还对被保险货物在运输途中由于外来原因造成的包括被偷窃、短少等全部或部分损失也负责赔偿。

五、除外责任

对下列损失不负赔偿责任：

（1）被保险人的故意行为或过失所造成的损失。

（2）属于发货人责任所引起的损失。

（3）在保险责任开始前，被保险货物已存在的品质不良或数量短差所造成的损失。

（4）被保险货物的自然损耗、本质缺陷、特性以及市价跌落、运输延迟所引起的损失或费用。

六、责任起讫

（1）海运险、陆运险、空运险和邮包险负“仓至仓”责任，自被保险货物运离保险单所载明的起运地仓库或储存处所开始运输时生效，包括正常运输过程中的海上、陆上、内河和驳船运输在内，直至该项货物到达保险单所载明目的地收货人的最后仓库或储存处所或被保险人用作分配、分派或非正常运输的其他储存处所为止。如未抵达上述仓库或储存处所，则以被保险货物在最后卸载地点全部卸离运输工具后满六十天（空运险为三十天）为止。如在上述六十天内被保险货物需转运到非保险单所载明的目的地时，则以该项货物开始转运时终止。

（2）由于被保险人无法控制的运输延迟、绕道、被迫卸货、重行装载、转载或承运人运用运输契约赋予的权限所作的任何运输上的变更或终止运输契约，致使被保险货物运到非保险单所载明目的地时，在被保险人及时将获知的情况通知保险人，并在必要时加缴保险费的情况下，本保险仍继续有效，保险责任按下列规定终止：

1）被保险货物如在非保险单所载明的目的地出售，保险责任至交货时为止，但不论任何情况，均以被保险货物在卸载地点全部卸离运输工具后满六十天（空运险为三十天）为止。

2）被保险货物如在上述六十天（空运险为三十天）期限内继续运往保险单所载原目的地或其他目的地时，保险责任仍按上述第1款的规定终止。

七、保险单的种类

目前，我国进出口业务中使用的保险单的种类主要有保险单、保险凭证、预约保险单、保险批单。

1．保险单（Insurance Policy）

保险单又称大保单，是保险人与被保险人之间订立保险合同的一种正式证明。保险单的正面印制了海上保险所需的基本事项，包括被保险人和保险人名称；保险标的名称、数量、包装；保险金额、保险费率和保险费；运输工具开航日期、装运港和目的港；承保险别；检验理赔人或代理人名称；赔款偿付地点；合同签订日期等。而保险单的背面则列明了一般保险条款，规定保险人与被保险人的各项权利和义务、保险责任范围、除外责任、责任起讫、损失处理、索赔理赔、保险争议处理、时效条款等各项内容。

2．保险凭证（Insurance Certificate）

保险凭证实质上是一种简化的保险单，保险凭证与海上保险单具有同等的法律效力，故又被称为小保单，用以证明海上货物运输保险合同的有效存在。现在实际业务中已经很少使用。保险凭证正面所列内容与海上保险单是一样的。但是，其背面是空白的，没有载明保险条款，而在正面声明以同类海上保险单所载条款为准。

3．预约保险单（Open Policy）

预约保险单又称开口保险单，它一般适用于经常有相同类型货物需要陆续装运的保险。这种事先预约的保险合同在我国的货物进出口中广泛适用，特别是我国进口货物基本上都采用预约保险单。许多贸易公司与保险公司订有预约保险合约，凡该公司出口或进口的货物均在预约保险的保障范围内。

4．保险批单（Endorsement）

保险批单是保险公司在保险单出立后，根据投保人的需求，对保险内容补充或变更而出具的一种凭证。批单是保险单的组成部分。保险单据应按信用证规定的内容提交。如信用证规定提交保险单，则只能接受保险单；如信用证规定是预约保险下的保险证明/声明，则保险单可做替代。除非信用证特别授权，否则保单是不能被接受的。

八、保险金额和保险费

保险金额是保险公司承担赔偿或给付保险金责任的最高限额，也是保险公司计算保险费的依据。保险金额的计算公式：

保险金额=CIF（CIP）价×（1+投保加成率）

保险费的计算公式：

保险费=保险金额×保险费率=CIF（CIP）价×（1+投保加成率）×保险费率

九、保险与 UCP600 条款的相关规定

（1）保险单据，如保险单或预约保险项下的保险证明书或者声明书，必须看似由保险公司或承保人或其代理人或代表出具并签署；代理人或代表的签字必须标明其系代表保险公司或承保人签字。

（2）如果保险单据表明其以多份正本出具，所有正本均须提交。

（3）暂保单将不被接受。可以接受保险单代替预约保险项下的保险证明书或声明书。

（4）保险单据日期不得晚于发运日期，除非保险单据表明保险责任不迟于发运日生效。

（5）保险单据必须表明投保金额并以与信用证相同的货币表示；信用证对于投保金额为货物价值、发票金额或类似金额的某一比例的要求，将被视为对最低保额的要求；如果信用证对投保金额未作规定，投保金额须至少为货物的 CIF 或 CIP 价格的 110%；如果从单据中不能确定 CIF 或者 CIP 价格，投保金额必须基于要求承付或议付的金额，或者基于发票上显示的货物总值来计算，两者之中取金额较高者；保险单据须标明承包的风险区间至少涵盖从信用证规定的货物监管地或发运地开始到卸货地或最终目的地为止。

（6）信用证应规定所需投保的险别及附加险（如有的话）。如果信用证使用诸如“通常风险”或“惯常风险”等含义不确切的用语，则无论是否有漏保之风险，保险单据将被照样接受。

（7）当信用证规定投保“一切险”时，如保险单据载有任何“一切险”批注或条款，无论是否有“一切险”标题，均将被接受，即使其声明任何风险除外。

（8）保险单据可以援引任何除外责任条款，保险单据可以注明受免赔率或免赔额（减除额）约束。

◆ 实训项目

【任务 1】制作投保单

2010 年 8 月 6 日，在完成托运手续确认船期后，浙江曼旎进出口有限公司外贸单证员王宁根据信用证中保险单条款“INSURANCE POLICY/CERTIFICATE IN DUPLICATE ENDORSED IN BLANK FOR 110% INVOICE VALUE, COVERING ALL RISKS AND WAR RISK OF CIC OF PICC (1/1/1981) INCL. WAREHOUSE TO WAREHOUSE AND I.O.P AND SHOWING THE CLAIMING CURRENCY IS THE SAME AS THE CURRENCY OF CREDIT.”等其他相关条款，以及商业发票和装箱单制作投保单。

货物运输保险投保单
APPLICATION FORM FOR CARGO TRANSPORTATION INSURANCE

投保单号：

被保险人：
INSURED：____

发票号（INVOICE NO.）
合同号（CONTRACT NO.）
信用证号（L/C NO.）
发票金额（INVOICE AMOUNT）____________投保加成（PLUS）______%

兹有下列物品向中国大地财产保险股份有限公司投保（INSURANCE IS REQUIRED ON THE FOLLOWING COMMODITIES：）

标　记 MARKS & NOS	包装及数量 QUANTITY	保险货物项目 DESCRIPTION OF GOODS	保险金额 AMOUNT INSURED

启运日期：　　　　　　装载工具
DATE OF COMMENCEMENT____________PER CONVEYANCE ____________

自　　　　经　　　　至
FORM____________VIA____________TO____________

提单号：　　　　　　赔款偿付地点：
B/L NO.____________CLAIM PAYABLE AT____________

投保险别：（PLEASE INDICATE THE CONDITIONS &/OR SPECIAL COVERAGES）

请如实告知下列情况：（如‘是’在（　）打‘×’）IF ANY, PLEASE MARK‘×’：

1．货物种类 袋装（　） 散装（　） 冷藏（　） 液体（　） 活动物（　） 机器/汽车（　） 危险品等级（　）
GOODS BAG/JUMBO BULK REEFER LIQUID LIVE ANIMAL MACHINE/AUTO DANGEROUS CLASS

2．集装箱种类 普通（　） 开顶（　） 框架（　） 平板（　） 冷藏（　）
CONTAINER ORDINARY OPEN FRAME FLAT REFRIGERATOR

3．转运工具 海轮（　） 飞机（　） 驳船（　） 火车（　） 汽车（　）
BY TRANSIT SHIP PLANE BARGE TRAIN TRUCK

4．船舶资料 船籍（　） 船龄（　）
PARTICULAR OF SHIP REGISTRY____________ AGE____________

备件：被保险人确认本保险合同条款和内容已经完全了解
THE ASSURED CONFIRMS HEREWITH THE TERMS AND CONDITIONS OF THESE INSURANCE CONTRACT FULLY UNDERSTOOD

投保人（签名盖章）APPLICANT'S SIGNATURE

电话（TEL）

投保日期（DATE）____________　　地址（ADD）____________

本公司自用（FOR OFFICE USE ONLY）

费率
RATE　AS ARRANGED____________

保费
PREMIUM　AS ARRANGED____________

备注：

经办人 BY________　核保人 ____________　负责人 ____________

总公司地址：上海市浦东南路 855 号　电话：021-58369588　邮政编码：200120　网址：www.ccic-net.com.cn

【任务 2】向保险公司办理保险

外贸单证员王宁制作好投保单后，向中国大地财产保险股份有限公司浙江省分公司办理保险。

项目九

制作附属单据操作

学习目标

能力目标

能根据信用证和/或外贸合同条款要求缮制附属单据，包括装运通知、受益人证明等。

知识目标

熟悉装运通知、受益人证明等附属单据的内容，了解船公司证明、船籍和航程证明、船龄证明等证明类附属单据的内容。

导入项目

上接项目八的导入项目。2010 年 4 月 15 日，浙江大同进出口有限公司外贸单证员桂小龙收到浙江双马国际货运有限公司寄来的如下海运提单。

<table>
<tr><td colspan="2">1. Shipper
ZHEJIANG DATONG IMPORT AND EXPORT CO., LTD.
NO.902 YILE ROAD, HANGZHOU, CHINA</td><td>B/L No. NGBFXT001568</td></tr>
<tr><td colspan="2">2. Consignee
TO ORDER</td><td>中海集装箱运输（香港）有限公司
CHINA SHIPPING CONTAINER LINES (HONGKONG)
Cable: CSHKAC Telex: 87986 CSHKAHX
Port-to-Port or Combined Transport
BILL OF LADING</td></tr>
<tr><td colspan="2">3. Notify Party (carrier not to be responsible for failure to notify)
CARK GMBH & CO. KG
DOMSTRASSE 55, D-20095 HAMBURG, GERMANY
TEL: 0049-40-3410967 FAX: 0049-40-3410966</td><td rowspan="3">RECEIVED in external apparent good order and condition, except otherwise noted. The total number of containers or other packages or units shown in the Bill of Lading receipt, is said by the shipper to contain the goods described above, which description the carrier has no reasonable means of checking and is not part of the Bill of Lading. One original Bill of Lading should be surrendered, except clause 22 paragraph 5, in exchange for delivery of the shipment. Signed by the consigned or duly endorsed by the holder in due course. Whereupon the other original(s) issued shall be void. In accepting this Bill of Lading, the Merchants agree to be bound by all the terms on the face and back hereof as if each had personally signed this Bill of Lading.
WHEN the place of Receipt of the Goods is an inland point and is so named herein, any notation of "ON BOARD", "SHIPPED ON BOARD" or words to like effect on this Bill of Lading shall be deemed to mean on board the truck, trail car, air craft or other inland conveyance (as the case may be), performing carriage form the Place or Receipt of the Goods to the Port of Loading.
SEE clause 4 on the back of this Bill of Lading (Terms continued on the back hereof Read Carefully).
ORIGINAL</td></tr>
<tr><td>4. Pre-carriage by</td><td>5. Place of Receipt</td></tr>
<tr><td>6. Ocean Vessel Voy. No.
XIN YA ZHOU V. 0023W</td><td>7. Port of Loading
SHANGHAI, CHINA</td></tr>
</table>

（续）

8. Port of Discharge HAMBURG, GERMANY		9. Place of Delivery	10. Final Destination (of the goods-not the ship)			
11. Marks & Nos. Container Seal No.	12. No. of Containers or Packages		13. Description of Goods		14. Gross Weight	15. Measurement
CARK DT1000033 HAMBURG CARTON NO：1-255	7 PALLETS FREIGHT PREPAID		FORGED BRASS BALL VALVES L/C NO.: LC-536-089075 DATE OF L/C: MARCH 17, 2010		5654.20KGS	6.776CBM
16. Description of Contents for Shipper's Use Only (CARRIER NOT RESPONSIBLE)						
17. Total Number of containers and/or packages (in words)：SEVEN PALLETS ONLY.						
18. Freight & Charges	19. Revenue Tons	20. Rate	21. Per	22. Prepaid	23. Collect	
24. Ex. Rate:	25. Prepaid at SHANGHAI	26. Payable at		27. Place and date of issue SHANGHAI APRIL 12, 2010		
	28. Total Prepaid	29. No. of Original B(s)/L THREE (3)		Signed for the Carrier CHINA SHIPPING CONTAINER LINES (HONGKONG) 王力		

【任务 1】制作装运通知

4 月 15 日，浙江大同进出口有限公司外贸单证员桂小龙根据海运提单、信用证相关条款、商业发票和装箱单制作并给 CARK GMBH & CO. KG 发装运通知。

SHIPPING ADVICE			
TO:		ISSUE DATE:	
		S/C. NO.:	
		L/C NO.:	
		L/C DATE:	
		NAME OF ISSUING BANK:	
Dear Sir or Madam:			
（a）We are Please to Advice you that the following mentioned goods has been shipped out, Full details were shown as follows:			
Invoice Number:			
Bill of loading Number:			
Ocean Vessel:			
Port of Loading:			
Date of shipment:			
Port of Destination:			
Estimated date of arrival:			
Containers/Seals Number:			
Description of goods:			
Shipping Marks:			
Quantity:			
Gross Weight:			
Net Weight:			
Total Value:			
Thank you for your patronage. We look forward to the pleasure of receiving your valuable repeat orders. Sincerely yours,			

【任务 2】制作受益人证明

4 月 15 日，浙江大同进出口有限公司外贸单证员桂小龙给 CARK GMBH & CO. KG 快递正本普惠制产地证，并制作受益人证明。

<table>
<tr><td colspan="4"></td></tr>
<tr><td colspan="4">BENEFICIARY'S CERTIFICATE</td></tr>
<tr><td rowspan="2">To:</td><td rowspan="2"></td><td>Invoice No.:</td><td></td></tr>
<tr><td>Date:</td><td></td></tr>
<tr><td colspan="4"></td></tr>
</table>

【任务 1】制作装运通知

浙江大同进出口有限公司外贸单证员桂小龙根据海运提单、信用证相关条款、商业发票和装箱单制作并给 CARK GMBH & CO. KG 发如下装运通知。

<table>
<tr><td colspan="4">ZHEJIANG DATONG IMPORT AND EXPORT CO., LTD.
NO.902 YILE ROAD, HANGZHOU, CHINA
TEL： 0086-571-87772409 FAX： 0086-571-87772407</td></tr>
<tr><td colspan="4">SHIPPING ADVICE</td></tr>
<tr><td rowspan="4">TO:</td><td rowspan="4">CARK GMBH & CO. KG
DOMSTRASSE 55, D-20095 HAMBURG, GERMANY</td><td>ISSUE DATE:</td><td>APRIL 15, 2010</td></tr>
<tr><td>S/C. NO.:</td><td>DT1000033</td></tr>
<tr><td>L/C NO.:</td><td>LC-536-089075</td></tr>
<tr><td>L/C DATE:</td><td>MARCH 17, 2010</td></tr>
<tr><td colspan="4">Dear Sir or Madam:</td></tr>
<tr><td colspan="4">（a）We are glad to advice you that the following mentioned goods has been shipped out, full details were shown as follows:</td></tr>
<tr><td colspan="2">Invoice Number:</td><td colspan="2">2010DT00101</td></tr>
<tr><td colspan="2">Bill of loading Number:</td><td colspan="2">NGBFXT001568</td></tr>
<tr><td colspan="2">Ocean Vessel:</td><td colspan="2">XIN YA ZHOU，V. 0023W</td></tr>
<tr><td colspan="2">Port of Loading:</td><td colspan="2">SHANGHAI</td></tr>
<tr><td colspan="2">Date of shipment:</td><td colspan="2">APRIL 12, 2010</td></tr>
<tr><td colspan="2">Port of Destination:</td><td colspan="2">HAMBURG, GERMANY</td></tr>
<tr><td colspan="2">Estimated date of arrival:</td><td colspan="2">MAY 7, 2010</td></tr>
<tr><td colspan="2">Containers/Seals Number:</td><td colspan="2"></td></tr>
<tr><td colspan="2">Description of goods:</td><td colspan="2">FORGED BRASS BALL VALVES</td></tr>
<tr><td colspan="2">Shipping Marks:</td><td colspan="2">CARK
DT1000033
HAMBURG
CARTON NO：1-255</td></tr>
<tr><td colspan="2">Quantity:</td><td colspan="2">14128SETS</td></tr>
<tr><td colspan="2">Gross Weight:</td><td colspan="2">5654.20KGS</td></tr>
<tr><td colspan="2">Net Weight:</td><td colspan="2">5584.20KGS</td></tr>
<tr><td colspan="2">Total Value:</td><td colspan="2">USD35862.40</td></tr>
<tr><td colspan="4">Thank you for your patronage. We look forward to the pleasure of receiving your valuable repeat orders.
Sincerely yours,</td></tr>
<tr><td colspan="4">ZHEJIANG DATONG IMPORT AND EXPORT CO., LTD.
桂大同</td></tr>
</table>

【任务 2】制作受益人证明

浙江大同进出口有限公司外贸单证员桂小龙给 CARK GMBH & CO. KG 快递正本普惠制产地证后，制作如下受益人证明。

<table>
<tr><td colspan="4">ZHEJIANG DATONG IMPORT AND EXPORT CO., LTD.
NO.902 YILE ROAD, HANGZHOU, CHINA
TEL：0086-571-87772409 FAX：0086-571-87772407</td></tr>
<tr><td colspan="4">BENEFICIARY'S CERTIFICATE</td></tr>
<tr><td rowspan="2">To:</td><td rowspan="2">WHOM IT MAY CONCERN.</td><td>Invoice No.:</td><td>2010DT00101</td></tr>
<tr><td>Date:</td><td>APRIL 15, 2010</td></tr>
<tr><td colspan="4">WE HEREBY CERTIFY THAT ORIGINAL GSP CERTIFICATE OF ORIGIN FORM A HAS BEEN SENT TO THE APPLICANT BY SPEED POST.

L/C NO.: LC-536-089075
L/C DATE：MARCH 17, 2010</td></tr>
<tr><td colspan="4">ZHEJIANG DATONG IMPORT AND EXPORT CO., LTD.
桂大同</td></tr>
</table>

一、受益人证明

受益人证明（Beneficiary's Certificate）是根据信用证条款，由出口商签发的用来证实有关内容的书面证明。证明的内容包括：寄出有关的副本单据、船样、样卡、码样、包装标签；货物已经检验；已发出装船通知等。

二、装运通知

装运通知（Shipping Advice）是出口商根据信用证规定在货物装船并取得提单后，以传真、电报或电传方式将与装船有关的情况及时告知收货人等有关当事人的单据。议付时，须提供该传真、电报或电传副本予以证明。装运通知一般包括发票号、提单号、船名航次、装运港、装运日期、目的港、预计到达日、货物品名及描述、唛头、信用证号等内容。

三、船公司证明

船公司证明（Shipping Company'S Certificate）是信用证受益人应开证申请人的要求，请船公司出具的不同认定内容的证明。

四、船籍和航程证明

船籍证明是说明载货船舶国籍的证明；航程证明是说明载货船舶航程中停靠的港口。阿拉伯世界国家开来的信用证通常要求提供非以色列船只、不得停靠以色列港口，不是黑名单船只，不得挂以色列国旗等。

五、船龄证明

船龄证明是说明载货船舶船龄的证明。有时信用证要求提供表明运输船舶的船龄不得超过多少年的证明。格式可参考前面几种。

◆ 实训项目 9-1

上接实训项目 8-1。2010 年 8 月 10 日，浙江曼旎进出口有限公司外贸单证员王宁收到浙江双马国际货运有限公司寄来的海运提单：

<table>
<tr><td colspan="4">MAERSK LINE</td><td colspan="2">BILL OF LADING FOR OCEAN TRANSPORT OR MULTIMODAL TRANSPORT</td><td colspan="2">SCAC　MAEU
B/L No.855966998</td></tr>
<tr><td colspan="4" rowspan="3">Shipper
ZHEJIANG MANNI IMPORT AND EXPORT CO., LTD.
99 XUEYUAN STREET, HANGZHOU, CHINA</td><td colspan="4">Booking No.
855966998</td></tr>
<tr><td colspan="2">Export references</td><td colspan="2">Svc Contract
229087</td></tr>
<tr><td colspan="4">Onward inland routing (Not part of Carriage as defined in clause 1. For account and risk of Merchant)</td></tr>
<tr><td colspan="4">Consignee (negotiable only if consigned "to order", "to order of" a named person or "to order of bearer")
TO ORDER</td><td colspan="4">Notify Party (see clause 22)
EMIRATES CLOTHES TRADER
P O BOX33, NO.12, SALAHUDDIN ROAD, DUBAI, U.A.E.</td></tr>
<tr><td colspan="2">Ocean Vessel
COLUMBINE MAERSK</td><td colspan="2">Voy. No.
1007</td><td colspan="4">Place of Receipt, Applicable only when document used as Multimodal Transport B/L (see clause 1)</td></tr>
<tr><td colspan="2">Port of Loading
NINGBO, CHINA</td><td colspan="2">Port of Discharge
DUBAI, U.A.E.</td><td colspan="4">Place of Delivery, Applicable only when document used as Multimodal Transport B/L (see clause 1)</td></tr>
<tr><td colspan="8">PARTICULARS FURNISHED BY SHIPPER</td></tr>
<tr><td colspan="6">Kind of Packages, Description of Goods, Marks & Numbers; Container No./Seal No.</td><td>Weight</td><td>Measurement</td></tr>
<tr><td colspan="6">1 CONTAINER SAID TO CONTAIN 5200 PIECES OF BOYS JACKET
MSKU8423308 ML-CM0181675 20' FCL

FREIGHT COLLECT　　　ORIGINAL

Above particulars as declared by Shipper, but without responsibility of or representation by Carrier (see clause 14)</td><td>2600 KGS</td><td>23.712M^3</td></tr>
<tr><td colspan="2">Freight & Charges</td><td>Rate</td><td>Unit</td><td colspan="2">Currency</td><td>Prepaid</td><td>Collect</td></tr>
<tr><td>Carrier's Receipt (see clause 1 and 14). Total number of containers or packages received by Carrier.
1 CONTAINER</td><td colspan="2">Place of issue of B/L
NINGBO, CHINA</td><td colspan="5" rowspan="3">SHIPPED, as far as ascertained by reasonable means of checking, in apparent good order and condition unless otherwise stated herein, the total number or quantity of Containers or other packages or units indicated in the box entitled "Carrier's Receipt" for carriage from the Port of Loading (or the Place of Receipt, if mentioned above) to the Port of Discharge (or the Place of Delivery, if mentioned above), such carriage being always subject to the terms, rights, defences, provisions, conditions, exceptions, limitations, and liberties hereof (INCLUDING ALL THOSE TERMS AND CONDITIONS ON THE REVERSE HEREOF NUMBERED 1-26 AND THOSE TERMS AND CONDITIONS IN THE CARRIER'S APPLICABLE TARIFF) and the Merchant's attention is drawn in particular to the Carrier's liberties …</td></tr>
<tr><td>No. & Sequence of Original B(s)/L
3/THREE</td><td colspan="2">date of issue of B/L
2010-08-09</td></tr>
<tr><td>Declared Value (see clause 7.3)</td><td colspan="2">Shipped on Board Date
2010-08-07</td></tr>
<tr><td colspan="3"></td><td colspan="5">Signed for the Carrier A.P.Moller-Maersk A/S trading as Maersk Line

Martina White
On behalf of the Carrier
Maersk Hong Kong Line</td></tr>
</table>

【任务 1】制作装运通知

8 月 10 日，外贸单证员王宁根据海运提单、信用证相关条款、商业发票和装箱单制作并给 Emirates Clothes Trader 发装运通知。

<table>
<tr><td colspan="4"></td></tr>
<tr><td colspan="4">SHIPPING ADVICE</td></tr>
<tr><td rowspan="5">TO:</td><td rowspan="5"></td><td>ISSUE DATE:</td><td></td></tr>
<tr><td>S/C. NO.:</td><td></td></tr>
<tr><td>L/C NO.:</td><td></td></tr>
<tr><td>L/C DATE:</td><td></td></tr>
<tr><td>NAME OF ISSUING BANK:</td><td></td></tr>
<tr><td colspan="4">Dear Sir or Madam:</td></tr>
<tr><td colspan="4">（b）We are Please to Advice you that the following mentioned goods has been shipped out, Full details were shown as follows:</td></tr>
<tr><td colspan="2">Invoice Number:</td><td colspan="2"></td></tr>
<tr><td colspan="2">Bill of loading Number:</td><td colspan="2"></td></tr>
<tr><td colspan="2">Ocean Vessel:</td><td colspan="2"></td></tr>
<tr><td colspan="2">Port of Loading:</td><td colspan="2"></td></tr>
<tr><td colspan="2">Date of shipment:</td><td colspan="2"></td></tr>
<tr><td colspan="2">Port of Destination:</td><td colspan="2"></td></tr>
<tr><td colspan="2">Estimated date of arrival:</td><td colspan="2"></td></tr>
<tr><td colspan="2">Containers/Seals Number:</td><td colspan="2"></td></tr>
<tr><td colspan="2">Description of goods:</td><td colspan="2"></td></tr>
<tr><td colspan="2">Shipping Marks:</td><td colspan="2"></td></tr>
<tr><td colspan="2">Quantity:</td><td colspan="2"></td></tr>
<tr><td colspan="2">Gross Weight:</td><td colspan="2"></td></tr>
<tr><td colspan="2">Net Weight:</td><td colspan="2"></td></tr>
<tr><td colspan="2">Total Value:</td><td colspan="2"></td></tr>
<tr><td colspan="4">Thank you for your patronage. We look forward to the pleasure of receiving your valuable repeat orders.
Sincerely yours,</td></tr>
<tr><td colspan="4"></td></tr>
</table>

【任务 2】制作受益人证明

8 月 10 日，外贸单证员王宁根据信用证要求，制作受益人证明。

<table>
<tr><td colspan="4"></td></tr>
<tr><td colspan="4">BENEFICIARY'S CERTIFICATE</td></tr>
<tr><td rowspan="2">To:</td><td rowspan="2"></td><td>Invoice No.:</td><td></td></tr>
<tr><td>Date:</td><td></td></tr>
<tr><td colspan="4"></td></tr>
</table>

◆ **实训项目 9-2**

上接实训项目 7-2。

【任务 1】制作受益人证明

2010 年 9 月 28 日，杭州维丰进出口有限公司外贸单证员叶丽把 1 份普惠制原产地证格

式 A 正本、1 份商业发票副本和 1 份装箱单副本快递给 Sri Russa E Johns SPA 后，根据信用证、商业发票和装箱单制作受益人证明。

BENEFICIARY'S CERTIFICATE			
To:		Invoice No.:	
		Date:	

【任务 2】制作装运通知

9 月 30 日，杭州维丰进出口有限公司外贸单证员叶丽收到浙江双马国际货运有限公司寄来的如下空运单：

999	HGH 1099 1589	1099 1589
Shipper's Name and Address Zhejiang Jinyuan Import And Export Co., Ltd. No.118 Xueyuan Street, Hangzhou, China	Shipper's Account Number	Not Negotiable **Air Waybill** Issued by AIR CHINA CARGO CO., LTD. BEIJING CHINA Member of IATA Copies 1, 2 and 3 of this Air Waybill are originals and have the same validity.
Consignee's Name and Address Sri Russa E Johns SPA 55, Corso Matteotti 20121, Milan, Italy Tel: 0039-02-98280909	Consignee's Account Number	It is agreed that the goods described herein are accepted for carriage in apparent good order and condition (except as noted) and subject to the conditions of contract on the reverse hereof. all goods may be carried by and other means including road or any other carrier unless specific contrary instructions are given hereon by the shipper. the shipper's attention is drawn to the notice concerning carrier's limitation of liability. shipper may increase such limitation of liability by declaring a higher value for carriage and paying a supplemental charge if required.
Issuing Carrier's Agent Name and City Shanghai Wecan Freight Forwarding Co., Ltd. Tel: 0086-571-86665451		Accounting Information FREIGHT PREPAID HGH/WNZ/NGB 2008-R009(I)
Agent's IATA Code 0831094	Account No.	
Airport of Departure (Addr. of First Carrier) and Requested Routing Hangzhou		

To	By First Carrier Routing and Destination	to	by	to	By	Currency	CHGS Code	WT/VAL PPD	WT/VAL COLL	Other PPD	Other COLL	Declared Value for Carriage	Declared Value for Customs
PVG	CA	MIL	CA			CNY		PP		PP		NVD	NCV

Airport of Destination	Flight/Date For carrier Use Only Flight/Date		Amount of Insurance	INSURANCE If Carrier offers insurance, and such insurance is requested in accordance with the conditions thereof, indicate amount to be insured in figures in box marked "Amount of Insurance."
MILAN	CA2304/27NOV	CA1069/29NOV	×××	

Handing Information

Sri Russa E Johns SPA

55, Corso Matteotti 20121, Milan, Italy

Tel: 0039-02-98280909

(For USA only) These commodities licensed by U.S. for ultimate destination …………………Diversion contrary to U.S. law is prohibited

No of Pieces RCP	Gross Weight	Kg lb	Rate Class	Commodity Item No.	Chargeable Weight	Rate Charge	Total	Nature and Quantity of Goods (incl. Dimensions or Volume)
260	1560	kg	Q		2600kgs	30.00	78000.00	2600 PIECES OF LAMB WAXY LADIES' JACKETS VOL:0.6×0.5×0.2×260＝15.6CBM
260	1560						78000.00	

（续）

Prepaid	Weight Charge Collect	Other Charges
3916.00		AWC:50.00 MYC: 2600.00×11＝28600.00 SCC: 3120.00
Valuation Charge		
Tax		
Total other Charges Due Agent		Shipper certifies that the particulars on the face hereof are correct and that insofar as any part of the consignment contains dangerous goods, such part is properly described by name and is in proper condition for carriage by air according to the applicable Dangerous Goods Regulations.
Total other Charges Due Carrier		Cherry
31770.00		Signature of Shipper or his Agent
Total Prepaid	Total Collect	Nov.26.2008 Hangzhou Cherry
109770.00		
Currency Conversion Rates	CC Charges in Dest. Currency	
		Executed on (date) at(place) Signature of Issuing Carrier or its Agent
For Carrier's Use only at Destination	Charges at Destination	Total Collect Charges 999－099 1589

ORIGINAL 3 (FOR SHIPPER)

9 月 30 日，外贸单证员叶丽根据空运单、信用证相关条款、商业发票和装箱单制作并给 Sri Russa E Johns SPA 发装运通知。

SHIPPING ADVICE			
TO:		ISSUE DATE:	
		S/C. NO.:	
		L/C NO.:	
		L/C DATE:	
		NAME OF ISSUING BANK:	
Dear Sir or Madam:			
（a）We are Please to Advice you that the following mentioned goods has been shipped out, Full details were shown as follows:			
Invoice Number:			
Bill of loading Number:			
Ocean Vessel:			
Port of Loading:			
Date of shipment:			
Port of Destination:			
Estimated date of arrival:			
Containers/Seals Number:			
Description of goods:			
Shipping Marks:			
Quantity:			
Gross Weight:			
Net Weight:			
Total Value:			
Thank you for your patronage. We look forward to the pleasure of receiving your valuable repeat orders. Sincerely yours,			

◆ **实训项目 9-3**

上接实训项目 7-3。

【任务 1】制作装运通知

2010 年 8 月 4 日，浙江大顺进出口有限公司外贸单证员朱丽娅根据出口合同、商业发票、装箱单和其他相关信息制作并给 Lina Trading Co., Ltd.发装运通知。

<table>
<tr><td colspan="4"></td></tr>
<tr><td colspan="4">SHIPPING ADVICE</td></tr>
<tr><td rowspan="5">TO:</td><td rowspan="5"></td><td>ISSUE DATE:</td><td></td></tr>
<tr><td>S/C. NO.:</td><td></td></tr>
<tr><td>L/C NO.:</td><td></td></tr>
<tr><td>L/C DATE:</td><td></td></tr>
<tr><td>NAME OF ISSUING BANK:</td><td></td></tr>
<tr><td colspan="4">Dear Sir or Madam:</td></tr>
<tr><td colspan="4">（b）We are Please to Advice you that the following mentioned goods has been shipped out, Full details were shown as follows:</td></tr>
<tr><td colspan="2">Invoice Number:</td><td colspan="2"></td></tr>
<tr><td colspan="2">Bill of loading Number:</td><td colspan="2"></td></tr>
<tr><td colspan="2">Ocean Vessel:</td><td colspan="2"></td></tr>
<tr><td colspan="2">Port of Loading:</td><td colspan="2"></td></tr>
<tr><td colspan="2">Date of shipment:</td><td colspan="2"></td></tr>
<tr><td colspan="2">Port of Destination:</td><td colspan="2"></td></tr>
<tr><td colspan="2">Estimated date of arrival:</td><td colspan="2"></td></tr>
<tr><td colspan="2">Containers/Seals Number:</td><td colspan="2"></td></tr>
<tr><td colspan="2">Description of goods:</td><td colspan="2"></td></tr>
<tr><td colspan="2">Shipping Marks:</td><td colspan="2"></td></tr>
<tr><td colspan="2">Quantity:</td><td colspan="2"></td></tr>
<tr><td colspan="2">Gross Weight:</td><td colspan="2"></td></tr>
<tr><td colspan="2">Net Weight:</td><td colspan="2"></td></tr>
<tr><td colspan="2">Total Value:</td><td colspan="2"></td></tr>
<tr><td colspan="4">Thank you for your patronage. We look forward to the pleasure of receiving your valuable repeat orders.
Sincerely yours,</td></tr>
<tr><td colspan="4"></td></tr>
</table>

项目十

制作汇票操作

学习目标

能力目标

能根据信用证或外贸合同条款填制信用证项下和托收项下的汇票。

知识目标

掌握汇票的定义、当事人、背书和承兑，熟悉汇票的种类，了解出票、提示、付款、拒付、追索等其他票据行为。

导入项目

上接项目九的导入项目。

制作汇票

2010 年 4 月 19 日，浙江大同进出口有限公司外贸单证员桂小龙制作好附属单据后，根据信用证和商业发票填制如下汇票。

<table>
<tr><th colspan="6">BILL OF EXCHANGE</th></tr>
<tr><td>凭
Drawn Under</td><td colspan="2"></td><td>不可撤销信用证
Irrevocable L/C No.</td><td colspan="2"></td></tr>
<tr><td>日期
Date</td><td></td><td>支取
Payable with interest</td><td colspan="3">@ % 按 息 付款</td></tr>
<tr><td>号码
No.</td><td></td><td>汇票金额
Exchange for</td><td></td><td>杭州
Hangzhou</td><td></td></tr>
<tr><td></td><td>见票
at</td><td></td><td colspan="3">日后（本汇票之副本未付）
sight of this FIRST of Exchange (Second of Exchange Being unpaid)</td></tr>
<tr><td colspan="2">付交
Pay to the order of</td><td colspan="4"></td></tr>
<tr><td>金额
the sum of</td><td colspan="5"></td></tr>
<tr><td>此致
To</td><td colspan="2"></td><td colspan="3"></td></tr>
</table>

示范操作

制作汇票

1．出票条款

这一栏按信用证的规定填写开证行名称、信用证号码和开证日期。

本业务填写：

Drawn Under: BANK OF CHINA, HAMBURG BRANCH
Irrevocable L/C No.: LC-536-089075
Date: MARCH 17, 2010

2．年息

这一栏由结汇银行填写，用以清算企业与银行间利息费用。出口公司不必填写此栏目。

3．号码

汇票号码，一般都以相应的发票号码兼作汇票号码。

本业务填写：2010DT00101。

4．汇票小写金额

填汇票小写金额。汇票小写金额，由货币名称缩写和阿拉伯数字组成。除非信用证另有规定，汇票金额应与发票金额一致，汇票上的金额大、小写必须一致，不得涂改，不允许更改后加盖校对章；若信用证规定汇票金额为发票金额的百分之几，例如 90%，那么发票金额应为 100%，汇票金额为 90%；若信用证规定部分信用证付款，部分托收，则分做两套汇票：信用证下支款的汇票按信用证允许的金额填制，其余部分为托收项下汇票的金额，两者之和等于发票金额。

本业务填写：USD35862.40。

5．汇票大写金额

填汇票大写金额。汇票大写金额由货币名称和货币金额组成。

本业务填写：U.S. DOLLARS THIRTY FIVE THOUSAND EIGHT HUNDRED AND SIXTY TWO AND CENTS FORTY ONLY.。

6．出票日期和出票地点

地点一般已印好，无需现填。出票地点后的横线填出票日期，信用证方式下，一般以议付日期作为出票日期。该日期不得早于随附的各种单据的出单日期，同时不能迟于信用证的交单/有效期。该日期一般由银行代填。

本业务填写：APRIL.19, 2010, HANGZHOU。

7．汇票付款期限

汇票付款期限分即期和远期两种。

（1）即期汇票的付款期限这一栏的填法较简单，只需在横线上用“***”或“——”或“×××”表示，也可直接打上“AT SIGHT”，但不能留空。

（2）远期汇票，按信用证的规定填入相应的付款期限。

例如，来证规定：“drafts at 90 days after sight”。

这是见票后 90 天付款的远期汇票，填写时，在此栏打上“90 DAYS AFTER”。

例如，来证规定：“drafts at 60 days after date”。

这是汇票出票日后 60 天付款的远期汇票，填写时，在此栏打上“60 DAYS AFTER DATE”，并把已印的 sight 划掉。

例如，来证规定：“drafts at 30 days after the B/L date”，B/L 日期为 JUNE 8, 2010。

这是提单日后 30 天付款远期汇票，填写时，在此栏打上“30 DAYS AFTER THE B/L DATE, JUNE 8, 2010”，并把已印的 sight 划掉。

本业务填写：AT SIGHT。

8．受款人/收款人

应从信用证的角度来理解这一栏目的要求。在信用证支付的条件下，汇票中受款人这一栏目中填写的应是银行名称和地址，一般都是议付行的名称和地址。究竟要哪家银行作为受款人，这要看信用证中是否有具体的规定。

本业务填写：PAY TO THE ORDER OF BANK OF CHINA, ZHEJIANG, CHINA.。

9．付款人

在信用证方式下，应按照信用证的规定，以开证行或其指定的付款行为付款人。倘若信用证中未指定付款人，应填写开证行。

本业务填写：BANK OF CHINA，NEW YORK。

10．出票人

一般填信用证的受益人，在可转让信用证情况下，也有可能为信用证的第二受益人。出票人应签署企业全称和负责人的签字或盖章。

汇票在没有特殊规定时，都打两张，一式两份。汇票一般都在醒目的位置上印着“1”、“2”字样，表示第一联和第二联。汇票的第一联和第二联在法律效力上无区别。第一联生效则第二联自动作废，第二联生效则第一联自动作废，即付一不付二，付二不付一。

制作好的汇票如下：

BILL OF EXCHANGE					
凭 Drawn Under	BANK OF CHINA, HAMBURG BRANCH		不可撤销信用证 Irrevocable L/C No.	LC-536-089075	
日期 Date	MARCH 17, 2010	支 取 Payable With interest	@ % 按 息 付款		
号码 No.	2010DT00101	汇票金额 Exchange for	USD35862.40	杭州 HANGZHOU	APRIL 19, 2010
	见票 at	***	日后（本汇票之副本未付） sight of this FIRST of Exchange (Second of Exchange Being unpaid)		
付交 Pay to the order of	BANK OF CHINA, ZHEJIANG BRANCH				
金额 the sum of	U.S. DOLLARS THIRTY FIVE THOUSAND EIGHT HUNDRED AND SIXTY TWO AND CENTS FORTY ONLY.				
此致 To	BANK OF CHINA, NEW YORK		ZHEJIANG DATONG IMPORT AND EXPORT CO., LTD. 桂大同		

知识支撑

一、汇票的定义

《英国票据法》对汇票的定义："汇票是由一人签发给另一人的无条件书面命令，要求受票人见票时或于未来某一规定的或可以确定的时间，将一定金额的款项支付给某一特定的人或其指定人或持票人。"

《中华人民共和国票据法》对汇票的定义："汇票是出票人签发的，委托付款人在见票时或在指定日期无条件支付确定的金额给收款人或其指定人或持票人的票据。"

二、汇票的种类

1. 按照出票人的不同，汇票可分为银行汇票和商业汇票

银行汇票的出票人是银行。商业汇票的出票人是工商企业或个人。在国际结算中，商业汇票通常是由出口商开立，向国外进口商或银行收取货款时使用的汇票。

2. 按照付款时间的不同，汇票可分为即期汇票和远期汇票

见票即付的是即期汇票，将来某一时间付款的是远期汇票。远期汇票的付款日期有记载方法，主要有：①规定某一个特定日期，即定日付款；②付款人见票后若干天；③出票日后若干天；④运输单据日后若干天，其中，较多用"提单日期后若干天"。

3. 按照承兑人的不同，汇票可分为商业承兑汇票和银行承兑汇票

商业承兑汇票是由工商企业或个人承兑的远期汇票。商业承兑汇票是建立在商业信用的基础之上，其出票人也是工商企业或个人。

银行承兑汇票是由银行承兑的远期商业汇票。银行承兑汇票通常由出口人签发，银行对汇票承兑后即成为该汇票的主债务人，而出票人则成为次债务人。所以银行承兑汇票是建立在银行信用的基础之上。

4. 按照是否附有货运单据，汇票可分为光票和跟单汇票

光票是指不附带货运单据的汇票。光票的流通全靠出票人、付款人或出让人（背书人）的信用。在国际结算中，除少量用于货款结算外，一般仅限于贸易从属费用、货款尾数、佣金等的托收或支付时使用。

跟单汇票是指附有货运单据的汇票。跟单汇票的付款以附交货运单据为条件，付款人要取得货运单据提取货物，必须付清货款或提供一定的担保。跟单汇票体现了钱款与单据对流的原则，对进出口双方提供了一定的安全保证。在国际结算中，大都采用跟单汇票作为结算工具。

三、汇票的票据行为

汇票的票据行为随汇票是即期还是远期而有所不同。即期汇票只需经过出票、提示和付款。远期汇票须经过承兑手续。如需流通转让，通常要经过背书。汇票遭到拒付时，还要涉及作成拒绝证明，依法行使追索权等法律问题。

1．出票

出票是指出票人签发票据并将其交付给收款人的票据行为。出票由两个动作组成，①由出票人写成汇票，并在汇票上签字；②由出票人将汇票交付给收款人。由于出票是设立债权债务的行为，所以，只有经过交付汇票才开始生效。

2．提示

提示是指收款人或持票人将汇票提交付款人要求付款或承兑的行为。提示可分为提示承兑和提示付款。提示承兑是指远期汇票持票人向付款人出示汇票，并要求付款人承诺付款的行为。提示付款是指汇票的持票人向付款人（或远期汇票的承兑人）出示汇票要求付款人（或承兑人）付款的行为。

3．承兑

承兑是指汇票付款人承诺在汇票到期日支付汇票金额的票据行为。汇票一经承兑，付款人就成为汇票的承兑人，并成为汇票的主债务人，而出票人便成为汇票的次债务人。承兑包括普通承兑和限制性承兑。

（1）普通承兑（General acceptance）。普通承兑是指汇票付款人对出票人的指示一概接受而不做任何保留。普通承兑一般包括以下内容：①承兑字样；②承兑日期；③承兑人签名。例如：

Accepted 10 September, 2010 For ABC Company Jack Smith

（2）限制性承兑（Qualified acceptance）。限制性承兑是一种付款人对汇票到期付款加注某些保留条件的承兑，也称保留承兑。常见的类型有：

1）有条件承兑（Conditional acceptance）。有条件承兑是指承兑人付款依赖于所述条件的完成。例如：

Accepted subject to to deduction for expenses 10 September, 2010 For ABC Company Jack Smith

2）部分承兑（Partial acceptance）。部分承兑是指对汇票所载金额的一部分作出承兑。例如：汇票上记载的金额为 HKD100,000.00，而作出如下承兑：

Accepted 10 September, 2010 Payable for amount of eighty thousand HK Dollar only For ABC Company Jack Smith

3）限制时间承兑（Qualified acceptance as to time）。限制时间承兑是指修改了付款期限。例如：汇票上载明的付款时间是承兑后 3 个月付款（payable in three months），而作出如下承兑：

Accepted 10 September, 2010 Payable in six months For ABC Company Jack Smith

4）限制地点承兑（Local acceptance）。限制地点承兑是指承兑时注明只能在某一特定指定地点付款。例如：

Accepted 10 September, 2010 Payable on the counter of HSBC, Hong Kong only For ABC Company Jack Smith

4．付款

付款是指付款人向持票人支付汇票金额的行为。即期汇票在付款人见票时照付；远期汇票于到期日在持票人作提示付款时由付款人付款。汇票一经付款，汇票上的一切债权债务即告结束。

5．背书

背书是一种以转让票据权利为目的的行为。背书通常由持票人在汇票的背面或粘单上签上自己的名字，或者再加上受让人即被背书人的名称，并把汇票交给受让人。汇票经过背书后，收款的权利就转让给了被背书人。背书主要分为指示性背书、限制性背书和空白背书。

指示性背书除操作示范中提到的指示性背书格式，还有以下另外两种表示方式：

PAY TO THE ORDER OF 被背书人 FOR 背书人 （签字）

或

PAY TO 被背书人 OR ORDER FOR 背书人 （签字）

限制性背书是限制被背书人继续转让的一种背书：

PAY TO 被背书人 ONLY(OR NOT NEGOTIABLE OR NOT TRANSFERABLE). FOR 背书人 （签字）

空白背书最简单，背书人仅在汇票的背面签名，而不记载谁是被背书人，因此空白背书也称为无记名背书：

FOR 背书人 （签字）

我国票据法认为空白背书无效。

6．拒付与追索

拒付包括拒绝付款和拒绝承兑两个内容。汇票被拒付，持票人除可向承兑人追索外，还有权向其前手，包括所有的背书人和出票人行使追索权。持票人进行追索时，应将拒付事实书面通知其前手，并提供被拒绝承兑或被拒绝付款的证明或退票理由。持票人不能出示拒绝证明、退票理由书的，丧失对其前手的追索权。追索的金额包括被拒付的汇票金额和自到期日或提示付款日起至清偿日止的利息，以及取得拒绝证书和向前手发出被拒绝通知的费用。

四、汇票的当事人

汇票有三个基本当事人，分别是出票人、付款人和收款人。在票据流通中又产生了流通当事人，如背书人和承兑人。根据当事人对汇票的权利和责任，又可分为债权人和债务人。汇票的债权人是指有权对债务人行使汇票权利的当事人，收款人和持票人均为汇票的债权人。汇票的债务人是指在汇票中承担付款责任的当事人，出票人、付款人、背书人和承兑人都是汇票的债务人。

1．出票人（Drawer）

出票人是开出并交付汇票的人。在汇票被承兑之前，出票人是主债务人；在汇票被承兑之后，出票人变为次债务人，承兑人成为主债务人。

汇票一经签发，出票人就负有担保付款和担保承兑的责任。如果汇票遭到拒付，只要持票人对退票采取了必要的法律程序，出票人被追索时，应偿付票款给持票人。如果出票人希望免受持票人的追索，在出票时可加注“无追索权”字样。但是如此操作会影响汇票的流通性，一般也不被收款人接受。

2．付款人（Drawee）

付款人也称受票人，是接受汇票并支付票款的人。付款人在未对汇票承兑之前，没有在汇票上签名，因此对汇票不承担法律责任，是汇票的次债务人；对汇票承兑之后，即在汇票上签名之后，付款人就要对汇票承担法律责任，从而成为汇票的主债务人。

3．收款人（Payee）

收款人也称受款人，是收取汇票的人，是汇票的主债权人。收款人有权向付款人要求付款，若遭拒绝，有权向出票人追索票款。

4．背书人（Endorser）

背书人是指在汇票背面签字，并将汇票交付给另一人的当事人。接受该汇票的人就被称为被背书人（Endorsee）。收款人可以通过背书成为背书人，并可以连续地进行背书来转让汇票的权利。背书人就成为其被背书人和随后的汇票权利被转让者的前手，被背书人就是背书人和其他更早的汇票权利转让者的后手。在这些背书人当中，收款人是第一背书人。背书人承担汇票的付款人付款或承兑的担保责任，一旦汇票遭拒付，后手向其追索时，应负责偿还票款，然后再向其前手追索偿还，直至追索到出票人。

5．承兑人（Acceptor）

付款人同意接受（accept）出票人的命令并在汇票正面签字，就成为承兑人。承兑人一经承兑，出票人就退居次债务人的地位，承兑人必须保证对其所承兑的文义付款，而不能以下述情况为借口拒绝向正当持票人付款：①出票人不存在；②出票人的签字是伪造的；③出票人没有签发票据的能力或授权。

6. 持票人（Holder）

持票人就是指持有汇票的当事人。持票人是票据权利的主体，享有以下权利：

（1）付款请求权。持票人可以享有向汇票的付款人或承兑人提示汇票要求付款的权利。

（2）追索权。持票人在得不到承兑或付款时，享有向其前手直至出票人要求清偿票款的权利。

（3）转让票据权。持票人享有依法转让其汇票的权利。

7. 正当持票人（Holder in due course）

正当持票人也称善意持票人（Bona fide holder），是善意地付出了对价，取得一张表面完整、合格、不过期汇票的持票人，并且未发现这张汇票曾被拒付，也未曾发现转让人在权利方面有任何缺陷。即要成为正当持票人，必须要满足以下所有条件：①汇票完整合格（completeness and regularity of the bill）；②不过期（not overdue）；③未发现汇票曾被拒付（without notice of previous dishonor）；④善意（good faith）；⑤付对价（for value）；⑥未发现转让人在权利方面的缺陷（without notice of any defective title of the transferor）。

对于以上正当持票人的定义，《中华人民共和国票据法》和英国《票据法》是一致的。而《日内瓦统一法》不要求必须给付对价，只要满足其他五个条件，就可成为合法持票人（lawful holder），享有与正当持票人同样的权利。

值得注意的是：收款人是不可能成为正当持票人的，因为汇票未经过流通转让。

正当持票人的权利优于前手，不受前手权利缺陷的影响，且不受汇票当事人之间债务纠葛的影响。

实训项目

◆ 实训项目 10-1

上接实训项目 9-1。

【任务 1】制作汇票

2010 年 8 月 10 日，浙江曼旋进出口有限公司外贸单证员王宁制作好附属单据后，根据信用证和商业发票填制如下汇票。

BILL OF EXCHANGE

凭 Drawn Under			不可撤销信用证 Irrevocable L/C No.		
日期 Date		支取 Payable With interest	@ % 按 息 付款		
号码 No.		汇票金额 Exchange for		杭州 Hangzhou	
	见票 at		日后（本汇票之副本未付） sight of this FIRST of Exchange (Second of Exchange Being unpaid)		
付交 Pay to the order of					
金额 the sum of					
此致 To					

◆ 实训项目 10-2

上接实训项目 9-3。

【任务 1】制作汇票

2010 年 8 月 9 日，浙江大顺进出口有限公司外贸单证员朱丽娅收到德莎国际货运代理（上海）有限公司寄来的如下海运提单。

<table>
<tr><td colspan="3" rowspan="2">MAERSK LINE</td><td colspan="2" rowspan="2">BILL OF LADING FOR OCEAN TRANSPORT OR MULTIMODAL TRANSPORT</td><td>SCAC MAEU</td></tr>
<tr><td>B/L No.855966330</td></tr>
<tr><td colspan="3" rowspan="3">Shipper
ZHEJIANG DASHUN IMPORT AND EXPORT CO., LTD.
808 JINGZHOU ROAD, HANGZHOU, CHINA</td><td colspan="3">Booking No.
855966330</td></tr>
<tr><td colspan="2">Export references</td><td>Svc Contract
229785</td></tr>
<tr><td colspan="3">Onward inland routing (Not part of Carriage as defined in clause 1. For account and risk of Merchant)</td></tr>
<tr><td colspan="3">Consignee(negotiable only if consigned "to order", "to order of" a named person or "to order of bearer")
TO ORDER</td><td colspan="3">Notify Party (see clause 22)</td></tr>
<tr><td>Ocean Vessel
MARIT MAERSK</td><td colspan="2">Voy. No.
1004</td><td colspan="3">Place of Receipt, Applicable only when document used as Multimodal Transport B/L (see clause 1)</td></tr>
<tr><td>Port of Loading
SHANGHAI, CHINA</td><td colspan="2">Port of Discharge
BARCELONA, SPAIN</td><td colspan="3">Place of Delivery, Applicable only when document used as Multimodal Transport B/L (see clause 1)</td></tr>
<tr><td colspan="6">PARTICULARS FURNISHED BY SHIPPER</td></tr>
<tr><td colspan="4">Kind of Packages, Description of Goods, Marks & Numbers; Container No./Seal No.</td><td>Weight</td><td>Measurement</td></tr>
<tr><td colspan="4">1 CONTAINER SAID TO CONTAIN 360 PIECES OF TIRES
MSKU8423399 ML-CM0181808 20' FCL

FREIGHT COLLECT   ORIGINAL

Above particulars as declared by Shipper, but without responsibility of or representation by Carrier (see clause 14)</td><td>4245KGS</td><td>29.052 CBM</td></tr>
<tr><td>Freight & Charges</td><td>Rate</td><td>Unit</td><td>Currency</td><td>Prepaid</td><td>Collect</td></tr>
<tr><td>Carrier's Receipt (see clause 1 and 14). Total number of containers or packages received by Carrier.
1 CONTAINER</td><td colspan="2">Place of issue of B/L
SHANGHAI, CHINA</td><td colspan="3" rowspan="3">SHIPPED, as far as ascertained by reasonable means of checking, in apparent good order and condition unless otherwise stated herein, the total number or quantity of Containers or other packages or units indicated in the box entitled "Carrier's Receipt" for carriage from the Port of Loading (or the Place of Receipt, if mentioned above) to the Port of Discharge (or the Place of Delivery, if mentioned above), such carriage being always subject to the terms, rights, defences, provisions, conditions, exceptions, limitations, and liberties hereof (INCLUDING ALL THOSE TERMS AND CONDITIONS ON THE REVERSE HEREOF NUMBERED 1-26 AND THOSE TERMS AND CONDITIONS IN THE CARRIER'S APPLICABLE TARIFF) and the Merchant's attention is drawn in particular to the Carrier's liberties …</td></tr>
<tr><td>No. & Sequence of Original B(s)/L
3/THREE</td><td colspan="2">date of issue of B/L
2010-08-06</td></tr>
<tr><td>Declared Value(see clause 7.3)</td><td colspan="2">Shipped on Board Date
2010-08-02</td></tr>
<tr><td colspan="3"></td><td colspan="3">Signed for the Carrier A.P.Moller-Maersk A/S trading as Maersk Line

Martina White
On behalf of the Carrier
Maersk Hong Kong Line</td></tr>
</table>

8 月 9 日，浙江大顺进出口有限公司外贸单证员朱丽娅根据出口合同和商业发票填制如下汇票。

<table>
<tr><th colspan="8">BILL OF EXCHANGE</th></tr>
<tr><td colspan="2">凭
Drawn Under</td><td colspan="3"></td><td>不可撤销信用证
Irrevocable L/C No.</td><td colspan="2"></td></tr>
<tr><td>日期
Date</td><td colspan="2"></td><td colspan="2">支取
Payable With interest</td><td colspan="3">@　　%　按　　息　　付款</td></tr>
<tr><td>号码
No.</td><td colspan="2"></td><td>汇票金额
Exchange for</td><td colspan="2"></td><td>杭州
Hangzhou</td><td></td></tr>
<tr><td></td><td>见票
at</td><td></td><td colspan="5">日后（本汇票之副本未付）
sight of this FIRST of Exchange (Second of Exchange Being unpaid)</td></tr>
<tr><td colspan="3">付交
Pay to the order of</td><td colspan="5"></td></tr>
<tr><td colspan="2">金额
the sum of</td><td colspan="6"></td></tr>
<tr><td>此致
To</td><td colspan="4"></td><td colspan="3"></td></tr>
</table>

项目十一

审单操作

能力目标

能根据信用证、UCP600 条款审核商业发票、装箱单、运输单据、保险单据、产地证、汇票等外贸单证，找出不符点。

知识目标

掌握审单原则和 UCP600 相关条款，熟悉审单方法、常见的单据不符点。

上接项目一的导入项目内容。2010 年 4 月 30 日，中国农业银行浙江省分行国际业务部同意浙江龙江机械有限公司的申请，开立如下信用证。

```
MT 700                          ISSUE OF A DOCUMENTARY CREDIT
SENDER: ABOCCNBJ110
        AGRICULTURE BANK OF CHINA, ZHEJIANG BRANCH
RECEIVER: BKCHJPJT××××
        BANK OF CHINA, TOKYO BRANCH
27:     SEQUENCE OF TOTAL
        1/1
40A:    FORM OF DOCUMENTARY CREDIT
        IRREVOCABLE
20:     DOCUMENTARY CREDIT NUMBER
        111LC1004690
31C:    DATE OF ISSUE
        100430
40E:    APPLICABLE RULES
        UCP LATEST VERSION
31D:    DATE AND PLACE OF EXPIRY
        100615 JAPAN
```

（续）

50: APPLICANT
ZHEJIANG LONGJIANG MACHINE CO., LTD.
NO. 88, WENHUI ROAD, HANGZHOU, CHINA

59: BENEFICIARY
TAKASHI MACHINERY CO., LTD.
NO.108, AZA SHINBO, OHAZA YAMAYA, OJIYA CITY, NIIGATA PREF., JAPAN

32B: CURRENCY CODE, AMOUNT
JPY5800000,00

41A: AVAILABLE WITH…BY…
ANY BANK IN JAPAN
BY NEGOTIATION

42C: DRAFTS AT…
AT SIGHT

42A: DRAWEE
ABOCCNBJ110

43P: PARTIAL SHIPMENTS
PROHIBITED

43T: TRANSSHIPMENT
PROHIBITED

44E: PORT OF LOADING/AIRPORT OF DEPARTURE
ANY PORT IN JAPAN

44F: PORT OF DISCHARGE/AIRPORT OF DESTINATION
SHANGHAI, CHINA

44C: LATEST DATE OF SHIPMENT
100531

45A: DESCRIPTION OF GOODS &/OR SERVICES
MICROSTAR TNC-L09 CNC LATHE, 1 SET, JPY5800000.00/SET CFR SHANGHAI, CHINA
COUNTRY OF ORIGIN AND MANUFACTURER: JAPAN/TAKASHI MACHINERY CO., LTD.
SHIPPING MARK: TM20100066/SHANGHAI, CHINA

46A: DOCUMENTS REQUIRED

1. SIGNED COMMERCIAL INVOICE IN 1 ORIGINAL AND 3 COPIES INDICATING CONTRACT NO. TM20100066 AND SHIPPING MARK NO.

2. PACKING LIST/WEIGHT MEMO IN 1 ORIGINAL AND 2 COPIES INDICATING GROSS AND NET WEIGHTS, MEASUREMENTS AND QUANTITY OF EACH ITEM.

3. FULL SET OF CLEAN ON BOARD BILLS OF LADING MADE OUT TO ORDER AND BLANK ENDORSED, MARKED "FREIGHT PREPAID" AND "CONTRACT NO." NOTIFYING THE APPLICANT.

4. CERTIFICATE OF QUANTITY AND QUALITY IN 1 ORIGINAL AND 2 COPIES ISSUED BY THE MANUFACTURER.

5. CERTIFICATE OF JAPANESE ORIGIN IN 1 ORIGINAL AND 1 COPIES ISSUED BY CHAMBER OF COMMERCE & INDUSTRY IN JAPAN.

6. BENEFICIARY'S CERTIFIED COPY OF FAX SEND TO THE APPLICANT WITHIN THREE DAYS AFTER SHIPMENT DATE ADVISING CONTRACT NO., NAME OF COMMODITY, QUANTITY, GROSS AND NET WEIGHT, INVOICE VALUE, NAME OF VESSEL, SHIPMENT DATE, AND ETA.

7. CERTIFICATE OF TREATMENT ISSUED BY J.P.Q.A. IF PACKING IS MADE WITH WOODEN CASE, OR, ONE ORIGINAL CERTIFICATE OF NON-WOODEN PACKING DECLARATION IF PACKING IS NOT MADE WITH WOODEN CASE.

47A: ADDITIONAL CONDITIONS

1. ALL DOCUMENTS MUST INDICATE THE L/C NO., DATE OF ISSUE AND THE NAME OF ISSUING BANK.

（续）

	2. A FEE OF USD50.00 OR EQUIVALENT WILL BE DEDUCTED FROM THE PROCEEDS FOR EACH PRESENTATION OF DISCREPANT DOCUMENTS UNDER THIS CREDIT. ACCEPTANCE OF ANY DISCREPANT DOCUMENTS THEREUNDER DOES NO WAY AMEND OUR L/C CONDITION, EACH SET OF DOCUMENTS UNDER THIS L/C BEARING SAME DISCREPANCY WILL BE DETERMINED ON A CASE-BY-CASE BASIS.
	3. DOCUMENTS PRESENTED WITH DISCREPANCIES WILL BE REJECTED. WE WILL HOLD THE DOCUMENTS UNTIL WE RECEIVE A WAIVER FROM THE APPLICANT AND AGREE TO ACCEPT IT OR RECEIVE YOUR FURTHER INSTRUCTIONS PRIOR TO AGREEING TO ACCEPT A WAIVER.
71B:	CHARGES
	ALL BANKING CHARGES OUTSIDE THE ISSUING BANK ARE FOR ACCOUNT OF BENEFICIARY.
48:	PERIOD FOR PRESENTATION
	DOCUMENTS MUST BE PRESENTED WITHIN 15 DAYS AFTER SHIPMENT DATE, BUT WITHIN THE VALIDITY OF THIS CREDIT.
49:	CONFIRMATION INSTRUCTION
	WITHOUT
78:	INSTRUCTION TO PAYING/ACCEPTING/NEGOTIATING BANK
	1. ALL DOCUMENTS TO BE SENT DIRECTLY TO THE AGRICULTURAL BANK OF CHINA, ZHEJIANG BRANCH, INTERNATIONAL DEPT., 30 QINGCHUN ROAD, HANGZHOU 310003, P.R.CHINA IN ONE LOT BY COURIER SERVICE.
	2. WE WILL HONOUR UPON RECEIPT OF THE STIPULATED DOCUMENTS WHICH CONSTITUTE A COMPLYING PRESENTATION.
	3. THIS CREDIT IS SUBJECT TO UCPDC (2007 REVISION) ICC PUBLICATION NO. 600.

2010 年 5 月 28 日，浙江龙江机械有限公司接到中国农业银行浙江省分行到单通知和以下单据。

1．商业发票

Takashi Machinery Co., Ltd.

NO.108, AZA SHINBO, OHAZA YAMAYA, OJIYA CITY, NIIGATA PREF., JAPAN

TEL: 0081-258-82-4309 FAX: 0081-258-83-1367

COMMERCIAL INVOICE

To:	ZHEJIANG LONGJIANG MACHINE CO., LTD. NO. 88, WENHUI ROAD, HANGZHOU, CHINA			Invoice No.: Invoice Date: Contract No.: Contract Date:	2010TM0111 MAY 19, 2010 TM20100066 APRIL 19, 2010
From:	YOKOHAMA, JAPAN		To:	SHANGHAI, CHINA	
Marks and Numbers		Number and kind of package Description of goods	Quantity （SET）	Unit Price （JPY/SET）	Amount （JPY）
TM20100066 SHANGHAI, CHINA		MICROSTAR TNC-L09 CNC LATHE	1	CFR SHANGHAI, CHINA 5800000.00	5800000.00
TOTAL:			1		5800000.00
SAY TOTAL:		JPY FIVE MILLION EIGHT HUNDRED THOUSAND ONLY			

TAKASHI MACHINERY CO., LTD.

山本桥一

2. 装箱单

Takashi Machinery Co., Ltd. NO.108, AZA SHINBO, OHAZA YAMAYA, OJIYA CITY, NIIGATA PREF., JAPAN TEL: 0081-258-82-4309 FAX: 0081-258-83-1367 PACKING LIST						
To: ZHEJIANG LONGJIANG MACHINE CO., LTD. NO. 88, WENHUI ROAD, HANGZHOU, CHINA			Invoice No.:	2010TM0111		
			Invoice Date:	MAY 19, 2010		
			Contract No.:	TM20100066		
			Contract Date:	APRIL 19, 2010		
From: YOKOHAMA, JAPAN		To:	SHANGHAI, CHINA			
Marks and Numbers	Number and kind of package Description of goods	Quantity （SET）	Package （CASE）	G.W. （KGS）	N.W. （KGS）	Meas. （CBM）
TM20100066 SHANGHAI, CHINA	MICROSTAR TNC-L09 CNC LATHE	1	2	2070	1540	9.196
	TOTAL:	1	2	2070	1540	9.196
SAY TOTAL:	TWO CASES ONLY.					

3. 一般原产地证

1. **Exporter** TAKASHI MACHINERY CO., LTD. NO.108, AZA SHINBO, OHAZA YAMAYA, OJIYA CITY, NIIGATA PREF., JAPAN	**CERTIFICATE OF ORIGIN** Issued by Chamber of Commerce & Industry Japan
2. **Consignee** ZHEJIANG LONGJIANG MACHINE CO., LTD. NO. 88, WENHUI ROAD, HANGZHOU, CHINA	*Printed ORIGINAL or COPY **ORIGINAL-1** 3. **No. and date of Invoice** 2010TM0111 MAY 19, 2010
5. **Transport details** FROM YOKOHAMA, JAPAN TO SHANGHAI, CHINA	4. **Country of Origin** JAPAN 6. **Remarks**
7. **Marks, numbers, number and kind of packages; description of goods**	8. **Quantity**
TM20100066 SHANGHAI, CHINA COMMODITY: CNC LATHE SPECIFICATION: MICROSTAR TNC-L09 PACKING: 2 CASES/1 CONTAINER	1 SET
9. **Declaration by the Exporter** The undersigned, as an authorized signatory, hereby declares that the above-mentioned goods were produced in the country shown in box 4.	10. **Certification** The undersigned hereby certifies, on the basis of relative invoice and other supporting documents, that the above-mentioned goods originate in the country shown in box 4 to the best of its knowledge and belief.
Place and Date: Ojiya, May 20, 2010 TAKASHI MACHINERY CO., LTD. 山本桥一	The Ojiya Chamber of Commerce & Industry M. Hoshino May 20, 2010 **Certificate No.** 1

The Japan Chamber of Commerce & Industry　　Japan CCI Form CO 2007.5

4. 海运提单

<table>
<tr><td colspan="3">SITC CONTAINER LINES CO., LTD.</td><td colspan="2">B/L No. SITSNYK814YS009</td></tr>
<tr><td colspan="3">1. Shipper
TAKASHI MACHINERY CO., LTD.
NO.108, AZA SHINBO, OHAZA YAMAYA, OJIYA CITY, NIIGATA PREF., JAPAN</td><td colspan="2" rowspan="7">BILL OF LADING
RECEIVED for shipment in external apparent good order and condition, unless otherwise indicated. The total number of packages or units stuffed in the container, the description of the goods and the weights shown in this Bill of Lading are furnished by the Merchants and the containers are already sealed by the Merchants, and which the carrier has no reasonable means of checking and is not a part of this Bill of Lading contract. The carrier has issued the number of Bills of Lading stated below, all of this tenor and date, one of the original Bills of Lading must be surrendered and endorsed or signed against the delivery of the goods or the delivery order and whereupon any other original Bills of Lading shall be void.
NOTE: Notwithstanding any customs or privileges to the contrary, the Merchants attention is drawn to the fact that the Merchant, in accepting this Bill of Lading …
ORIGINAL</td></tr>
<tr><td colspan="3">2. Consignee
TO ORDER</td></tr>
<tr><td colspan="3">3. Notify Party</td></tr>
<tr><td colspan="3">ZHEJIANG LONGJIANG MACHINE CO., LTD.
NO. 88, WENHUI ROAD, HANGZHOU, CHINA
TEL: 0086-571-86739270 FAX: 0086-571-86739271</td></tr>
<tr><td>4. *Precarriage by</td><td colspan="2">5. *Place of Receipt
YOKOHAMA PORT CY</td></tr>
<tr><td>6. Vessel/Voy. No.
SINOTRANS，0814W</td><td colspan="2">7. Port of Loading
YOKOHAMA PORT, JAPAN</td></tr>
<tr><td>8. Port of Discharge
SHANGHAI, CHINA</td><td colspan="2">9. Port of Destination
SHANGHAI CY</td></tr>
<tr><td>Marks & Nos.
Container / Seal No.</td><td colspan="2">No. and Kind of Packages; Description of Goods</td><td>Gross Weight</td><td>Measurement</td></tr>
<tr><td>TM20100066
SHANGHAI, CHINA

CN: GESU2975766
SN: SITJ218907</td><td colspan="2">"SHIPPER'S LOAD & COUNT" "SAID TO CONTAIN"
COMMODITY: CNC LATHE
SPECIFICATION: MICROSTAR TNC-L09
QUANTITY: 1 SET
1 CONTAINER (2 CASES)
FREIGHT COLLECT</td><td>2070KGS</td><td>9.196CBM</td></tr>
<tr><td colspan="5">Description of Contents for Shipper's Use Only (Not part of This B/L Contract)</td></tr>
<tr><td colspan="5">Total Number of containers and/or packages (in words)：ONE (1) CONTAINER ONLY.</td></tr>
<tr><td>Ex. Rate:</td><td>Prepaid at</td><td>Payable at</td><td colspan="2">No. of Original B(s)/L
THREE (3)</td></tr>
<tr><td colspan="3">Place and date of issue
YOKOHAMA, MAY 20, 2010</td><td colspan="2">Signed
OAITO CORPORATION
J. Kitty</td></tr>
<tr><td colspan="3">FOR DELIVERY OF GOODS, PLS APPLY TO: TEL: 021-51166954/56/57
SITC CONTAINER LINES(SHANGHAI) CO., LTD. FAX: 021-63602930</td><td colspan="2">AS AGENT FOR THE CARRIER
SITC CONTAINER LINES CO., LTD.</td></tr>
</table>

注：背面空白

5. 装运通知

Takashi Machinery Co., Ltd.

NO.108, AZA SHINBO, OHAZA YAMAYA, OJIYA CITY, NIIGATA PREF., JAPAN

TEL: 0081-258-82-4309 FAX: 0081-258-83-1367

SHIPPING ADVICE

TO: ZHEJIANG LONGJIANG MACHINE CO., LTD. ISSUE DATE: MAY 21, 2010
NO. 88, WENHUI ROAD, HANGZHOU, CHINA S/C. NO.: TM20100066

（续）

DEAR SIR OR MADAM:

WE ARE PLEASED TO ADVICE YOU THAT WE SHIPPED THE FOLLOWING MACHINE ON MAY 20, 2010 UNDER VIA "SINOTRANS，0814W".

COMMODITY: CNC LATHE
SPECIFICATION: MICROSTAR TNC-L09
QUANTITY: 1 SET
UNIT PRICE: JPY5800000.00/SET CFR SHANGHAI, CHINA
PACKING: 2 CASES/1 CONTAINER
GROSS/NET WEIGHT: 2070KGS/1540KGS
SHIPPING MARK: TM20100066
SHANGHAI, CHINA

AT YOUR REQUEST WE COURIERED TODAY COPIES OF OUR INVOICE, BILL OF LADING, PACKING LIST, CERTIFICATE OF QUALITY AND QUANTITY, BENEFICIARY'S CERTIFICATE AND ORIGINAL OF JAPANESE ORIGIN, CERTIFICATE OF TREATMENT FOR THE ABOVE.

SINCERELY YOURS,
TAKASHI MACHINERY CO., LTD.
山本桥一

6．植物检疫证书

JAPAN PLANT QUARANTINE ASSOCIATION
3-4-3 UCHIKANDA, CHIYODA-KU, TOKYO, JAPAN
CERTIFICATE OF TREATMENT

NO.: 25-07689
DATE OF ISSUE: MAY 21, 2010

THIS IS TO CERTIFY THAT THE GOODS DESCRIBED BELOW HAVE BEEN TREATED AS FOLLOWS.
DATE: MAY 14, 2010-5-22 TREATMENT: HEAT TREATMENT
CHEMICAL(ACTIVE INGREDIENT): NIL DURATION: A MINIMUM OF 30 MINUTES
CONCENTRATION: NIL TEMPERATURE: ABOVE 56° C
ADDITIONAL INFORMATION: THESE SOLID WOOD PACKING MATERIALS MEET THE REQUIREMENT OF ISPM 15.

DESCRIPTION OF THE CONSIGNMENT

DECLARED NUMBER AND DESCRIPTION OF PACKAGES OR GOODS: WOOD PACKAGE MATERIAL
LASHING: 30 KGS
PACKING: 2 CASES 530 KGS

NAME AND ADDRESS OF EXPORTER: TAKASHI MACHINERY CO., LTD.
NO.108, AZA SHINBO, OHAZA YAMAYA, OJIYA CITY, NIIGATA PREF., JAPAN
NAME AND ADDRESS OF CONSIGNEE: ZHEJIANG LONGJIANG MACHINE CO., LTD.
NO. 88, WENHUI ROAD, HANGZHOU, CHINA

SHIPPING MARK: TM20100066
SHANGHAI, CHINA

WOOD PACKING MATERIAL OF THIS CONSIGNMENT IS STAMPED AS UNIQUE GRAPHIC SYMBOL, NATIONAL CODE, "HT" AND THE OFFICIAL NO. 0001123.

EIJU IMAIZUMI
YOKOHAMA PLANT PROTECTION ASSOCIATION
ON BEHALF OF: YOICHI SEKIGUCHI
PRESIDENT
JAPAN PLANT QUARANTINE ASSOCIATION

7. 质量与数量证明

Takashi Machinery Co., Ltd.

NO.108, AZA SHINBO, OHAZA YAMAYA, OJIYA CITY, NIIGATA PREF., JAPAN

TEL: 0081-258-82-4309 FAX: 0081-258-83-1367

CERTIFICATE OF QUALITY AND QUANTITY

TO: WHOM IT MAY CONERN DATE: MAY 21, 2010

WE HEREBY CERTIFY THAT THE FOLLOWING GOODS ARE ASSEMBLED AND INSPECTED UNDER OUR FACTORY SATANDARD, AND THEY PROVED GOOD QUALITY.

COMMODITY: CNC LATHE

SPECIFICATION: MICROSTAR TNC-L09

QUANTITY: 1 SET

8. 汇票

BILL OF EXCHANGE

NO. 2010TM0111 Date: MAY 24, 2010

FOR JP￥5800000.00

At ****** Sight of This Second Bill of Exchange

（First of the tenor and date being unpaid）Pay to BANK OF CHINA, TOKYO BRANCH or order

the sum of JPY FIVE MILLION EIGHT HUNDRED THOUSAND ONLY

Drawn under AGRICULTURE BANK OF CHINA, ZHEJIANG BRANCH

L/C NO. 111LC1004690 Dated APRIL 30, 2010

TO:

AGRICULTURE BANK OF CHINA, ZHEJIANG BRANCH

TAKASHI MACHINERY CO., LTD.

山本桥一

【任务 1】审核进口单据

外贸单证员季华须根据信用证、UCP600 审核各种进口单据，找出不符点。

示范操作

第一步：根据信用证条款审核商业发票。

通过审核发现商业发票中存在以下不符点：

（1）货物描述错误，缺货物的产地国和制造商名称。

（2）缺信用证号码、开证日期和开证行名称。

第二步：根据信用证条款、商业发票审核装箱单。

通过审核发现装箱单中存在的不符点是，缺信用证号码、开证日期和开证行名称。

第三步：根据信用证条款、商业发票和装箱单审核一般原产地证。

通过审核发现一般原产地证中存在的不符点是，缺信用证号码、开证日期和开证行名称。

第四步：根据信用证条款、商业发票和装箱单审核海运提单。

通过审核发现海运提单中存在以下不符点：

（1）海运提单背面缺空白背书。

（2）运费的支付方式 FREIGHT COLLECT 错误，正确的是 FREIGHT PREPAID。

（3）缺已装船批注。

（4）缺信用证号码、开证日期和开证行名称。

第五步：根据信用证条款、商业发票、装箱单和海运提单审核装运通知。

通过审核发现装运通知中存在以下不符点：

（1）缺 ETA，即预计到达目的港的时间。

（2）缺信用证号码、开证日期和开证行名称。

第六步：根据信用证条款、商业发票、装箱单审核植物检疫证书。

通过审核发现植物检疫证书中存在的不符点是，缺信用证号码、开证日期和开证行名称。

第七步：根据信用证条款、商业发票、装箱单审核质量与数量证明。

通过审核发现质量与数量证明中存在以下不符点：

（1）缺制造商的盖章和签名。

（2）缺信用证号码、开证日期和开证行名称。

第八步：根据信用证条款、商业发票审核汇票。

通过审核发现汇票中无不符点。

综上所述，全套结汇单据存在以下不符点：

1. 所有商业单据都缺信用证号码、开证日期和开证行名称。

2. 商业发票的货物描述错误，缺货物的产地国和制造商名称。

3. 海运提单中，背面缺空白背书；运费的支付方式 FREIGHT COLLECT 错误，正确的是 FREIGHT PREPAID；缺已装船批注。

4. 装运通知缺 ETA。

5. 质量与数量证明缺制造商的盖章和签名。

一、审单原则

在信用证结算方式下，外贸单证员审单的原则是单货一致、单证一致、单单一致；银行审单的原则是单证一致、单单一致。在托收结算方式下，外贸单证员审单的原则是单货一致、单约一致、单单一致；银行审单的原则是审核单据的名称、份数是否与托收申请书一致，并无审核单据内容的义务；在汇款结算方式下，外贸单证员审单的原则是单货一致、单约一致、单单一致。

1. 单证一致

“单证一致”是指所提交的单据在种类、份数和内容上都要与信用证的要求一致。单证一致具体体现在：①单据与信用证条款相符；②单据与 UCP 与 ISBP 等信用证国际惯例相符。

2. 单单一致

“单单一致”是指所提交单据内容之间要一致。“单单一致”审核时，要以发票为中心来审核各单据之间的一致情况。

3．单约一致

“单约一致”是指各单据要与合同条款一致。

4．单货一致

“单货一致”是指单据要与实际装运货物一致。

二、主要单据的审核要点

1．汇票的审核要点

①汇票载有正确的信用证参考号码；②载有当前的日期；③签字及/或出票人的名称与受益人的名称一致；④填写正确的付款人，不能是开证申请人；⑤金额大小写一致，并与信用证规定、发票相符；⑥汇票的期限就是信用证所要求的；⑦收款人应是受益人或交单银行；⑧如果需要背书，是否已被正确地背书；⑨是否有限制性背书；⑩是否包含信用证要求的条款；⑪所开立的金额不超过信用证可以使用的余额。

2．商业发票的审核要点

①除非信用证另有规定，商业发票的出具人与汇票的出票人应相同，在绝大多数情况下为信用证的受益人；②除非信用证另有规定，抬头为开证申请人；③不得为“形式发票”或“临时发票”；④货物描述和信用证的货物描述相符；⑤没有表现出来任何附加的、不利的涉及物状态或价值的货物描述；⑥发票上包括信用证所提及的货物细节、价格条款；⑦发票上提供的其他资料如唛头、号码、运输通知等与其他单据一致；⑧发票上的货币与信用证一致；⑨发票金额与汇票金额一致；⑩发票金额不超过信用证可使用的余额；如不允许分批装运，发票应包括信用证要求的整批装运金额，如允许分批装运，金额在总、分之间互不矛盾，并与信用证规定、汇票相符；⑪按照信用证要求发票已被签字（或公证人证实、合法化、签证等）；⑫有些资料关于装运、包装、重量、运费或其他有关的运输费用符合其他单据上所载明的；⑬提交正确张数的正本及副本；⑭显示的合同号与信用证规定一致；⑮注意上下浮动幅度，如信用证的金额、单价、货物数量前有“大约”（About，circa）字样，则有关金额、单价、数量允许有 10%上下浮动幅度；除信用证规定货物的数量不得增减外，在所支付款项不超过信用证金额的条件下，货物的数量准许有 5%上下的浮动幅度，但当信用证规定数量以包装单位或个体计数时，此项浮动不适用。

3．运输单据的审核要点

①运输单据的种类必须与信用证规定相符；②运输单据应具备法定条件并由运输公司（如船公司、航空公司等）或其代理人签名；③除非信用证另有规定，必须提交全套提单；④收货人和被通知人名称、地址、起运港、目的港、装运日期等，应符合信用证规定；⑤除非信用证另有规定，发货人（Shipper）通常为受益人或转让信用证中的受让人，但若是受益人以外的一方作为发货人，也可接受；⑥提单货物描述一般符合信用证所说明的货物描述，货名可以用统称（General term），唛头、数量、重量、船名、线路等应与信用证相符，并与其他单据一致；⑦提单上价格条款或有关运费的记载必须与信用证及其他单据一致。如 CIF、CFR，相应的费用记载应为“Freight prepaid”（运费已预付），或“Freight paid”（运费已付）；FOB，相应的费用记载应为“Freight collect”（运费到付）或“Freight payable at destination”（目的地

支付运费)；⑧提单抬头若为"To order of shipper"、"To shipper's Order"、"To order"，均应作背书；⑨收妥备运提单（Received B/L），必须于货物实际装船后，加注"On board"（已装船）字样及已装船日期；⑩修改提单，必须在更正处加盖更正章及船公司或其代理人或船长的小签（Initial signature，即签上姓氏，也叫简签）。⑪运输单据上没有条款能够使其瑕疵或不清洁（见 UCP600 第 32 条 a 款）。

4．保险单的审核要点

①应明确保险单的全套正本份数，并且除非信用证另有规定，必须提交全套正本保险单；②保险单据必须由保险公司（Insurance company）或承保人（Underwriters）或他们的代理人（Agents）开立及签署，除非信用证另有规定，银行不接受由保险经纪人（Broker）签发的暂保单（Cover note）；③保险单日期必须早于或等于提单日期；④除非信用证另有规定，保险单显示的金额、币别必须与信用证要求一致；⑤投保的险种必须符合信用证的要求，若信用证使用了含义不明确的条款，如"通常险别"（Usual risks）或"惯常险别"（Customary risks），银行应当按照所提示的保险单予以接受；⑥除非信用证另有规定，银行将接受证明受免赔率（Franchise）或免赔额约束的保险单据；⑦当信用证规定"投保一切险"时，银行应接受含有任何"一切险"批注或条文的保险单据，不论其有无"一切险"标题，甚至表明不包括某种险别；⑧保险单的船名、航程、装运港、目的港、唛头等应与提单、发票等其他单据一致；⑨应表明赔付地、在目的地的支付赔款代理人、支付的货币种类，信用证如无此项规定，赔付地点可以选择在进出口人的任何一方；⑩信用证要求保险单（Insurance policy）时，不得以保险凭证（Insurance certificate）代替，反之则可以；⑪份数完全符合信用证规定的数量。

5．产地证的审核要点

①它是独立的单据，不要与其他单据联合起来，必须由信用证指定的机构出具，若信用证无此规定，可以由包括受益人在内的任何人出具。②按照信用证要求，它已被签字、公证人证实、合法化、签证等。③内容必须符合信用证的要求，并与其他单据不矛盾；如信用证规定货物为某地生产，则产地证必须表明为某地生产。④载明原产地国家，应该符合信用证的要求。⑤含有检验意义的产地证的日期不能迟于提单；特殊产地证的格式必须符合进口国惯例的要求。⑥份数不能少于信用证规定的数量。

6．装箱单、重量单的审核要点

①单据的名称和份数必须和信用证要求相符；②货物的名称、规格、数量及唛头等，必须与其他单据相符，可以相互补充，不可互相矛盾；③数量、重量及尺码的小计必须吻合，并与信用证、提单、发票等单据相符；④提供的单据份数不能少于信用证规定的数量。

三、单据的主要不符点

1．单据的共同不符点

（1）过效期（L/C expired）：单据提交时已超过了信用证规定的有效期。

（2）过装期（Late shipment）：运输单据的装运日期超过了信用证规定的最迟装船期。

（3）过交单期（Late presentation）：单据提交的日期超过信用证规定的货物装船后向指定银行提示单据的期限。如果信用证要求汇票，则汇票出具日应是单据提示日，如果信用证未要求汇票，且无特殊说明，则寄单行的索汇面函日期将被认为是交单日期。

2．汇票的主要不符点

①非由受益人出具；②未经签署；③未经背书或背书不正确；④未按信用证规定显示“Drawn under”条款；⑤金额与发票或信用证不符；⑥金额大小写不一致；⑦期限显示不正确；⑧发票号码、信用证号码等其他需要显示的号码不符。

3．商业发票的主要不符点

①非由受益人出具；②未经签署（若信用证规定要签署）；③抬头不符，未给出信用证的申请人（信用证规定做成其他人抬头的除外）；④货物描述与信用证不一致，单价不符；⑤超金额与或短装；⑥唛头与信用证或海运提单等其他单据不一致；⑦未按信用证要求显示特殊内容，如需经过使馆认证而未认证，信用证要求显示扣减或增加附属费用而发票未显示；⑧其他如开证行名、装运港、目的港与信用证规定或其他单据不一致。

4．海运提单的主要不符点

①正本提单份数不符；②抬头（Consignee）名址不符；③被通知人名址不符；④货物描述与信用证规定或发票等其他单据不符；⑤未显示“On board”；⑥重量、体积与装箱单等其他单据不一致；⑦提交了不清洁提单；⑧未经背书或背书不正确；⑨签发人不符，未显示承运人（Carrier）或签发人身份不明。

5．保险单据的主要不符点

①未提交全套正本保险单据/证明；②被保险人不符；③保险标的金额不符，币种、大小写不符；④保险标的物与发票等其他单据不符；⑤保险险别不符；⑥出单日迟于运输单据日期；⑦偿付地、币种不符；⑧未经背书或背书不正确；⑨其他如发票号码、航运路线与发票、提单不符。

四、审单与UCP600的部分相关条款

（1）按照指定行事的被指定银行、保兑行（如有）以及开证行必须对提示的单据进行审核，并仅以单据为基础，以决定单据在表面上看来是否构成相符提示；按照指定行事的被指定银行、保兑行（如有）以及开证行，自其收到提示单据的翌日起算，应各自拥有最多不超过五个银行工作日的时间以决定提示是否相符。该期限不因单据提示日适逢信用证有效期或最迟提示期或在其之后而被缩减或受到其他影响。

单据中内容的描述不必与信用证、信用证对该项单据的描述以及国际标准银行实务完全一致，但不得与该项单据中的内容、其他规定的单据或信用证相冲突；除商业发票外，其他单据中的货物、服务或行为描述若需规定，可使用统称，但不得与信用证规定的描述相矛盾。

如果信用证要求提示运输单据、保险单据和商业发票以外的单据，但未规定该单据由何人出具或单据的内容。如信用证对此未做规定，只要所提交单据的内容看来满足其功能需要，银行将对提示的单据予以接受。

提示信用证中未要求提交的单据，银行将不予置理。如果收到此类单据，可以退还提示人；如果信用证中包含某项条件而未规定需提交与之相符的单据，银行将认为未列明此条件，并对此不予置理。

单据的出单日期可以早于信用证开立日期，但不得迟于信用证规定的提示日期。

当受益人和申请人的地址显示在任何规定的单据上时，不必与信用证或其他规定单据中显示的地址相同，但必须与信用证中述及的各自地址处于同一国家内。用于联系的资料（电传、电话、电子邮箱及类似方式）如作为受益人和申请人地址的组成部分将被不予置理。然而，当申请人的地址及联系信息作为按照 UCP600 的第 19 条、20 条、21 条、22 条、23 条、24 条或 25 条出具的运输单据中收货人或通知方详址的组成部分时，则必须按照信用证规定予以显示。

显示在任何单据中的货物的托运人或发货人不必是信用证的受益人。

假如运输单据能够满足 UCP600 的第 19 条、20 条、21 条、22 条、23 条或 24 条的要求，则运输单据可以由承运人、船东、船长或租船人以外的任何一方出具。

（2）当开证行确定提示相符时，就必须予以兑付；当保兑行确定提示相符时，就必须予以兑付或议付并将单据寄往开证行；当被指定银行确定提示相符并予以兑付或议付时，必须将单据寄往保兑行或开证行。

（3）信用证中规定的各种单据必须至少提供一份正本；除非单据本身表明其不是正本，银行将视任何单据表面上具有单据出具人正本签字、标志、图章或标签的单据为正本单据；除非单据另有显示，银行将接受单据作为正本单据：如果该单据表面看来由单据出具人手工书写、打字、穿孔签字或盖章，或表面看来使用单据出具人的正本信笺，或声明单据为正本，除非该项声明表面看来与所提示的单据不符。

如果信用证要求提交副本单据，则提交正本单据或副本单据均可；如果信用证使用诸如“一式两份”、“两张”、“两份”等术语要求提交多份单据，则可以提交至少一份正本，其余份数以副本来满足。但单据本身另有相反指示的除外。

实训项目

◆ **实训项目**

上接实训项目 1-1。

2010 年 8 月 20 日，中国农业银行浙江省分行开立了号码为 111LC0900879 的信用证，具体内容如下。

MT 700 ISSUE OF A DOCUMENTARY CREDIT

SENDER: ABOCCNBJ110

AGRICULTURAL BANK OF CHINA ZHEJIANG BRANCH

RECEIVER: BKCHHKHHXXXXN

BANK OF CHINA (HONG KONG) LIMITED

27:	Sequence of Total 1/1
40A:	Form of Documentary Credit IRREVOCABLE
20:	Documentary Credit Number 111LC1000879
31C:	Date of Issue 100820

（续）

40E: Applicable Rules
UCP LATEST VERSION
31D: Date and Place of Expiry
101022HONGKONG
50: Applicant
ZHEJIANG ANNIE IMPORT & EXPORT CO., LTD.
1298 HUAXING ROAD, HANGZHOU, CHINA
59: Beneficiary
U.A.C.C. (PACIFIQUE) S.A.
18TH FLOOR, TACWOOD PLAZA, 32 DES VOEUX ROAD, CENTRAL, HONG KONG
32B: Currency Code, Amount
EUR55500,00
41A: Available With…By…
ANY BANK IN HONG KONG
BY NEGOTIATION
42C: Drafts at…
AT SIGHT
42A: Drawee
AGRICULTURAL BANK OF CHINA ZHEJIANG BRANCH
43P: Partial Shipments
PROHIBITED
43T: Transshipment
ALLOWED
44E: Port of Loading/Airport of Departure
DOUALA, CAMEROON
44F: Port of Discharge/Airport of Destination
ZHANGJIAGANG, CHINA
44C: Latest Date of Shipment
101001
45A: Description of Goods &/or Services
150CBM SAPELLI LOGS, DIAMETER: 60-80CM, LENGTH: 5M AND UP, SLICING GRADE,
ORIGIN: CAMEROON, UNIT PRICE: EUR370,00/CBM FOB DOUALA, CAMEROON.
46A: Documents Required

1. SIGNED COMMERCIAL INVOICE IN QUINTUPLICATE INDICATING THIS L/C NO.

2. PACKING LIST IN QUINTUPLICATE INDICATING THE DIAMETER, LENGTH AND MEASUREMENT OF EACH LOG.

3. FULL SET OF CLEAN 'ON BOARD' OCEAN BILLS OF LADING MADE OUT TO ORDER AND BLANK ENDORSED, MARKED 'FREIGHT COLLECT' AND NOTIFY APPLICANT.

4. CERTIFICATE OF ORIGIN IN TRIPLICATE ISSUED BY THE MANUFACTURER.

5. ONE ORIGINAL AND TWO COPIES OF PHYTOSANITARY CERTIFICATE ISSUED BY THE COMPETENT GOVERNMENT QUARANTINE AUTHORITY OF THE EXPORT COUNTRY.

47A: Additional Conditions

1. A FEE OF USD50.00 OR EQUIVALENT WILL BE DEDUCTED FROM THE PROCEEDS FOR EACH PRESENTATION OF DISCREPANT DOCUMENTS UNDER THIS CREDIT. ACCEPTANCE OF ANY DISCREPANT DOCUMENTS THEREUNDER DOES NO WAY AMEND OUR L/C CONDITION, EACH SET OF DOCUMENTS UNDER THIS L/C BEARING SAME DISCREPANCY WILL BE DETERMINED ON A CASE-BY-CASE BASIS.

2. DOCUMENTS PRESENTED WITH DISCREPANCIES WILL BE REJECTED. WE WILL HOLD THE DOCUMENTS UNTIL WE RECEIVE A WAIVER FROM THE APPLICANT AND AGREE TO ACCEPT IT OR RECEIVE YOUR FURTHER INSTRUCTIONS PRIOR TO AGREEING TO ACCEPT A WAIVER.

（续）

3. PLS RELEASE THIS L/C TO BENEFICIARY AFTER ALL YOUR ADVISING COMMISSIONS COLLECTED.

4. THIRD PARTY DOCUMENTS EXCEPT INVOICE AND DRAFT ARE ACCEPTANCE.

5. ALL DOCUMENTS MUST SHOW THE L/C NO.

71B: Charges

ALL BANKING CHARGES OUTSIDE THE ISSUING BANK ARE FOR ACCOUNT OF BENEFICIARY.

48: Period for Presentation

DOCUMENTS MUST BE PRESENTED WITHIN 21 DAYS AFTER SHIPMENT DATE, BUT WITHIN THE VALIDITY OF THIS CREDIT.

49: Confirmation Instruction

WITHOUT

78: Instruction to Paying/Accepting/Negotiating Bank

1. ALL DOCUMENTS TO BE SENT DIRECTLY TO THE AGRICULTURAL BANK OF CHINA, ZHEJIANG BRANCH, INTERNATIONAL DEPT., 30 QINGCHUN ROAD, HANGZHOU 310003, P.R.CHINA IN ONE LOT BY COURIER SERVICE.

2. WE WILL HONOUR UPON RECEIPT OF THE STIPULATED DOCUMENTS WHICH CONSTITUTE A COMPLYING PRESENTATION.

3. THIS CREDIT IS SUBJECT TO UCPDC (2007 REVISION) ICC PUB. NO. 600.

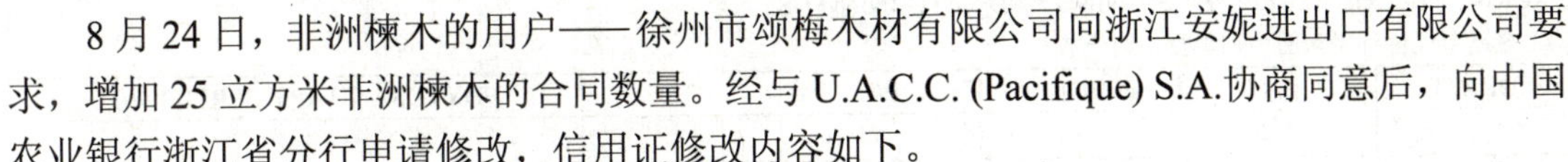

8 月 24 日，非洲楝木的用户——徐州市颂梅木材有限公司向浙江安妮进出口有限公司要求，增加 25 立方米非洲楝木的合同数量。经与 U.A.C.C. (Pacifique) S.A.协商同意后，向中国农业银行浙江省分行申请修改，信用证修改内容如下。

MT 707 AMENDMENT TO A DOCUMENTARY CREDIT

SENDER: ABOCCNBJ110

AGRICULTURAL BANK OF CHINA ZHEJIANG BRANCH

RECEIVER: BKCHHKHHXXXXN

BANK OF CHINA (HONG KONG) LIMITED

SENDER'S REFERENCE	20 :	111LC1000879
RECEIVER'S REFERENCE	21 :	NON
DATE OF ISSUE	31C:	100820
DATE OF AMENDMENT	30 :	100827
NUMBER OF AMENDMENT	26E:	01
BENEFICIARY(BEFORE THIS AMENDMENT)	59 :	U.A.C.C. (PACIFIQUE) S.A. 18TH FLOOR, TACWOOD PLAZA, 32 DES VOEUX ROAD, CENTRAL, HONG KONG
NEW DATE AND PLACE OF EXPIRY	31E:	101022HONGKONG
INCREASE OF DOC CREDIT AMOUNT	32B:	CURRENCY EUR AMOUNT 9250,00
NEW DOC. CREDIT MOUNT AFTER AMENDMENT	34B:	CURRENCY EUR AMOUNT64750,00
LATEST DATE OF SHIPMENT	44C:	101001
NARRATIVE	79 :	FOR FIELD 45A, THE QUANTITY OF SAPELLI LOG.IS INCREASED BY 150CBM TO 175CBM. OTHER TERMS AND CONDITIONS REMAIN UNCHANGED. AMENDMENT FEE USD14,00 AND CABLE FEE USD30,00 ARE FOR A/C OF APPLICANT. SUBJECT TO UCPDC (2007 REVISION) ICC PUB. NO.600.

10 月 15 日，浙江安妮进出口有限公司外贸单证员马金春接到中国农业银行浙江省分行到单通知，具体单据如下：

1. 到单通知

中国农业银行
AGRICULTURAL BANK OF CHINA
进口信用证到单通知
ADVICE OF BILL ARRIVAL

To: 致	ZHEJIANG ANNIE IMPORT & EXPORT CO., LTD. 浙江安妮进出口有限公司	Date: 日期	2010-10-15
Contract No.: 合同号	ANNIE10029	Draft Amount 汇票金额	EUR64750.00
L/C No.: 信用证号	111LC1000879	AB No.: 到单编号	AB9876545647
Tenor Type: 即期/远期	AT SIGHT	Maturity Date 到期日	2010-10-22
Negotiating Bank: 议付行	BANK OF CHINA (HONG KONG) LIMITED		
Doc. Mail Date: 寄单日期	2010-10-12		

PLEASE FIND HEREWITH ENCLOSED THE FOLLOWING DOCUMENTS SENT FROM NEGOTIATING BANK AND ACKNOWLEDGE RECEIPT BY SIGNING AND RETURNING US.
兹附奉议付行寄来的下列单据，请查收。

DRAFT	B/L	INVOICE	P/L	C/O	PHYTOSANITARY CERTIFICATE
1	3/3	5	5	3	1+2

DISCREPANCIES (IF ANY):
单据不符点：

REMARKS:
备注（客户）

NOTE:
1. 该单据将于上述付款日对外付款，请贵司于接本通知后三日内将所附《对外付款/承兑通知书》签署意见及核销单一式三联填妥加盖公章后交我行，以便及时对外付款。否则，我行将于上述付款日对外付款，不再另行通知。
2. 如贵司因单据有不符点需拒付，请于接本通知后三日内将所附的拒付通知交我行，并退回全套单据。

（银行盖章）

2. 汇票

BILL OF EXCHANGE

NO. UACC-10-039　　　　DATE: OCT. 9, 2010 HONG KONG

FOR EUR63322.54

AT +++ SIGHT OF THIS FIRST BILL OF EXCHANGE (SECOND OF THE SAME TENOR AND DATE BEING UNPAID) PAY TO BANK OF CHINA (HONG KONG) LIMITED OR ORDER THE SUM OF EURO SIXTY THREE THOUSAND THREE HUNDRED TWENTY TWO AND CENTS FIFTY FOUR ONLY.

VALUE RECEIVED.

DRAWN UNDER AGRICULTURAL BANK OF CHINA, ZHEJIANG BRANCH

L/C NO. 111LC1000897　　DATED AUG. 20, 2010

TO: ABOCCNBJ110
AGRICULTURAL BANK OF CHINA
ZHEJIANG BRANCH

JACKIE WANG
U.A.C.C. (PACIFIQUE) S.A.

3. 海运提单

<table>
<tr><td colspan="3">MAERSK LINE</td><td colspan="3">BILL OF LADING FOR OCEAN TRANSPORT OR MULTIMODAL TRANSPORT</td><td colspan="2">SCAC MAEU
B/L No.855954779</td></tr>
<tr><td colspan="3" rowspan="3">Shipper
U.A.C.C. (PACIFIQUE) S.A.
18TH FLOOR, TACWOOD PLAZA, 32 DES VOEUX ROAD, CENTRAL, HONG KONG</td><td colspan="5">Booking No.
855954779</td></tr>
<tr><td colspan="5">Export references / Svc Contract 229785</td></tr>
<tr><td colspan="5">Onward inland routing (Not part of Carriage as defined in clause 1. For account and risk of Merchant)</td></tr>
<tr><td colspan="3">Consignee(negotiable only if consigned "to order", "to order of" a named person or "to order of bearer")
TO ORDER</td><td colspan="5">Notify Party (see clause 22)</td></tr>
<tr><td colspan="2">Ocean Vessel
CLAES MAERSK</td><td>Voy. No.
0804</td><td colspan="5">Place of Receipt, Applicable only when document used as Multimodal Transport B/L (see clause 1)</td></tr>
<tr><td colspan="2">Port of Loading
DOUALA, CAMEROON</td><td>Port of Discharge
ZHANGJIAGANG, CHINA</td><td colspan="5">Place of Delivery, Applicable only when document used as Multimodal Transport B/L (see clause 1)</td></tr>
<tr><td colspan="8">PARTICULARS FURNISHED BY SHIPPER</td></tr>
<tr><td colspan="6">Kind of Packages, Description of Goods, Marks & Numbers; Container No./Seal No.</td><td>Weight</td><td>Measurement</td></tr>
<tr><td colspan="6">7 CONTAINERS SAID TO CONTAIN 44 PIECES OF SAPELLI LOGS
MSKU8423386 ML-CM0181881 40 DRY 9'6 7 PIECES 21426KGS 25.207CBM
MSKU0522994 ML-CM0181882 40 DRY 9'6 7 PIECES 21040KGS 24.753CBM
TCNU9315452 ML-CM0181883 40 DRY 9'6 6 PIECES 20109KGS 23.658CBM
CLHU8019323 ML-CM0181884 40 DRY 9'6 6 PIECES 19502KGS 22.943CBM
PONU8113159 ML-CM0181885 40 DRY 9'6 6 PIECES 21108KGS 24.833CBM
PONU7267252 ML-CM0181886 40 DRY 9'6 6 PIECES 21277KGS 25.032CBM
PONU7267253 ML-CM0181887 40 DRY 9'6 6 PIECES 21128KGS 24.716CBM
FREIGHT COLLECT ORIGINAL
Above particulars as declared by Shipper, but without responsibility of or representation by Carrier (see clause 14).</td><td>145590 KGS</td><td>171.142 CBM</td></tr>
<tr><td colspan="2">Freight & Charges</td><td colspan="2">Rate</td><td>Unit</td><td>Currency</td><td>Prepaid</td><td>Collect</td></tr>
<tr><td colspan="2">Carrier's Receipt (see clause 1 and 14). Total number of containers or packages received by Carrier.
7 CONTAINERS</td><td colspan="2">Place of issue of B/L
HONG KONG</td><td colspan="4" rowspan="3">SHIPPED, as far as ascertained by reasonable means of checking, in apparent good order and condition unless otherwise stated herein, the total number or quantity of Containers or other packages or units indicated in the box entitled "Carrier's Receipt" for carriage from the Port of Loading (or the Place of Receipt, if mentioned above) to the Port of Discharge (or the Place of Delivery, if mentioned above), such carriage being always subject to the terms, rights, defences, provisions, conditions, exceptions, limitations, and liberties hereof (INCLUDING ALL THOSE TERMS AND CONDITIONS ON THE REVERSE HEREOF NUMBERED 1-26 AND THOSE TERMS AND CONDITIONS IN THE CARRIER'S APPLICABLE TARIFF) and the Merchant's attention is drawn in particular to the Carrier's liberties …</td></tr>
<tr><td colspan="2">No. & Sequence of Original B(s)/L
3/THREE</td><td colspan="2">date of issue of B/L
2010-10-06</td></tr>
<tr><td colspan="2">Declared Value(see clause 7.3)</td><td colspan="2">Shipped on Board Date
2010-09-21</td></tr>
<tr><td colspan="4"></td><td colspan="4">Signed for the Carrier A.P.Moller-Maersk A/S trading as Maersk Line

Martina White
On behalf of the Carrier
Maersk Hong Kong Line</td></tr>
</table>

4. 植物检疫证明

RE-EXPORTATION PHYTOSANITARY CERTIFICATE No. 0006297	REPUBLIC OF CAMEROON MINISTRY OF AGRICULTURE AND RURAL DEVELOPMENT ****** DEPARTMENT OF REGULATION AND QUALITY CONTROL OF INPUTS AND AGRICULTURAL PRODUCTS
Name and address of exporter TRANSIBOIS P/C VICWOOD CENTRAFRIQUE BP.2578 BANGUI/RCA	
Name and address of consignee ZHEJIANG ANNIE IMPORT AND EXPORT CO., LTD. 1298 HUAXING ROAD, HANGZHOU, CHINA	Plant Protection Organisation of Cameroon To Plant Protection Organisation of CHINA
Declared means of transport BY VESSEL "CLAES MAERSK"	Origin: REPUBLIC OF CAMEROON
Port of entry ZHANGJIAGANG, CHINA	
Distinguishing marks, number and description of packages; name of produce; botanical name of plants 44 SAPELLI LOGS	Declared quantity 171.142 CBM 146590 KGS

This is to certify that the plants, plant products or other regulated articles described above have been imported in to Cameroon, covered by the phytosanitary certificate: the original ☒ certified true copy of which is attached to this certificate. They are packaged ☐, repackaged in original ☐, new containers ☐; that based on the original phytosanitary certificate ☐ and on additional inspection☒,they are considered to comply with the current phytosanitary requirements of the contracting importing party and that during storing in Cameroon the consignment has not been subjected to the risk of infestation or infection.

Additional declaration:

TREATMENT CARRIED OUT		Place of issue: DOUALA, CAMEROON Date of issue: SEPTEMBER 19, 2010
Type of treatment	Fumiation ☒ Desinfection ☐	
Chemical product (Active matter) PULVERISATION	Duration and temperature 3 HOURS	Name of authorized officer: GOUROUMAHA SLLOUETTE
Concentration KOATGRUME 5%+EAU95%		Signature: *GOUROUMAHA SLLOUETTE*
Additional information		

5. 商业发票

U.A.C.C. (PACIFIQUE) S.A.

18TH FLOOR, TACWOOD PLAZA, 32 DES VOEUX ROAD, CENTRAL, HONG KONG

Tel: 00852-2581-3097 Fax: 00852-2581-3099

INVOICE

SOLD TO ZHEJIANG ANNIE IMPORT AND EXPORT CO., LTD. 1298 HUAXING ROAD, HANGZHOU, CHINA		**INVOICE NO.** UACC-10-039	**DATE** 8 OCT., 2010
		CONTRACT NO. ANNIE10029	**L/C NO.** 111LC1000879
VESSEL NAME CLAES MAERSK	**VOYAGE NO.** 0804	**SAILING DATE** SEP. 21, 2009	
PORT OF LOADING DOUALA,CAMEROON	**PORT OF DISCHARGE** ZHANGJIAGANG, CHINA	**TERMS OF PAYMENT** L/C AT SIGHT	

（续）

DESCRIPTN OF GOODS	NUMBER OF PACKAGES	QUANTITY	UNIT PRICE	AMOUNT
			FOB DOUALA, CAMEROON	
SAPELLI LOGS DIAMETER: 60-80CM LENGTH: 5M AND UP SLICING GRADE ORIGIN: CAMEROON	44 LOGS	171.142 CBM	EUR370.00/CBM	EUR63322.54
SAY: EURO SIXTY THREE THOUSAND THREE HUNDRED TWENTY TWO AND CENTS FIFTY FOUR ONLY.			INVOICE TOTAL	EUR63322.54

For and on behalf of
U.A.C.C. (Pacifique) S.A.
Jackie Wang

Authorized Signature(s)

6．装箱单

U.A.C.C. (PACIFIQUE) S.A.

18TH FLOOR, TACWOOD PLAZA, 32 DES VOEUX ROAD, CENTRAL, HONG KONG

Tel: 00852-2581-3097　Fax: 00852-2581-3099

PACKING LIST

SOLD TO		INVOICE NO.	DATE
ZHEJIANG ANNIE IMPORT AND EXPORT CO., LTD. 1298 HUAXING ROAD, HANGZHOU, CHINA		UACC-10-039	8 OCT., 2010
		CONTRACT NO. ANNIE10029	L/C NO. 111LC1000879
VESSEL NAME CLAES MAERSK	VOYAGE NO. 0804	SAILING DATE SEP. 21, 2010	
PORT OF LOADING DOUALA,CAMEROON	PORT OF DISCHARGE ZHANGJIAGANG, CHINA	DESCRIPTN OF GOODS T APELLI LOGS	

CONTAINER NO.	LOG NO.	WEIGHT	TOTAL VOLUME OF EACH LOG
MSKU8423386	1-7	21426KGS	25.207CBM
MSKU0522994	8-14	21040KGS	24.753CBM
TCNU9315452	15-20	20109KGS	23.658CBM
CLHU8019323	21-26	19502KGS	22.943CBM
PONU8113159	27-32	21108KGS	24.833CBM
PONU7267252	33-38	21277KGS	25.032CBM
PONU7267253	39-44	21128KGS	24.716CBM
TOTAL	44 LOGS	145590 KGS	171.142 CBM

SHIPPED IN 7×40' CONTAINERS/44 LOGS
THE DETAILS OF THE LOGS SEE THE PAGE 2-4 OF 4.

For and on behalf of
U.A.C.C. (Pacifique) S.A.
Jackie Wang

Authorized Signature(s)

PAGE NO.: 1 OF 4

U.A.C.C. (PACIFIQUE) S.A.

18TH FLOOR, TACWOOD PLAZA, 32 DES VOEUX ROAD, CENTRAL, HONG KONG

Tel: 00852-2581-3097 Fax: 00852-2581-3099

PACKING LIST

SOLD TO ZHEJIANG ANNIE IMPORT AND EXPORT CO., LTD. 1298 HUAXING ROAD, HANGZHOU, CHINA	INVOICE NO. UACC-10-039	DATE 8 OCT., 2010
	CONTRACT NO. ANNIE10029	L/C NO. 111LC1000879

CONTAINER NO.	LOG NO.	LENGTH	DIAMETER	TOTAL VOLUME OF EACH LOG
MSKU8423386	1	7.50M	68CM	2.724CBM
	2	6.10M	73CM	2.553CBM
	3	7.20M	69CM	2.692CBM
	4	11.10M	64CM	3.571CBM
	5	11.20M	76CM	5.081CBM
	6	10.60M	76CM	4.809CBM
	7	10.40M	68CM	3.777CBM
				25.207CBM
MSKU0522994	8	10.10M	76CM	4.582CBM
	9	9.50M	71CM	3.761CBM
	10	6.20M	67CM	2.186CBM
	11	9.30M	74CM	4.000CBM
	12	9.90M	72CM	4.031CBM
	13	6.60M	69CM	2.468CBM
	14	8.00M	77CM	3.725CBM
				24.753CBM
TCNU9315452	15	10.30M	73CM	4.311CBM
	16	8.30M	75CM	3.667CBM
	17	7.80M	77CM	3.632CBM
	18	7.20M	71CM	2.851CBM
	19	11.40M	73CM	4.771CBM
	20	11.50M	70CM	4.426CBM
				23.658CBM

PAGE NO.: 2 OF 4

U.A.C.C. (PACIFIQUE) S.A.

18TH FLOOR, TACWOOD PLAZA, 32 DES VOEUX ROAD, CENTRAL, HONG KONG

Tel: 00852-2581-3097 Fax: 00852-2581-3099

PACKING LIST

SOLD TO ZHEJIANG ANNIE IMPORT AND EXPORT CO., LTD. 1298 HUAXING ROAD, HANGZHOU, CHINA	INVOICE NO. UACC-10-039	DATE 8 OCT., 2010
	CONTRACT NO. ANNIE10029	L/C NO. 111LC1000879

CONTAINER NO.	LOG NO.	LENGTH	DIAMETER	TOTAL VOLUME OF EACH LOG
CLHU8019323	21	10.20M	74CM	4.387CBM
	22	10.00M	76CM	4.537CBM
	23	6.40M	72CM	2.606CBM
	24	11.40M	74CM	4.903CBM
	25	7.90M	76CM	3.584CBM
	26	8.30M	67CM	2.926CBM
				22.943CBM

（续）

PONU8113159	27	10.00M	75CM	4.418CBM
	28	8.90M	74CM	3.828CBM
	29	9.90M	77CM	4.610CBM
	30	9.30M	76CM	4.219CBM
	31	9.20M	74CM	3.957CBM
	32	9.60M	71CM	3.801CBM
				24.833CBM
PONU7267252	33	7.90M	74CM	3.398CBM
	34	9.40M	76CM	4.265CBM
	35	11.30M	72CM	4.601CBM
	36	11.70M	76CM	5.308CBM
	37	9.00M	77CM	4.191CBM
	38	7.60M	74CM	3.269CBM
				25.032CBM

PAGE NO.: 3 OF 4

U.A.C.C. (PACIFIQUE) S.A.

18TH FLOOR, TACWOOD PLAZA, 32 DES VOEUX ROAD, CENTRAL, HONG KONG

Tel: 00852-2581-3097 Fax: 00852-2581-3099

PACKING LIST

SOLD TO ZHEJIANG ANNIE IMPORT AND EXPORT CO., LTD. 1298 HUAXING ROAD, HANGZHOU, CHINA	INVOICE NO. UACC-10-039	DATE 8 OCT., 2010
	CONTRACT NO. ANNIE10029	L/C NO. 111LC1000879

CONTAINER NO.	LOG NO.	LENGTH	DIAMETER	TOTAL VOLUME OF EACH LOG
PONU7267253	39	10.00M	76CM	4.537CBM
	40	9.50M	71CM	3.761CBM
	41	10.20M	74CM	4.387CBM
	42	9.90M	72CM	4.031CBM
	43	7.20M	69CM	2.692CBM
	44	11.70M	76CM	5.308CBM
				24.716CBM

PAGE NO.: 4 OF 4

【任务】审核进口单证

外贸单证员马金春需根据信用证 111LC1000879 及其修改、UCP600 的条款，按照“单证相符，单单相符”的审单原则，对以上进口单据进行审核，并写出审单结果。

项目十二

交单收汇和单证归档操作

能力目标

能按信用证或外贸合同条款进行交单，能处理不符单据，能按业务的要求将各类单证归档。

知识目标

掌握信用证结算方式下的交单收汇操作方法，熟悉电汇、托收结算方式下的交单收汇操作方法和单证归档要求。

上接项目十的导入项目。

【任务 1】办理交单

2010 年 4 月 19 日，浙江大同进出口有限公司外贸单证员桂小龙通过审核，认为各单据都单证一致、单单一致。然后，把准备好的结汇单据以及原信用证、信用证修改书的正本向中国银行浙江省分行国际业务部进行交单。交单时，填写交单联系单。

中国银行浙江省分行

客户交单联系单

致：中国银行浙江省分行

兹随附下列信用证项下出口单据一套，请按国际商会第 600 号出版物《跟单信用证统一惯例》办理寄单索汇。

开证行：　　信用证号：

通知行：　　通知行编号：

最迟装期：　　效期：　　交单期限：

汇票付款期限：　　汇票金额：

发票编号：　　发票金额：

单据	名称	汇票	发票	海关发票	海运提单正本	海运提单副本	航空运单	货物收据	保险单	装箱/重量单	数量/质量/重量证	产地证	GSP FORM A	检验/分析证	受益人证明	船公司证明	电抄	装运通知	
	份数																		

委办事项：打（“×”者）

□附信用证及修改书共__页。

□单据中有下列不符点：

□请向开证行寄单，我公司承担一切责任。　　□请电提不符点，待开证行同意后再寄单。

□寄单方式：□特快专递 □航空挂号　　□索汇方式：□电索 □信索 （□特快专递 □航空挂号）

核销单编号：____________

公司联系人：____________联系电话：____________公司签章：

第一联 交寄单行（一）

银行审单记录：

银行接单日期：　　寄单日期：

汇票/发票金额：　　BP No:

银行费用：
- 通知/保兑：
- 议/承/付：
- 修改费：
- 邮费：
- 电传：
- 小计：

费用由　　承担

银行经办：

银行复核：

退单记录：

【任务 2】处理不符单据

4 月 26 日，中国银行浙江省分行国际业务部工作人员通知浙江大同进出口有限公司外贸单证员桂小龙，开证行中国银行汉堡分行发来拒付电，拒付理由是，所提交的海运提单不是已装船提单。请分析开证行的拒付理由是否成立，为什么？如果拒付理由成立，请设计拒付的救济措施。

【任务 3】收汇后的业务处理

如果通过采取不符单据救济措施后，2010 年 5 月 7 日，浙江大同进出口有限公司收到中国银行浙江省分行国际业务部的通知，开证行中国银行汉堡分行已在当日兑付。收汇之后，外贸单证员需做好哪些业务处理？

【任务 1】办理交单

2010 年 4 月 19 日，如果浙江大同进出口有限公司外贸单证员桂小龙填写客户交单联系单各栏目内容，填写完毕后签字并交单。

中国银行浙江省分行

客户交单联系单

致：中国银行浙江省分行

兹随附下列信用证项下出口单据一套，请按国际商会第 600 号出版物《跟单信用证统一惯例》办理寄单索汇。

开证行：BANK OF CHINA，HAMBURG BRANCH　　信用证号：LC-536-089075

通知行：BANK OF CHINA，ZHEJIANG BRANCH　　通知行编号：AD91005302299

最迟装期：100417　　效期：100508　　交单期限：21 天

汇票付款期限：AT SIGHT　　汇票金额：USD35862.40

发票编号：2010DT00101　　发票金额：USD35862.40

单据 名称	汇票	发票	海关发票	海运提单正本	海运提单副本	航空运单	货物收据	保险单	装箱/重量单	数量/质量/重量证	产地证	GSP FORM A	检验/分析证	受益人证明	船公司证明	电抄	装运通知	
份数	2	3		3	1			2	3			1		1			1	

委办事项：打（“×”者）

☒附信用证及修改书共 2 页。

☐单据中有下列不符点：

☐请向开证行寄单，我公司承担一切责任。　　☐请电提不符点，待开证行同意后再寄单。

☐寄单方式：☒特快专递 ☐航空挂号　　☐索汇方式：☐电索 ☐信索 （☐特快专递 ☐航空挂号）

核销单编号：338667889

公司联系人：________ 联系电话：________ 公司签章：

第一联　交寄单行（一）

银行审单记录：

退单记录：

银行接单日期：

汇票/发票金额：

银行费用：

- 通知/保兑：
- 议/ 承/ 付：
- 修 改 费：
- 邮　　费：
- 电　　传：
- 小　　计：

费用由　　　　承担

寄单日期：

BP No:

银行经办：

银行复核：

【任务 2】处理不符单据

1．分析开证行的拒付理由是否成立

针对开证行中国银行汉堡分行的拒付进行分析，由于从海运提单事先印就的文字 "received in external apparent good order and condition…" 看，该提单是属于收妥备运提单，因此开证行的拒付理由成立。

2．拒付的救济措施

针对这一不符点，外贸单证员可以采取补交单据的救济方法，即马上向船公司出具保函并申请出具加盖已装船批注的海运提单，然后在信用证规定的交单期内（不迟于 2010 年 5 月 3 日）向议付行——中国银行浙江省分行补交正确的海运提单，转交给开证行，并要求开证行退还错误的海运提单，从而实现相符交单。

【任务 3】收汇后的业务处理

收汇后，外贸单证员必须要注意催促货代公司尽快退回出口货物报关单（收汇核销联）、出口货物报关单（出口退税专用联）、出口收汇核销单（正联和出口退税专用联）、场站收据等相关单据。等收到这些单据，复印副本存档后，把正本单据移交财务部门，办理出口收汇核销和退税手续。重要单据的移交，要用专门本子登记，由接收人签收。

顺利收汇后，外贸单证员按照发票号码的顺序进行单据归档工作。对于每票业务，外贸单证员需归档的单据一般包括信用证、商业发票、装箱单、订舱委托书、报检单、出口收汇核销单存根、报关单、报关委托书、产地证、运输单据、保险单据、其他结汇单据等。

一、信用证结算方式下的交单收汇

信用证结算方式下，受益人在按信用证要求发运完货物后，应随即缮制信用证规定的全套单据，连同信用证正本（如经修改的还需连同修改通知书）在信用证规定的交单期和信用证的有效期内，向开证行的指定银行交单请求议付或兑付。

1．交单时间的限制

受益人制单后，应在规定的交单期内，向信用证中指定的银行交付全套单据。若信用证中没有规定交单期限，银行将不接受自装运日起 21 天内提交的单据，但在任何情况下，单据的提交不得迟于信用证的有效期。若信用证到期日或交单日的最后一天，适逢接受单据的银行终止营业日，则规定的到期日或交单期的最后一天将延至该银行开业的第一个营业日。但若该银行中断营业是因为天灾、暴动、骚乱、叛乱、战争、罢工、停工或银行本身无法控制的任何其他原因，则信用证规定的到期日或交单期的最后一天不能顺延。

2．交单地点的限制

所有信用证必须规定一个付款或承兑的交单地点，或在议付信用证的情况下须规定一个交单议付的地点，但自由议付信用证除外。若开证行将信用证的到期地点定在其本国或其自己的营业柜台，而不是受益人国家，这对受益人极为不利，因为他必须保证于信用证的有效期内在开证行营业柜台前提交单据。

3．议付行对单据的处理

议付行审核单据，若单证相符、单单一致，就会办理议付（或押汇），并向开证行寄单请求付款。议付行对不符点单据主要采取以下处理办法：

（1）凭保函议付。如果单据有非实质性的不符点，且受益人信誉较好，银行可凭受益人出具的保函议付，并向开证行寄单索汇。在这种情况下，有的议付行会表提不符点（即在面函上注明单据的所有不符点），通知开证行此信用证凭受益人出具的担保议付，请求开证行接受不符点；国内大多数银行则是将受益人出具的保函存档，不表提不符点，与处理相符单据一样，向开证行寄单索汇。

（2）电提不符点。如果单据金额较大，不符点较严重，为保证收汇安全，银行可以采取电报、电传、SWIFT 等方式把不符点告知开证行，要求其回电授权付款、承兑或议付不符点单据。在取得开证行同意并授权付款、承兑或议付时，议付行可按单据相符的方式，直接议付单据并照常索汇。采取电提不符点，可较快地明确开证人是否接受不符点，有利于受益人及时处理。受益人应配合议付行与开证行联系、加快沟通速度。不过，即使开证行授权议付，在偿付时，仍可能从偿付货款中扣除不符点费（Discrepancy fee）和电报费（Cable charges）。

（3）托收寄单或征求意见寄单。若单据中含有严重不符点，受益人征得进口商同意，且进口商资信较好的情况下，寄单行可将单据寄给开证行作托收处理，并在寄单面函上列明不符点。这种托收寄单方式可减少业务手续和费用，但也使得受益人完全失去开证行的付款保证，单据是否被接受，取决于开证申请人的商业信用。

寄单行也可向开证行寄单，征求其意见，在远期交易的情形下，如开证行通知单据已被接受，应负到期付款的责任。

（4）退单。若单据严重不符，受益人或受益人所在地银行不愿作托收处理，议付行可将单据退回。

4．信用证项下不符单据的处理与救济

（1）审核开证行提出不符点的前提条件是否成立。开证行提出不符点的前提条件包括：

1）在合理的时间内提出不符点，即在开证行收到单据次日起的 5 个工作日之内向单据的提示者提出不符点。

2）无延迟地以电信方式将不符点通知提示者。

3）不符点必须一次性提出，即如第一次所提不符点不成立，即使单据还存在实质性不符点，开证行也无权再次提出。

4）通知不符点的同时，必须说明单据代为保管听候处理，或退交单者。

以上条件必须同时满足，否则，开证行便无权声称单据有不符点而拒付。

(2)审核开证行所提的不符点是否成立。外贸单证员应根据信用证条款、UCP600 和 ISBP 认真审核开证行所提的不符点，判断其是否成立。若不成立，应通过议付行与开证行据理力争，直至开证行付款。

（3）若不符点成立，且条件允许，可补交相符单据。信用证项下不符单据的救济是指当单据由于不符而遭开证行拒付之后，受益人可在规定的时间内及时将替代或更正后的相符单据补交给银行。根据 UCP600 的规定，单据经审核存在不符点且银行决定拒付时，则开证行所承担的信用证项下的付款责任得以免除；但当受益人在规定时间内补交了符合信用证规定的单据，开证行必须承担其付款责任。如果受益人在前期操作过程中浪费了大量时间，就会丧失补交单据时间。

（4）若不符点成立，且无法补交相符单据，要积极与开证申请人洽谈。开证行拒付并不意味着开证申请人拒付，如果开证申请人最终放弃不符点，尽管开证行并不受开证申请人决定的约束，但一般会配合开证申请人付款。所以开证行拒付后，如果不符点确实成立，且无法补交相符单据，应分析与开证申请人之间的关系以及此笔交易的实际情况，以决定怎样与其交涉，说服开证申请人接受不符点并付款。只要货物质量过关，货物市场价格较好，开证申请人一般不会以此为借口拒绝接受单据。另外，也可以采取降价的方式，使开证申请人能付款赎单。

（5）若不符点成立，且开证申请人拒绝接受单据，则可在进口国另寻买主。若开证申请人拒绝接受不符点单据，受益人可以设法在进口国另寻买主，毕竟受益人拥有对单据的处理权。但其前提是信用证要求递交全套正本提单，若 1/3 正本提单已寄给开证申请人，2/3 正本提单提交给银行，则可能会面临钱货两失困境。

（6）退单退货。如果受益人无法在进口国寻找到新买主，就只有退单退货了。不过在作出此决定之前，一定要仔细核算运回货物所需的费用和货值之间是否有利可图。有利益即迅速安排退运，因为时间拖得愈久，费用（港杂、仓储等）就越高；若运回货物得不偿失，还不如将货物放在目的港，由目的港海关处理。

二、T/T 结算方式下的交单收汇

如果是装运前 T/T 的结算方式，出口商在装运前已全部收到进口商电汇的合同金额。在装运之后，就直接把包括海运提单在内的所有单据寄给进口商，或指示船公司把提单电传给进口商。

如果是装运后凭提单传真件 T/T 的结算方式，出口商在装运后，把海运提单传真给进口商，等进口商将合同金额电汇到出口商银行账户之后，才把包括海运提单在内的所有单据寄给进口商。

如果是后 T/T 的结算方式，出口商在装运后就把包括海运提单在内的所有单据寄给进口商，等进口商收到货物之后的一段时间内采用电汇方式把合同款项付给出口商。

三、托收结算方式下的交单收汇

选择托收结算方式时，出口商装运货物后，应及时将有关托收单据交托收行办理托收。

托收交单较灵活，单据种类、单据内容、交单时间由出口商根据合同和进口商情况决定。交单时，出口商应向托收行提供明确的托收指示书。

值得注意的是，托收行没有审核单据的义务，只是根据委托人的指示和国际商会托收统一规则办理，不能擅自超越、修改、疏漏、延误委托人的指示。

代收行是指接受托收行（或中间行）的委托，向付款人办理收款并交单的银行。如果进口商没有付款或承兑的情况下，代收行在未得到出口商授权擅自交单，将由其承担损失责任。

四、单证归档

外贸单证是外贸活动的重要资料，是货物流通的原始凭证。它反映了整个货物流转过程，是业务档案资料的主要组成部分，具有重要的分析参考价值。因此，加强单证归档管理是一项非常重要的工作。

每套单证都应有一套副本留存档卷备查。单证副本的归档方法可分为分散归档和集中归档两种。分散归档是由各分管环节各自将本环节缮制和经营的副本单证分类归档。例如提单由办理运输的环节按运输日期归档，商业发票按发票号码分别由制单环节归档等。集中归档是在交单后将全套副本集中起来进行保管。一般地说，业务量大、部门多、分工细的单位适宜于分散归档；业务量不大，工作线条比较简单的单位适宜于集中归档。

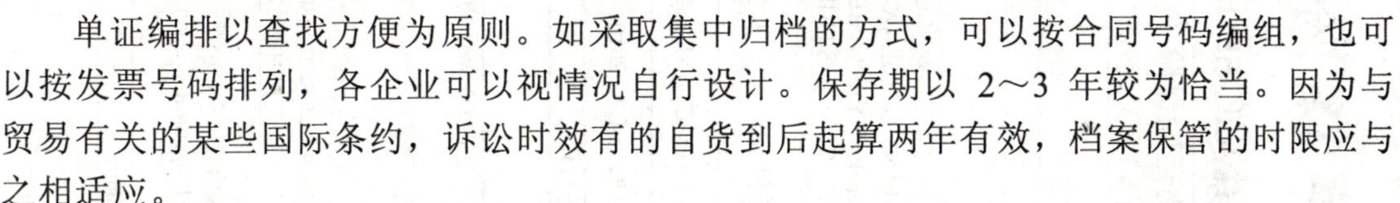

单证编排以查找方便为原则。如采取集中归档的方式，可以按合同号码编组，也可以按发票号码排列，各企业可以视情况自行设计。保存期以 2～3 年较为恰当。因为与贸易有关的某些国际条约，诉讼时效有的自货到后起算两年有效，档案保管的时限应与之相适应。

另外，除保留必要的书面资料以外，还要充分利用电脑存储电子单证信息，以加强单证工作的管理。

实训项目

◆　**实训项目 12-1**

上接实训项目 10-1。

2010 年 8 月 6 日，浙江曼旎进出口有限公司收到中国大地财产保险股份有限公司如下保险单。

中国大地财产保险股份有限公司
China Continent Property&Casualty Insurance Company Ltd.

货物运输保险单
CARGO TRANSPORTATION INSURANCE POLICY

发票号（INVOICE NO.）	2010MN05015	保单号次 POLICY NO.	SS98456
合同号（CONTRACT NO. ）	MN10066		
信用证号（L/C NO. ）	KKK101090		
被保险人： INSURED:	ZHEJIANG JINYUAN IMPORT AND EXPORT CO.，LTD.		

中国人民保险公司（以下简称本公司）根据被保险人的要求，由被保险人向本公司缴付约定的保险费，按照本保险单承保险别和背面所载条款与下列特款承保下述货物运输保险，特立本保险单。

THIS POLICY OF INSURANCE WITNESSES THAT THE PEOPLE'S INSURANCE COMPANY OF CHINA （HEREINAFTER CALLED "THE COMPANY" ） AT THE REQUEST OF THE INSURED AND IN CONSIDERATION OF THE AGREED PREMIUM PAID TO THE COMPANY BY THE INSURED，UNDERTAKES TO INSURE THE UNDERMENTIONED GOODS IN TRANSPORTATION SUBJECT TO THE CONDITIONS OF THIS OF THIS POLICY AS PER THE CLAUSES PRINTED OVERLEAF AND OTHER SPECIAL CLAUSES ATTACHED HEREON.

标记 MARKS&NOS	包装及数量 QUANTITY	保险货物项目 DESCRIPTION OF GOODS	保险金额 AMOUNT INSURED
AS PER INVOICE NO. 2010MN05015	260CTNS	BOYS JACKET	USD84656.00

总保险金额 TOTAL AMOUNT INSURED:	SAY U.S. DOLLARS EIGHTY FOUR THOUSAND SIX HUNDRED AND FIFTY SIX ONLY

保费： PERMIUM:	AS ARRANGED	启运日期 DATE OF COMMENCEMENT：	AUGUST 7，2010	装载运输工具： PER CONVEYANCE:	AS PER B/L
自 FROM:	NINGBO	经 VIA ＊＊＊	至 TO	DUBAI	

承保险别：
CONDITIONS:

COVERING ALL RISKS AND WAR RISK OF CIC OF PICC （1/1/1981） INCL. WAREHOUSE TO WAREHOUSE AND I.O.P AND SHOWING THE CLAIMING CURRENCY IS THE SAME AS THE CURRENCY OF CREDIT.

所保货物，如发生保险单项下可能引起索赔的损失或损坏，应立即通知本公司下述代理人查勘。如有索赔，应向本公司提交保单正本（本保险单共有 2 份正本）及有关文件。如一份正本已用于索赔，其余正本自动失效。

IN THE EVENT OF LOSS OR DAMAGE WITCH MAY RESULT IN A CLAIM UNDER THIS POLICY，IMMEDIATE NOTICE MUST BE GIVEN TO THE COMPANY'S AGENT AS MENTIONED HEREUNDER. CLAIMS，IF ANY，ONE OF THE ORIGINAL POLICY WHICH HAS BEEN ISSUED IN **TWO** ORIGINAL（S） TOGETHER WITH THE RELEVANT DOCUMENTS SHALL BE SURRENDERED TO THE COMPANY. IF ONE OF THE ORIGINAL POLICY HAS BEEN ACCOMPLISHED. THE OTHERS TO BE VOID.

赔款偿付地点 CLAIM PAYABLE AT	DUBAI IN USD	中国大地财产保险股份有限公司 China Continent Property & Casualty Insurance Company Ltd. 杨燕
出单日期 ISSUING DATE	AUGUST 6，2010	Authorized Signature:

杭 州 银 行

客户交单联系单

致：杭州银行

兹随附下列信用证项下出口单据一套，请按国际商会第 600 号出版物《跟单信用证统一惯例》办理寄单索汇。

开证行：	信用证号：
通知行：	通知行编号：

最迟装期：	效期：	交单期限：

汇票付款期限：	汇票金额：
发票编号：	发票金额：

单据	名称	汇票	发票	海关发票	海运提单正本	海运提单副本	航空运单	货物收据	保险单	装箱/重量单	数量/质量/重量证	产地证	GSP FORM A	检验/分析证	受益人证明	船公司证明	电抄	装运通知	
	份数																		

委办事项：打（“×”者）

□附信用证及修改书共__页。

□单据中有下列不符点：

□请向开证行寄单，我公司承担一切责任。　　□请电提不符点，待开证行同意后再寄单。

□寄单方式：□特快专递　□航空挂号　　□索汇方式：□电索　□信索　（□特快专递　□航空挂号）

核销单编号：______________

公司联系人：______________联系电话：______________公司签章：

第一联　交寄单行（一）

银行审单记录：	银行接单日期：		寄单日期：
	汇票/发票金额：		BP No:
	银行费用	通知/保兑：	银行经办：
		议/承/付：	
		修改费：	
		邮费：	
		电传：	银行复核：
		小计：	
退单记录：	费用由　　　　承担		

【任务 1】办理交单

8 月 10 日，如果浙江曼旎进出口有限公司外贸单证员王宁通过审核，认为各单据都单证一致、单单一致。然后，就把准备好的结汇单据以及原信用证、信用证修改书的正本向杭州银行国际业务部进行交单。交单时，填写交单联系单。

【任务 2】处理不符单据

8 月 11 日，杭州银行国际业务部工作人员通知浙江曼旎进出口有限公司外贸单证员王宁，存在以下不符点：

（1）商业发票：未进行商会和阿联酋使领馆认证。

（2）一般原产地证：未进行商会和阿联酋使领馆认证。

（3）受益人证明：未注出信用证号码、开证日期和开证行名称。

（4）海运提单：运费支付方式错误。

请分析这些不符点是否成立，为什么？如果弥补不符点后 8 月 23 日向银行交单办理出口收汇，是否过交单期，为什么？

【任务 3】收汇后的业务处理

8 月 30 日，浙江曼旎进出口有限公司收到杭州银行收账通知（银行水单）如下：

外汇结汇收账通知（人民币）		hzbank 杭州银行
□日期　2010 年 8 月 30 日		第五联
□户名　浙江曼旎进出口有限公司		
□账号　767081009999		
□外汇金额　USD72990.80	□牌价　USD1=￥6.7895	□人民币金额　￥495571.04
□摘要	□净额　USD72990.80	
业务编号：111BP1001245 发票金额：USD76960.00 国外扣佣：USD3848.00 国外扣费：USD25.00 国内扣费：USD96.20 扣除合计：USD3969.20	发票号码：2010MN05015 备注：	核销单号：338599087
□会计：　王力	□复核：　李健	□记账：　张林荣

收汇之后，外贸单证员王宁需做好哪些业务处理？

◆ **实训项目 12-2**

上接实训项目 9-2。

2010 年 9 月 25 日，Sri Russa E Johns SPA 的 QC 检验商品合格后，出具以下检验证书：

SRI RUSSA E JOHNS SPA

55，CORSO MATTEOTTI 20121，MILAN，ITALY

TEL：0039-02-98280909　FAX：0039-02-98280900

INSPECTION　CERTIFICATE

ISSUE DATE	：NOV. 25，2008
ORDER NO.	：77315
CONTRACT NO.	：ZJJY08199
L/C NO.	：59340I015228

THE SELLER : ZHEJIANG JINYUAN IMPORT AND EXPORT CO.，LTD.

COMMODITY : LAMB WAXY LADIES' JACKETS，STYLE NO.DE5，COLOR：　COFFEE BEAN

QUANTITY :2600PCS

THIS IS TO CERTIFY THAT THE SHIPMENT OF THE ABOVE MENTIONED ORDER HAS BEEN INSPECTED AND ARE IN ACCORDANCE WITH THE QUALITY OF THE CONFIRMED SAMPLE OF 080723.

BIN LI

THE QC OF SRI RUSSA E JOHNS SPA

【任务 1】办理交单

9 月 30 日，如果杭州维丰进出口有限公司外贸单证员叶丽通过审核，认为各单据都单证一致、单单一致。然后，就把准备好的结汇单据以及原信用证、信用证修改书的正本向中国银行浙江省分行国际业务部进行交单。交单时，填写交单联系单。

中国银行浙江省分行

客户交单联系单

致：中国银行浙江省分行

兹随附下列信用证项下出口单据一套，请按国际商会第 600 号出版物《跟单信用证统一惯例》办理寄单索汇。

开证行：	信用证号：	
通知行：	通知行编号：	
最迟装期：	效期：	交单期限：
汇票付款期限：	汇票金额：	
发票编号：	发票金额：	

单据	名称	汇票	发票	海关发票	海运提单正本	海运提单副本	航空运单	货物收据	保险单	装箱/重量单	数量/质量/重量证	产地证	GSP FORM A	检验/分析证	受益人证明	船公司证明	电抄	装运通知	
	份数																		

委办事项：打（“×”者）

□附信用证及修改书共__页。

□单据中有下列不符点：

□请向开证行寄单，我公司承担一切责任。　□请电提不符点，待开证行同意后再寄单。

□寄单方式：□特快专递　□航空挂号　□索汇方式：□电索　□信索（□特快专递　□航空挂号）

核销单编号：______

公司联系人：　联系电话：　公司签章：

第一联　交寄单行（一）

银行审单记录：	银行接单日期：		寄单日期：
	汇票/发票金额：		BP No:
	银行费用	通知/保兑：	银行经办：
		议/承/付：	
		修改费：	
		邮　费：	
		电　传：	银行复核：
		小　计：	
退单记录：	费用由　承担		

【任务 2】处理不符单据

9 月 30 日，假如你是中国银行浙江省分行国际业务部工作人员，对杭州维丰进出口有限公司所交的单据进行审核，你认为存在哪些不符点？杭州维丰进出口有限公司外贸单证员叶丽应采取哪些措施弥补这些不符点？

【任务 3】收汇后的业务处理

杭州维丰进出口有限公司外贸单证员叶丽弥补不符点后向中国银行浙江省分行交单收汇。2010 年 10 月 27 日顺利收汇之后，外贸单证员叶丽需做好哪些业务处理？

◆ 实训项目 12-3

上接实训项目 10-2。

【任务 1】办理交单

2010 年 8 月 9 日，浙江大顺进出口有限公司外贸单证员朱丽娅填写如下跟单托收委托书并向中国银行浙江省分行交单办理出口托收。

<table>
<tr><td colspan="3" align="center">中 国 银 行
BANK OF CHINA
跟 单 托 收 委 托 书
Documentary Collection Instruction</td></tr>
<tr><td>TO：BANK OF CHINA</td><td colspan="2">DATE：____________</td></tr>
<tr><td>We enclose the following draft（s）/documents as specified under which please collect in Collecting Bank（Full name & address）accordance with the instructions indicated herein. This collection is subject to URC522.</td><td colspan="2">Collecting Bank　（Full name & address）</td></tr>
<tr><td>Drawer　（Full name & address）</td><td colspan="2">Tenor</td></tr>
<tr><td>Drawee　（Full name & address）</td><td>Draft/Inv. No.</td><td>Amount</td></tr>
<tr><td colspan="3">DOCUMENTS</td></tr>
</table>

（续）

Draft	Commercial Invoice.	Packing List	B/L	N/N B/L	AWB.	C/O	Insurance Policy	Inspection Certificate	Certificate	Cable Copy

SPECIAL INSTRUCTIONS：

☐ Please deliver documents against ☒payment/ ☐acceptance

☐ All your charges are to be borne by the drawee.

☐ In case of a time bill，please advise us of acceptance giving maturity date.

☐ In case of dishonour，please do not protest but advise us of non-payment/ non acceptance giving reasons.

☐ Please instruct the collecting bank to deliver documents upon receipt of all their banking charges.

☐

联系人： 电话： 公司盖章：

【任务 2】收汇后的业务处理

2010 年 8 月 16 日，浙江大顺进出口有限公司顺利收汇之后，外贸单证员朱丽娅需做好哪些业务处理？

参 考 文 献

[1] 中国国际贸易学会商务专业培训考试办公室．外贸业务理论与实务[M]．北京：中国商务出版社，2007.

[2] 章安平．国际结算[M]．杭州：浙江大学出版社，2010.

[3] 国际商会中国国家委员会．ICC 跟单信用证统一惯例（UCP600）[M]．北京：中国民主法制出版社，2006.

[4] 全国国际商务单证培训认证考试办公室．国际商务单证理论与实务[M]．北京：中国商务出版社，2005.